Language Testing and Validation

Research and Practice in Applied Linguistics

General Editors: **Christopher N. Candlin** and **David R. Hall**.

All books in this series are written by leading researchers and teachers in Applied Linguistics, with broad international experience. They are designed for the MA or PhD student in Applied Linguistics, TESOL or similar subject areas and for the language professional keen to extend their research experience

Titles include:

Cyril J. Weir
LANGUAGE TESTING AND VALIDATION

Forthcoming titles:

Martin Bygate and Virginia Samuda
TASKS IN LANGUAGE LEARNING

Francesca Bargiela, Catherine Nickerson and Brigitte Planken
BUSINESS COMMUNICATION

Sandra Gollin and David R. Hall
LANGUAGE FOR SPECIFIC PURPOSES

Sandra Hale
COMMUNITY INTERPRETING

Geoff Hall
LITERATURE IN LANGUAGE EDUCATION

Richard Kiely and Pauline Rea-Dickins
PROGRAM EVALUATION IN LANGUAGE EDUCATION

Martha Pennington
PRONUNCIATION

Devon Woods and Emese Bukor
INSTRUCTIONAL STRATEGIES IN LANGUAGE EDUCATION

Tony Wright
LANGUAGE EDUCATION AND CLASSROOM MANAGEMENT

Research and Practice in Applied Linguistics
Series Standing Order ISBN 1–4039–1184–3 hardcover
Series Standing Order ISBN 1–4039–1185–1 paperback
(*outside North America only*)

You can receive future titles in this series as they are published by placing a standing order. Please contact your bookseller or, in case of difficulty, write to us at the address below with your name and address, the title of the series and one of the ISBNs quoted above.

Customer Services Department, Macmillan Distribution Ltd, Houndmills, Basingstoke, Hampshire RG21 6XS, England

---

Language Testing and Validation

An Evidence-based Approach

Cyril J. Weir
*Centre for Research in English Language Learning
and Assessment (CRELLA)
University of Luton*

First published 2005 by
PALGRAVE MACMILLAN
Houndmills, Basingstoke, Hampshire RG21 6XS and
175 Fifth Avenue, New York, N.Y. 10010
Companies and representatives throughout the world

PALGRAVE MACMILLAN is the global academic imprint of the Palgrave
Macmillan division of St. Martin's Press, LLC and of Palgrave Macmillan Ltd.
Macmillan® is a registered trademark in the United States, United Kingdom
and other countries. Palgrave is a registered trademark in the European
Union and other countries.

ISBN 1–4039–1188–6 hardback
ISBN 1–4039–1189–4 paperback

This book is printed on paper suitable for recycling and made from fully
managed and sustained forest sources.

A catalogue record for this book is available from the British Library.

A catalog record for this book is available from the Library of Congress.

10   9   8   7   6   5   4   3   2   1
14   13   12   11   10   09   08   07   06   05

Printed and bound in Great Britain by
Antony Rowe Ltd, Chippenham and Eastbourne

To Shigeko, Jamie and Mary, and to my friends

Contents

General Editors' Preface

Research and Practice in Applied Linguistics is an international book series from Palgrave Macmillan which brings together leading researchers and teachers in Applied Linguistics to provide readers with the knowledge and tools they need to undertake their own practice-related research. Books in the series are designed for students and researchers in Applied Linguistics, TESOL, Language Education and related subject areas, and for language professionals keen to extend their research experience.

Every book in this innovative series is designed to be user-friendly, with clear illustrations and accessible style. The quotations and definitions of key concepts that punctuate the main text are intended to ensure that many, often competing, voices are heard. Each book presents a concise historical and conceptual overview of its chosen field, identifying many lines of enquiry and findings, but also gaps and disagreements. It provides readers with an overall framework for further examination of how research and practice inform each other, and how practitioners can develop their own problem-based research.

The focus throughout is on exploring the relationship between research and practice in Applied Linguistics. How far can research provide answers to the questions and issues that arise in practice? Can research questions that arise and are examined in very specific circumstances be informed by, and inform, the global body of research and practice? What different kinds of information can be obtained from different research methodologies? How should we make a selection between the options available, and how far are different methods compatible with each other? How can the results of research be turned into practical action?

The books in this series identify some of the key researchable areas in the field and provide workable examples of research projects, backed up by details of appropriate research tools and resources. Case studies and exemplars of research and practice are drawn on throughout the books. References to key institutions, individual research lists, journals and professional organizations provide starting points for gathering information and embarking on research. The books also include annotated lists of key works in the field for further study.

The overall objective of the series is to illustrate the message that in Applied Linguistics there can be no good professional practice that isn't based on good research, and there can be no good research that isn't informed by practice.

Christopher N. Candlin
Macquarie University, Sydney
and Open University, UK

David R. Hall
Macquarie University, Sydney

Acknowledgements

I am especially grateful to Chris Candlin of Macquarie University for his encouraging and insightful comments at each stage in the preparation of the manuscript. His sure and encyclopedic grasp of the field of Applied Linguistics helped in the development of many of the ideas this book contains.

A number of my PhD students and attachments at Roehampton University contributed to the conceptualization of testing as evidence-based validity in Part 2 of this book during their studies in the Centre for Research in Testing, Evaluation and Curriculum in ELT (CRTEC) at Roehampton University; in particular, Akmar Saidatul, Tony Green and Xiu Xudong, and Jessica Wu, Rachel Wu and Joyce Shao Chin of the LTTC in Taiwan. My colleague (in CRTEC) Barry O'Sullivan contributed substantially to the framework for speaking. Glenn Fulcher was the source for many of the website references in Chapter 12. Jin Yan from the CET in China helped with the proof reading and commented reflectively on the text. Roger Hawkey read the typescript and made a number of useful suggestions. Akmar Saidatul helped with the index.

Cambridge ESOL funded part of the research that this book is based on and staff in their Research and Validation Group commented critically on the ms at a number of stages.

The publishers are grateful to the following for permission to reproduce copyright material:

TOEFL materials are reprinted by permission of Educational Testing Service, the copyright owner. However the test questions and any other testing information are provided in their entirety by Palgrave Macmillan. No endorsement of this publication by Educational Testing Service should be inferred.

LTTC GEPT materials are printed by permission of the Language Training and Testing Centre in Taiwan.

USAID for the materials from the *Student Achievement Test Development Manual*, ed. H. Khalifa (2003), produced for use by teachers in Egypt.

Abbreviations

AAAL	American Association of Applied Linguistics
ACTFL	American Council on the Teaching of Foreign Languages
AERA	American Educational Research Association
AERT	Advanced English Reading Test
AILA	International Association of Applied Linguistics
ALTE	Association of Language Testers in Europe
ANOVA	Analysis of Variance
APA	American Psychological Association
BAAL	British Association of Applied Linguistics
CALS	Centre for Applied Language Studies, University of Reading
CB	Computer-based
CBT	Computer-based Test
CEF	Common European Framework of Reference for Languages
CET	College English Test
CLA	Communicative Language Ability
CPE	Certificate of Proficiency in English
CR	Criterion-referenced
CRTEC	Centre for Research in Testing Evaluation and Curriculum
CUEFL	Communicative Use of English as a Foreign Language
EALTA	European Association for Language Testing and Assessment
EAP	English for Academic Purposes
EFL	English as a Foreign Language
ELBA	English Language Battery
ELT	English Language Teaching
EPTB	English Proficiency Test Battery
EPQ	Eysenck Personality Questionnaire
ERIC	Educational Resources Information Center
ESL	English as a Second Language
ESOL	English for Speakers of Other Languages
ESP	English for Specified Purposes
ETS	Educational Testing Service
FCE	First Certificate in English
FL	Foreign Language
FSI	Foreign Service Institute
GCE	General Certificate of Education
GCSE	General Certificate of Secondary Education

GEPT	General English Proficiency Test
IATEFL	International Association for Teaching English as a Foreign Language
IELTS	International English Language Testing System
ILR	Interagency Language Roundtable
ILTA	International Language Testing Association
IRT	Item Response Theory
JMB	Joint Matriculation Board (Northern Universities)
KR	Kudar Richardson
L1	First Language
L2	Second Language
LTM	Long-term Memory
LTRC	Language Testing Research Colloquium
LTTC	Language Training and Testing Centre
LTU	Language Testing Update
MCQ	Multiple-choice Question
MFR	Multi-faceted Rasch Analysis
MTMM	Multi-trait, Multi-method
NCME	National Council on Measurement in Education
NNS	Non-native Speaker
OPI	Oral Proficiency Interview
PBT	Paper-Based Test
PLAB	General Medical Council's Professional and Linguistic Assessments Board (Test of overseas doctors' language proficiency), United Kingdom
RSA	Royal Society of Arts
SAQ	Short-answer Question
SATD	Student Achievement Test Development
SD	Standard Deviation
SEM	Standard Error of Measurement
STM	Short-term Memory
SLA	Second Language Acquisition
SOPI	Simulated Oral Proficiency Interview
SPSS	Statistical Package for the Social Sciences
TEEP	Test of English for Educational Purposes
TEM	Test for English Majors
TL	Target Language
TLU	Target Language Use
TOEFL	Test of English as a Foreign Language
TOEIC	Test of English for International Communication
TSE	Test of Spoken English
TSWE	Test of Standard Written English
TWE	Test of Written English
UCLES	University of Cambridge Local Examinations Syndicate

UCRN	University of Cambridge Research Notes
UK	United Kingdom
USAID	United States Agency for International Development

Introduction

In language testing we are concerned with the extent to which a test can be shown to produce scores that are an accurate reflection of a candidate's ability in a particular area, e.g., careful reading to extract main ideas from a text, writing an argumentative essay, breadth of vocabulary knowledge, or spoken interaction with peers. It demands an understanding of both trait and method. Trait is concerned with the underlying constructs/abilities we wish to measure in students, the *what* of language testing. Method deals with the *how*, the instruments we develop to provide us with the information about these construct(s).

Test validation is the process of generating evidence to support the well-foundedness of inferences concerning trait from test scores, i.e., essentially, testing should be concerned with evidence-based validity. Test developers need to provide a clear argument for a test's validity in measuring a particular trait with credible evidence to support the plausibility of this interpretative argument (see Kane 1992). This is similar in a number of respects to a defence lawyer acting in the courtroom. As we will see below, this necessarily involves providing data relating to *context-based, theory-based* and *criterion-related* validities, together with the various *reliabilities*, or *'scoring validity'* as we prefer to call it.

Testing also has an ethical dimension in so far as it affects people's lives (see Davies (ed.) 1997). This leads us into the area of consequential validity where we are concerned with a test's impact on individuals, institutions and society, and with the use that is made of test results. Getting it right, ensuring test fairness, is a necessity not an ideal for testing. In developing assessment tools a decision must be taken on what is criterial in the particular domain under review, and this decision and the test measures used for operationalizing it must be ethically defensible. Test developers must be made accountable for their products.

Language testing is not just about creating the instruments for data generation – as it may seem from a number of practical books on the market, which deal principally with the mechanics of test production. Test development needs to go deeper than this, even when these are low-stake tests for use in the classroom for formative purposes. We want to show that testing must always be concerned with evidence-based validity, i.e., the relationships between the testing instrument and the construct(s) it attempts to measure.

The core of this book is concerned with exploring a framework for establishing the validity of the interpretation of scores on tests produced by Exam Boards or by teachers for use in their classrooms. This is what testing should be concerned with. Until it is, we can have little confidence in our interpretation of the test scores that are available to us. We offer below a blueprint of the types of evidence we must provide if we are to justify the correctness of our interpretations of abilities from test scores. Though specifically framed with English for Speakers of Other Languages (ESOL) in mind, the blueprint has implications for all forms of educational assessment.

This book follows the rationale and structure of the *Research and Practice in Applied Linguistics Series* in first providing a theoretical overview of the field, followed by detail of how this works in practice and then suggesting focuses and methods for researching key areas. In Part 1 we map out the types of validation evidence we need to provide if we are to have any confidence that the results of performance on a test give us an accurate picture of the underlying abilities or constructs we are attempting to measure. In Part 2 we unpack validity further in relation to actual examples and procedures taken from tests from around the world and provide an evidence-based validity framework for asking questions of any exam or form of assessment. In Part 3 we suggest a number of research activities, which will generate data on whether a test matches up to various criteria in the framework. Lastly, in Part 4, we detail a number of electronic and paper-based resources.

The first chapter sets the scene by tracing the development of language tests over the last century. It will attempt to describe the different stages in Western approaches to language testing, variously labelled by Bernard Spolsky (ed., 1978: v–x) as the 'pre-scientific' which lasted up to the Second World War and the 'psychometric-structuralist' that took us into the 1970s in Britain (but, as we will see, much later in the USA). Finally, we deal with the 'psycholinguistic-sociolinguistic' era covering the late 1970s until the present day in Britain (but really only taking off in the 1990s in the USA). More provocatively, these stages were described by Keith Morrow (1979) as 'the Garden of Eden, the Vale of Tears and the Promised Land'.

Part 1
Testing as Validity

1
Language Testing Past and Present

Language tests from the distant past to the present are important historical documents. They can help inform us about attitudes to language, language testing and language teaching when little alternative evidence of what went on in the bygone language classroom remains. Seeing where we have come from also helps us better understand where we are today. The Cambridge ESOL Certificate of Proficiency in English (CPE) has by far the longest track record of any serious EFL examination still in existence, so it is a particularly useful vehicle for researching where we have come from in European approaches to language teaching and testing over the last century. We will trace some significant events in its history to exemplify the developments in the field during that period (see Weir 2003 for a full history of the CPE).

1.1   The Cambridge Proficiency Examination 1913–1945: 'The Garden of Eden', 'the pre-scientific era'

Weir (2003: 2) describes how Cambridge's formal entry into testing the English of foreign students took place in 1913, when it first offered the Certificate of Proficiency in English (CPE). The examination was based on the traditional, essay-based, native-speaker language syllabus including an English literature paper, the same as that sat by native speakers for university matriculation, and an essay, but also a compulsory phonetics paper, a grammar section and translation from and into French and German. These were complemented by an oral component with dictation, reading aloud and conversation.

The emphasis in this early pre-scientific era was thus on language use, though some attention was paid to form in the grammar and phonetics sections. The 'scientific' issue of test reliability was still relatively little understood, at least outside the United States (see Spolsky 1995) and the notion of the 'connoisseurship' of an elite group of examiners prevailed. All was thought to be well in this testing Garden of Eden.

1913 CPE Examination

(i) Written:

(a) Translation from English into French or German		2 hours
(b) Translation from French or German into English, and questions on English Grammar		2 ½ hours
(c) English Essay		2 hours
(d) English Literature (The paper on English Language and Literature [Group A, Subject 1] in the Higher Local Examination)		3 hours 1½ hours
(e) English Phonetics		

(ii) Oral:

Dictation	½ hour
Reading and Conversation	½ hour

The 1913 test corresponded closely to the contents of Sweet's (1899) *The Practical Study of Languages: A Guide for Teachers and Learners* (see Howatt 1984 for details) and mirrored a concern with pronunciation as well as translation. Phonetics occupied a central position in the field of linguistics and language studies which was to survive until the 1960s in tests such as the English Language Battery Version A (ELBA) and the English Proficiency Test Battery (EPTB) used in university admissions (see Davies 2005 for a detailed account of these exams) and even later in the Professional and Linguistic Assessments Board (PLAB) test for overseas doctors wishing to practise in Britain. Grammar translation as a basis for testing proficiency was also to endure into the 1970s in most foreign language testing in the UK and still lingers on in the university sector. In contrast, the testing of English as a foreign language was to progress more quickly.

It is also interesting to note that an oral test (reading aloud and conversation) with associated dictation, was present in an international English as a Foreign Language (EFL) test at such an early stage. This multi-componential approach with a variety of discrete point, integrative and communicative tasks was to differentiate the Cambridge main suite examinations from most of its competitors through the twentieth century. It marks a British/European preoccupation with the trait, with *what* we are testing, as against an American preference for the method, the *how* of testing. This contrast was to last throughout the twentieth century until the Test of English as a Foreign Language (TOEFL) Next Generation programme.

Weir (2003: 14) points out how the approach in the first half of the century was to aim for construct validity and work on reliability, 'rather than through the single-minded pursuit of objectivity seriously curtail what CPE would be able to measure. A valid test that might not present perfect psychometric qualities was preferred to an objective test which though

Concept 1.1   Reliability and validity: competing paradigms in test development?

In these early days of language testing, reliability and validity were often seen as dichotomous concepts, a question of where priorities were to be placed. The cardinal guiding principle for Cambridge was construct validity, i.e., appropriateness in what was being measured, followed closely by utility for the teaching community. This does not mean they did not seek to achieve reliability, i.e., consistency of measurement, but reliability was not the overriding determinant of what went into the examination. According to Spolsky (1995), until the work of Roach in the 1940s on improving rater reliability, they appear to have remained relatively immune to psychometric influences from across the Atlantic.

always reliable might not measure that much of value, e.g., not test speaking or writing.'

In America the reverse was true and some aspects of validity were sometimes sacrificed in the pursuit of reliability. It is only with the recent development of TOEFL Next Generation that an attempt has been made to redress the situation by focusing on test activities more relevant to the demands of real-life academic study. Similarly in mainstream education in the USA, there is now increasing public concern over several aspects of validity of a number of the standardized tests that proliferate in school assessment despite their undoubted claims to reliability, i.e., measurement consistency.

We return to the issues of validity in Chapters 2, 3 and 4.

1.2   Developments in the 1960s: the move towards a language-based examination

Concept 1.2   Language tests should only test language

In the early 1960s we see the beginnings of a critical shift in the language testing tradition in Britain towards a view that language might be divorced from testing literary or cultural knowledge. It is thus possible in this period to date the start of a gradual but critical change of the English language examination to one which focuses on language as against an assortment of language, literature and culture.
(Weir 2003: 17–18)

Up to this point, the case for a language-based test had been hampered by the desire of linguists to gain academic respectability and recognition for language degree programmes in the older universities by injecting a heavy dose of literature and culture into their courses and examinations.

Weir (2003:19) describes how:

> candidates still have to take two other papers in addition to the compulsory 'English Language' paper. However, unlike the previous major revision in 1953, candidates can choose both 'Use of English' and 'Translation from and into English' as two additional papers, which means they do not have to take anything from (b) 'English Literature' or its alternatives.

1966

Oral: Dictation, Reading and Conversation
Written: Candidates must offer (a) English Language and **two** other papers chosen from (b), (c) or (d). No candidate may offer more than one of the alternatives in (b).

(a) English Language (composition and a passage or passages of English with language questions. The choice of subjects set for composition will include some for candidates who are specially interested in commerce)	(3 hours)
(b) Either English Literature	(3 hours)
Or Science Texts	
Or British Life and Institutions	
Or Survey of Industry and Commerce	
(c) Use of English	(3 hours)
(d) Translation from and into English	(3 hours)

In section (b) of the Use of English paper 3 option, multiple-choice items are introduced. This marks a growing interest in improving the reliability of the test overall, at least in terms of the internal consistency of the discrete item components (see Chapter 9). The more consistent the items were with each other in terms of how candidates performed on them, the higher this internal reliability. Spolsky (1978), in line with wider developments in the fields of statistics and linguistics, labelled this the 'psychometric-structuralist' era and Morrow (1979) 'The Vale of Tears'. The latter title was a reaction to an obsessive pursuit of objectivity, not just in tests of micro-linguistic knowledge (e.g., vocabulary) but also, for example, in the Multiple-Choice Question (MCQ) structure and written expression section in TOEFL. This indirect measure was used as an estimate of academic writing ability until the introduction of the bolt-on Test of Written English (TWE) paper in response to consumer wishes in 1986. Breaking language down into its elements also fitted well with the immediate constituent analysis of sentences in vogue with linguists in this period.

1.3 The 1975 and 1984 revisions: 'The Promised Land'?

The 1975 revisions saw the CPE examination taking a shape that, in its broad outline, is familiar to the Cambridge candidate of today and largely represents the content coverage of language tests at this level across the world. Weir (2003: 24) describes how

> the new CPE listening, reading and speaking tests in particular represented major developments on the 1966 revision and echoed the burgeoning interest in communicative language teaching in the 1970s; an increasing concern with language in use as against language as a system for study.... The 1970s saw a change from teaching language as a system to teaching it as a means of communication as set out and discussed in Widdowson (1978).

In the UK it was reflected in the teaching and publications emerging from CALS at the University of Reading under the influence of Ron White, Don Porter, Keith Morrow and Keith Johnson, and at Lancaster University under the influence of Chris Candlin, Michael Breen and colleagues.

The increased reliance on multiple-choice formats (in papers 2–4) acknowledged the attention international examinations felt they must pay to the demands of objectivity. The concern to improve marker reliability, particularly from the 1980s onwards, also aimed to improve the dependability of the scores in productive tests (papers 1 and 5).

The direct connection between the exam and British culture was completely broken and this potential source of test bias much reduced.

Content of the 1975 Certificate of Proficiency in English

PAPER 1 Composition	(3 hours)
PAPER 2 Reading Comprehension	(1¼ hours)
PAPER 3 Use of English	(3 hours)
PAPER 4 Listening Comprehension	(30 minutes)
PAPER 5 Interview	(approx. 12 minutes)

Weir (2003: 26) describes how

> the five papers have replaced the old division of Oral and Written and indicate some movement to recognizing further the need to address the notion that language proficiency is not unitary but partially divisible. It was to take a number of American applied linguists rather longer to discard their firmly held convictions that language proficiency was unitary and that therefore it mattered little what was tested as long as it was done reliably (see Oller 1979).

During the 1980s and 1990s there was, however, a degree of convergence of views on testing internationally, helped in no small part by the growing influence of the Language Testing Research Colloquium, which annually brought together researchers and scholars interested in language testing from around the world. The birth of the journal *Language Testing* as a result of a weekend meeting of a small group of British testers at Lancaster University in 1980 (see Alderson and Hughes (eds.) 1981) was to promote further the exchange of views across the Atlantic. The advent of the Language Testing list-serve, a web-based discussion forum in the 1990s, similarly promoted the exchange of views and an understanding of different traditions. The growing acceptance, or at least recognition, of international standards for language testing spawned by the drawing up of the American Educational Research Association *et al.* (1974, 1985, 1999) standards made an equally positive contribution. Full details of links to all of these can be found in Part 4.

Now that the channels of communication are open and earlier entrenched positions have softened, the future development of the field will depend on clarifying, codifying and disseminating a framework for test development, administration and analysis that all test developers can buy into. The rest of this book explores what might go into such a framework.

Further reading

Spolsky (1995) is an impressive, scholarly history of the development of ESOL examinations in the USA and Britain, if somewhat predisposed to the psychometric orientation of the former.

Weir and Milanovic (eds.) (2003) gives a full history of the development over a century of a major international ESOL examination the CPE looked at from a British perspective with its humanistic/sociolinguistic leanings.

2
The Nature of Test Validity

Quote 2.1   Hughes, Porter and Weir on the need for validity evidence

The provision of satisfactory evidence of validity is indisputably necessary for any serious test.
(1988: 4)

By the end of the twentieth century Cambridge ESOL was addressing the reliability as well as the more traditional validity aspects of its examinations. Their earlier concern with construct validity was now matched by an equal regard for reliability, at least from the 1980s, in the UK. In the wider testing world, exam providers such as TOEFL had also begun to acknowledge the legitimacy of the socio-cognitive elements of validity and devoted the attention to them that they had always paid to the reliability aspect. The commitment to continually improve validity exhibited by Cambridge ESOL and Educational Testing Service (ETS) TOEFL examinations is encouraging, but the picture is very different for many other examining boards.

Quote 2.2   On the lack of validity evidence for many tests

[M]any test makers acknowledge a responsibility for providing general validity evidence of the instrumental value of the test but very few actually do it.
(Messick 1992: 89)

Alderson and Buck (1993) demonstrated how many UK language examinations failed to show evidence of meeting criteria, which were essential, if we were to have any faith in the results they produced. The situation is depressingly similar ten years on from their study. In response to this situation, a desire to improve the fairness of all testing procedures is the rationale for this book.

Concept 2.1   A reform agenda for the twenty-first century

To improve test fairness we need an agenda for reform, which sets out clearly the basic minimum requirements for sound testing practice. Stakeholders in the testing process, in particular students and teachers, need to be able to ask the right questions of any examinations, commercial or classroom-based. Examination providers should be able and required to provide appropriate evidence in response to these questions.

In Part 1 we map out the types of validation evidence we need to provide if we are to have any guarantee that the results of performance on a test give us an accurate picture of the underlying abilities or constructs we are attempting to measure. The focus in validation is therefore primarily on the examination score or grade as a reliable measure of a trait or 'construct'. In Part 2 we will unpack these concepts further in relation to actual examples and procedures taken from tests around the world and provide a framework for asking questions of any exam or form of assessment. In Part 3 we offer a methodology for investigating further whether a test matches up to a criterion in the framework.

Concept 2.2   Validity in general

The concept of validity has been around for a long time. Kelly (1927: 14) noted, 'The problem of validity is that of whether a test really measures what it purports to measure.' Lado (1961: 321) similarly asked, 'Does a test measure what it is supposed to measure? If it does, it is valid.' Cronbach (1971: 463) took a similar position: 'Every time an educator asks "but what does the instrument really measure?" he is calling for information on construct validity.'

Though some writers have found this too vague (Loevinger 1957), it continues to appear as a useful generalization in many books on testing or measurement: for example, in Davies (1990: 21), Hatch and Lazaraton (1997: 540), Henning (1987: 89).

We would wish to modify this general view of validity slightly.

Concept 2.3   Validity resides in test scores

Validity is perhaps better defined as the extent to which a test can be shown to produce data, i.e., test scores, which are an accurate representation of a candidate's level of language knowledge or skills. In this revision, validity resides in the scores on a particular administration of a test rather than in the test *per se*.

It is inaccurate to talk of a test such as TOEFL or the International English Language Testing System (IELTS) as being valid or not. It is the scores produced by a particular administration of a test on a particular sample of candidates that we are concerned with. Obviously, over time, if various versions of a test or administrations of the same test provide similar results, then synthetically a case may be made for X or Y test being valid over time and across versions and population samples.

Concept 2.4   Validity is multifaceted

Validity is multifaceted and different types of evidence are needed to support any claims for the validity of scores on a test. These are not alternatives but complementary aspects of an evidential basis for test interpretation.

No single validity can be considered superior to another. Deficit in any one raises questions as to the well-foundedness of any interpretation of test scores.

Quote 2.3   Messick's unified view of validity

Validity is broadly defined as nothing less than an evaluative summary of both the evidence for and the actual – as well as the potential – consequences of score interpretation and use (i.e., construct validity conceived comprehensively). This comprehensive view of validity integrates considerations of content, criteria and consequences into a comprehensive framework for empirically testing rational hypotheses about score meaning and utility.
(1995: 742)

He thus sees the complementarity of the different sources of evidence formerly considered as separable validities. As such he came to be seen as representing a new orthodoxy on approaching construct validity as a superordinate category for test validities. Bachman had made the point earlier in a similar fashion.

Quote 2.4   Bachman on the inclusiveness of validity

[I]t is important to recognize that none of these by itself is sufficient to demonstrate the validity of a particular interpretation or use of test scores.
(1990: 237)

In fact, the view that construct validity should be regarded as a superordinate concept embracing all other forms of validity has a longer pedigree (see Anastasi 1988, Weir 1988a). The notion of contributory validity evidence as against distinct validities began to emerge in the 1980s.

There is perhaps a potential for confusion in the literature with respect to the term *construct validity* itself. It is often used as a superordinate term for all the validities and also to refer more specifically to the theoretical construct, in the past often expressed in terms of individual cognitive ability, on which the test is based. We prefer instead to reinstate the term *validity* as the superordinate category of description and accordingly we discuss below what the elements of validity are and what evidence they can generate in support of interpretation of the test scores produced.

In addition, the traditional polarization of reliability and validity as illustrated in Chapter 1 is unhelpful and reliability would be better regarded as one form of validity evidence. We accordingly will employ a more apposite term, *scoring validity*, to emphasize its part in the wider validity concept. Again, we are not alone in this as earlier work by Alderson (1991a) shows.

Quote 2.5   Alderson on validity and reliability

I have long found it difficult to see that item homogeneity (internal consistency) can be seen as a matter of reliability, rather than as one of validity...parallel form reliability is simply concurrent validation.
(Alderson1991a: 61–3)

A test should always be constructed on an explicit specification, which addresses both the cognitive and linguistic abilities involved in activities in the language use domain of interest, as well as the context in which these abilities are performed (theory-based validity and context validity). In our view, construct validity is a function of the interaction of these two aspects of validity and is not just a matter of ability within the individual in isolation (see McNamara 1997, Johnson 2001, Fulcher 2003: 44–6, for discussion of this interactional competence perspective).

Next, in the implementation stage when the test has been administered, we need to look at the data generated and apply statistical analyses to these to tell us the degree to which we can depend on the results (scoring validity).

Finally, we can collect data on events after the test has been developed and administered to shed further light on the well-foundedness of the inferences we are making about underlying abilities on the basis of test results. The focus here is on the value of the test for end-users of the information provided and the extent to which such use can be justified (see Chapelle

1999, Messick 1989). This takes us into the area of criterion-related validity evidence where a test is measured against other external measures of the construct, and also that of *consequential* validity where the impact of the test on society and individuals or institutions is investigated. This consideration further modifies the general view we started with by emphasizing that validity does not just reside in the test itself or rather in the scores on the test but also in the inferences that are made from them.

Concept 2.5   Validity is a matter of degree

Messick (1989:33) emphasizes that 'it is important to note that validity is a matter of degree, not all or none'.

In respect of one single aspect of validity, e.g., content coverage, a test may not provide a perfect fit in terms of appropriate operations and conditions. Another version of the test may demonstrate a stronger match with the test specification. A test's claims to validity may also differ across the types of validity evidence generated in relation to a single administration of one version of the test. For example, Version A of a writing test may be strong in content coverage and theory related validity but have a marker reliability coefficient of less than 0.9. It may also vary on the same aspect of validity from administration to administration of the same or different forms. Validity should then be viewed as a *relative* concept.

Most examinations lay claim to the numerous aspects of validity. However, what are often lacking are *validation* studies of actual tests that demonstrate this. Validation can be seen as a form of evaluation where a variety of quantitative and qualitative methodologies (see Part 3) are used to generate evidence to support inferences from test scores. The validity of a test does not lie in what the test designers claim; rather, they need to produce evidence to support such claims starting from the initial design process. We first specify the different types of validity evidence before unpacking these with examples element by element in Part 2, and then suggest a variety of methodological procedures for generating data on each element in Part 3.

Further reading

Bachman (1990) is the significant book in the field, which tackles modern language testing in a serious and rigorous fashion. Hard-going in parts, but well worth the effort.

Bachman and Palmer (1996) is an update on 1990, but with a more practical focus.

Hughes, Porter and Weir (1988) provide an early but still useful discussion of validation in relation to the British Council ELTS test.

Kunnan (ed.) (1998) is a useful collection of papers on validation in language assessment. Kunnan (Chapter 1) provides an overview of validation studies in language assessment carried out up to 1996, categorized in relation to Messick's (1989) progressive matrix of validity.

Nitko (2001) discusses these concepts in an educational measurement context.

3
Before the Test Event:
A Priori Validity Evidence

3.1 Theory-based validity

There are two aspects to theory-based validity. One concerns <u>*a priori*</u> evidence collected before the test event, the other <u>*a posteriori*</u> evidence generated after the test has been administered (Weir 1988a).

The language tester can empirically investigate after the test event what language skills have been operationalized through statistical analysis of the data generated to determine underlying patterns, and through criterion-related studies to relate information produced by this test to that produced by others with known properties. In the past, relatively little attention was paid to the non-statistical aspects of theory-based validity. In the earlier psychometric–structuralist approach to language testing (see Chapter 1) the prevailing theoretical paradigm lent itself easily to testing discrete elements of the target language (lexical or grammatical items) and little need was seen for much *a priori* deliberation on the match between theory and test.

Construct validity was viewed from a purely statistical perspective in much of the American testing literature of the 1980s (see Bachman and Palmer 1981). It was seen principally as a matter of the *a posteriori* statistical validation of whether a test had measured a construct in individuals, which had a reality independent of other constructs. The concern was much more with the *a posteriori* relationship between a test and psychological abilities, traits, constructs it had measured than with *a priori* investigation of what *should* be elicited by the test before its actual administration.

Quote 3.1 Bachman and Palmer on the construct validation of tests of communicative competence

An empirical investigation into the construct validity of tests of speaking and reading English as a second language was performed. . . . An analysis of variance . . . supported the hypothesis that speaking and reading abilities are independently measurable. (1981: 149–50)

17

\digm, in order to show the validity of a test, it is necessary to
t correlates highly with indices of behaviour that one might
...oretically expect it to correlate with, and also that it does not correlate
significantly with variables that one would *not* expect it to correlate with
(see Bachman 1990: 250, Campbell and Fiske 1959). Fulcher (2003: 207–21)
provides a clear worked example of a multi-trait, multi-method study.

Statistical analysis after the event was seen as an adequate basis for determining the existence or non-existence of a number of language ability
constructs, for example, in Quote 3.1 speaking and reading.

However, is there not a problem if we do not have a clear idea of what we
want to measure before we construct and administer a test to students? Is
there a problem with a 'suck-it-and-see' approach?

Concept 3.1   Defining the construct from the start

There is a need for validation at the *a priori* stage of test development. The more fully
we are able to describe the construct we are attempting to measure at the *a priori* stage
the more meaningful might be the statistical procedures contributing to construct
validation that can subsequently be applied to the results of the test. Statistical data do
not in themselves generate conceptual labels. We can never escape from the need
to define what is being measured, just as we are obliged to investigate how adequate
a test is in operation.

There are two major threats to validity: 'construct under-representation' and
'construct irrelevance' (see Messick 1989 and 1992). We need to ensure the
constructs we are eliciting are precisely those we intend to and that these
are not contaminated by other irrelevant variables, such as method effect.
If important constructs are under-represented in our tests, this may have an
adverse washback effect on the teaching that precedes the test, teachers may
simply not teach certain important skills if they are not in the test: for
example, listening to English skills in Egyptian schools, when not tested, is
not taught. If we only test careful reading and not expeditious reading (see
Urquhart and Weir 1998), are we measuring all of reading ability?

Test developers also need to be aware of prevailing theories concerning
the language processing which underlies the various operations required in
real-life language use. Where such use is to be operationalized in a test the
underlying processing should be replicated as far as is possible, i.e., we must
demonstrate *theory-based validity*. (See Levelt 1993 and Hughes 2002 for the
theory of the cognitive processes involved in speaking; Grabe and Kaplan
1996 and Hyland 2002 for writing; Urquhart and Weir 1998 and Grabe and
Stoller 2002 for reading; and Rost 1990, 2002 for listening.) In Chapter 7 we
present outlines of what seem to be appropriate internal processing models
for each of the four skills.

Obviously, this language processing does not take place in a vacuum, so testers also need to specify the context in which this processing takes place. They need to provide empirically-based descriptions of the conditions under which these language operations are usually performed. Such descriptions of both operations and performance conditions should match target situation use as closely as possible, i.e., they should demonstrate *context validity* (see Weir 1993). In short, a socio-cognitive theoretical model is required which helps identify the elements of both context and processing and the relationships between them.

We have briefly outlined our view of theory-based validity and next we turn to context validity, the second pillar in our definition of construct. We return to these concepts in Chapters 6 and 7 where we try to unpack each in turn and provide categories of description for the elements that make up both. In this way, we hope to establish what we as test developers need to consider in order for us to be clearer about the constructs we are attempting to measure through our tests.

3.2   Context validity

Traditionally described as *content* validity, we feel that the term *context* better accounts for the social dimension of language use. Though we will retain the use of the term *content* in referring to the work of others, in keeping with the socio-cognitive approach to testing advocated in this book we will here refer to the *context validity* of the test tasks.

Concept 3.2   Context validity

Context validity is concerned with the extent to which the choice of tasks in a test is representative of the larger universe of tasks of which the test is assumed to be a sample. This coverage relates to linguistic and interlocutor demands made by the task(s) as well as the conditions under which the task is performed arising from both the task itself and its administrative setting.

Quote 3.2   Anastasi on content validity

Essentially the systematic examination of the test content to determine whether it covers a representative sample of the behaviour domain to be measured.
   Anastasi outlined (p.132) the following guidelines for establishing content validity:

1. the behaviour domain to be tested must be systematically analysed to make certain that all major aspects are covered by the test items, and in the correct proportions;

> 2. the domain under consideration should be fully described in advance, rather than being defined after the test has been prepared;
> 3. content validity depends on the relevance of the individual's test responses to the behaviour area under consideration, rather than on the apparent relevance of item content.
>
> (1988: 131)

We would strongly endorse point 3. It is obviously crucial for a test supposedly targeting specified enabling skills, functional use and/or knowledge areas and the conditions under which these are elicited to establish that the test conforms to the specification, especially if claims are made for this being representative of the domain in question. Actual as well as intended operationalizations are necessary. O'Sullivan *et al.* (2002) provide a detailed example of how Cambridge ESOL is attempting to achieve this for its oral examinations using an observation checklist. Verbal protocol analysis as described by Lazaraton (2002) has a similar intent. See Part 3 for further exemplification of pertinent methodologies.

Achieving context validity is not without its problems, given the difficulty we have in characterizing language proficiency with sufficient precision to ensure the validity of the representative sample we include in our tests, and the further threats to validity arising out of any attempts to operationalize real-life behaviours in a test. The difficulties involved do not, however, absolve us from attempting to make our tests as relevant in terms of context as is possible; see Chapter 6 for ways in which we might address this.

Bachman and Palmer (1996: 23) see test authenticity as 'the degree of correspondence of the characteristics of a given language test to the features of a TLU (target language use) task'. The greater the fit, the more confidence we may have in relating test performance to likely real-life behaviour, given that the test task also meets the demands of the other validities referred to in this Part – for example, theory-based validity and appropriate cognitive processing.

There is a symbiotic relationship between context- and theory-based validity and both are influenced by, and in turn influence, the criteria used for marking which are dealt with as part of scoring validity in our evidence-based framework below. In Part 2 we illustrate how decisions taken with regard to context validity dimensions have important effects on the mental processing that results when candidates perform the tasks in the test situation. For example, in a writing test decisions operationalized in the rubric about addressee, purpose and explicit criteria for marking can have profound effects on the goal-setting and monitoring parts of the executive processing dimension of written production (see Part 2, Figure 5.4 below p. 47). The criteria used in marking (an important element of scoring validity) are an important element of the construct a test is attempting to measure.

Where these criteria are known, they impact directly on both context validity and, through the task, on the meta-cognitive processing at the heart of
theory-based validity. In this view, context validity, theory-based validity
and scoring validity, particularly in terms of marking criteria, are inextricably
linked and together represent attempts to make a test construct valid. In
Part 2 we describe what we need to take into account in a socio-cognitive
approach to test validation at the *a priori* stage. We address the various
elements of context- and theory-based validity that are currently discussed
in the literature. If the test passes the first *a priori* validity hurdle, it is worth-
while establishing its validity against external criteria, through confirmatory
a posteriori statistical analysis. If the first stage, with its emphasis on context-
and theory-based validity, is bypassed, then we should not be too surprised
if the type of test available for external validation procedures does not suit
the purpose for which it was intended.

Further reading

Bachman (1990) gives good coverage of the cognitive aspects of 'construct validity'.
Bachman and Palmer (1996) is an update on Bachman 1990, but with more practical exemplification.
Messick (1989) provides a much referred to and important discussion of validity, if
somewhat opaque in parts.

4
After the Test Event: *A Posteriori* Validity Evidence

4.1 Scoring validity

In Quote 2.5, Alderson (1991a) noted how his students were often confused when they came to deal with internal consistency estimates of reliability and also parallel forms of reliability. He argued that these may be equally well regarded as evidence of validity. You may well ask, 'So, what is reliability? How or does it in fact differ at all from validity?' We propose to use the term *scoring validity* as the superordinate for all the aspects of reliability discussed below in line with the growing consensus that it is a valuable part of a test's overall validity. When referring to specific reliabilities and in quoting the work of others we will retain the traditional labelling.

Quote 4.1   Jones on reliability

Reliability is a word whose everyday meaning adds powerful positive connotations to its technical meaning in testing. Reliability is a highly desirable quality in a friend, a car or a railway system. Reliability in testing also denotes dependability, in the sense that a reliable test can be depended on to produce very similar results in repeated uses.

(2001: 1)

Quote 4.2   Anastasi on reliability

[T]he consistency of scores obtained by the same persons when reexamined with the same test on different occasions, or with different sets of equivalent items, or under variable examining conditions ... [it] indicates the extent to which individual differences in test scores are attributable to 'true' differences in the characteristics under consideration and the extent to which they are attributable to chance errors ... measures of test reliability make it possible to estimate what proportion of total variance of test scores is *error variance* .... Essentially, any condition that is irrelevant to the

---

purpose of the test represents error variance. Thus when examiners try to maintain uniform testing conditions by controlling the testing environment, instructions, time limits, rapport and other similar factors, they are reducing error variance and making the test scores more reliable...
(1988: 109)

Scoring validity concerns the extent to which test results are *stable over time, consistent in terms of the content sampling* and *free from bias*. In other words, it accounts for the degree to which examination marks are free from errors of measurement and therefore the extent to which they can be depended on for making decisions about the candidate.

In the past, advocates of different aspects of validity often found themselves in opposing camps. Each side espoused the rightness of their cause. One side argued for focusing on reliability. They resolutely maintained that without reliability validity is threatened (Loevinger 1957) and that a test that is unreliable can never yield valid inferences from test scores.

The other side argued the case for focusing on other aspects of validity.

Quote 4.3   Various testing authorities on the limitations of reliability

Cronbach (1990: 121) argued that theory- and content-based validity are the qualities that affect the test the most and that without such validity a test and all other criteria including reliability are worthless (Bachman 1990: 289).

Wood (1993: 132) similarly quotes Feldt and Brennan: 'No body of reliability data, regardless of the elegance of the methods used to analyse it, is worth very much if the measure to which it applies is irrelevant or redundant.'

Fred Davidson recently brought the following quotation to the attention of L-Test list serve: 'Despite some exceptional instances, the first logical step in the development of psychometrics seems to be to devise a series of instruments each of which measures something accurately, regardless of what that something may be; and the second, and following step, to discover what that something is.' (J. O'Connor (1934) *Psychometrics: A Study of Psychological Measurements*. Cambridge, Mass.: Harvard University Press, p. xvi)

How does the field regard these concepts in the twenty-first century? In recent years there has certainly been a modification of the polarized view. Following Alderson (1991a), reliability is now increasingly seen as a type of validity evidence (Chapelle 1999: 258) and accordingly we need another superordinate term for it to reflect this. We would suggest that *scoring validity* seems to be the most suitable, and if a test lacks this its validity is seriously threatened. However, while scoring validity is a *necessary* quality of a good test it is by no means *sufficient* evidence of a test's validity and must be balanced in relation to the other aspects of validity. It seems sensible to seek to enhance a test's scoring validity as far as possible without compromising the other validities.

Accepting that scoring validity now merits due consideration along with traditional validities, will any reliability figure do for all administrations of a test? If an Exam Board calculates a reliability figure for this year's test, will it do for next year's as well? Will a figure for this year's June First Certificate in English (FCE) be sufficient for the December FCE as well? The short answer to all these questions is 'no'.

Quote 4.4   Sawilovsky on constraints on reliability estimates

[S]tatements about the reliability of a certain test must be accompanied by an explanation of what type of reliability was estimated, how it was calculated, and under what conditions or for which sample characteristics the result was obtained. (2000: 159)

So when we talk of a test having a specified reliability (as with other validity estimates) we should do so with reference to the scores obtained on that particular version of the test by a specific sample of examinees. Aeroplanes have to be checked before, during and after each flight; the same applies to the language tests we use. The next obvious question is, what types of scoring validity should we address?

Types of scoring validity

Within language testing, much of the literature to do with computing the scoring validity of language test scores has been based on work in educational and psychological testing more generally, e.g., the APA *Standards* between 1954 and 1985. In the new volume of the American Educational Research Association, American Psychological Association and National Council on Measurement in Education *Standards* (AERA/APA/NCME 1999) the revised chapter on 'Reliability and Errors of Measurement' (Part 1, section 2) still identifies the broad categories of reliability which have traditionally been recognized in the field:

- test–retest reliability;
- parallel forms reliability;
- internal consistency;
- marker reliability.

Concept 4.1   Test–retest reliability

One obvious way of demonstrating that a test is measuring ability consistently is to give the same test twice to the same group of learners. The scores obtained by the same persons on the two test administrations are correlated to give a reliability coefficient (see Chapter 9 for the formula for calculating this). This number can range from –1 to +1 on a continuous scale. 0 indicates total lack of reliability or complete inconsistency; 1 is the ideal value and indicates perfect reliability or complete consistency. Popham (1990: 123) notes that 'such stability estimates of test reliability are based on the consistency of a test's measurement over time'. The error variance corresponds to the random changes in performance from the first to the second implementation. If the test were to award the same or very similar score or grade to each learner on both occasions, it would be a consistent – i.e., reliable – measure. Such a test would not be susceptible to random fluctuation in the condition of the examinees or the test environment. Reliability that is demonstrated in this way is known as *test–retest reliability*. It is concerned essentially with the dependability of test scores *over different occasions*.

However, this type of reliability is problematic: for example, the learners' performance on the second occasion is likely to be influenced by their experience on the first occasion with varying amounts of improvement for different individuals; memory may also play a part. Anastasi (1988: 117) points out that the 'nature of the test itself may change with repetition'. For example, in a language test, once inferences have been worked out or the main ideas established or a jumbled text reassembled, the correct response might be reproduced without many of the intervening processing steps. (See also Alderson 1991a for further detailed criticism.)

Anastasi (1988: 117) notes that correlations are likely to decrease progressively the longer the interval, so there may be a number of different correlations obtained dependent on the gaps between various administrations. She suggests that the interval should never be longer than six months between the two administrations and the length of the interval should always be reported. With longer intervals scores are likely to be influenced by intervening experiences or environmental effects.

Given its problems, this type of reliability is seldom carried out and parallel forms reliability is the preferred choice.

Concept 4.2   Parallel forms reliability

The administration of parallel (alternate) forms of a test in independent sessions provides us with alternate-form coefficients. The tests must be as similar as possible in terms of the operations tested and the performance conditions of code complexity, cognitive complexity and communicative demand, i.e., they should meet the same test specifications in every respect. Thus the same language skills/sub-skills would be tested

Concept 4.2   (Continued)

on the same breadth of items and any input would be the same in length, degree of topic familiarity and difficulty level, etc. The tests would have been constructed to be equivalent but not identical. Such equivalent but not identical tests are known as *parallel forms*.

N.B. Case study 4 on ways to establish parallel forms reliability is located in Chapter 11.

The results achieved by the learners on the first parallel form would be compared statistically with the results achieved by them on the second parallel form (the context- and theory-based validities would also need to be comparable). The resulting correlation would be the *parallel forms reliability* of each of the two forms, i.e., it would be an estimate of the extent to which each of the two forms was awarding the same marks as the other. It would tell us how much error variance had resulted due to the content sampling of the two forms. By squaring the correlation we can provide an estimate of the degree of overlap between the two; see Fulcher (2003: 201–3) for discussion of problems of using correlation to determine equivalence. Again, a crossover design would be necessary to avoid a practice effect on the second version.

Though such procedures are not without practical problems and suffer some of the problems outlined for test–retest reliability, exam boards have been the subject of criticism where the parallelness of forms used in and across administrations is not demonstrated. Spolsky (1995) makes this criticism of Cambridge ESOL examinations echoing Bachman *et al.* (1995) and later repeated in Chalhoub-Deville and Turner (2000). Fortunately, advances in statistical sophistication have enabled commercial test providers to address the problem of test equivalence in novel ways.

Concept 4.3   Item-response theory (IRT)

Item-response theory models have become increasingly popular measurement tools in the past 35 years. These models use responses to items on a test or survey questionnaire to simultaneously locate both the items and the respondents on the same latent continuum (or latent space in the case of multidimensional IRT). This enables one to measure individuals on the latent trait defined by the set of items (e.g., ability, attitude, craving, satisfaction, quality of life, etc.) while simultaneously scaling each item on the very same dimension (e.g., easy versus hard items in the case of an ability test, unfavourable versus favourable statements in the case of an attitude questionnaire).

http://www.education.umd.edu/Depts/EDMS/tutorials/Intro.html

Having placed both individual and items on the same scale, one can estimate the probability of a candidate of known ability responding correctly to an item of known difficulty.

By the 1990s the processes used by Cambridge ESOL to produce examination papers included *item-banking* for storing the test materials and constructing test papers with known measurement characteristics (see Weir and Milanovic (eds.) 2003: 91–3 for an extended discussion). An underlying scale is constructed (using IRT analysis) onto which the difficulty of all the test items can be mapped across the five examination levels (from KET to CPE). This is achieved by routine pre-testing of new items alongside items or test components with known difficulty values (i.e., anchor tests). All new items are now calibrated in this way using Rasch analysis, and are put into the item-bank with values linking them to the common scale.

If you want to establish such difficulty estimates by employing Rasch analysis on the items in your own tests, ETA is a good-value, windows-based IRT analysis package, which also provides classical analysis. It is available at http://www.stet.co.uk.

Concept 4.4   Using a latent trait model: Rasch analysis

The purpose of a performance examination is to infer candidate abilities that go beyond the particular sample of tasks, items and judges encountered. Whether the goal is to make reproducible pass/fail decisions or to position candidates according to demonstrated ability, the performance examination must measure candidate ability consistently. This is most efficiently accomplished by using a latent trait model to give examinees an ability estimate which is independent of the current value of individual facet elements, such as judges, tasks and items. Thus candidate ability estimates are comparable regardless of the particular judge or examination encountered.
(Lunz and Wright 1997)

These test construction procedures ensure that tasks selected for a particular examination (such as CPE at Level 5) fall within the specified range of difficulty and achieve the targeted average for the paper as a whole. These procedures help to ensure comparability of difficulty and maintenance of standards across different forms of the paper and between sessions (June–December, etc.). This applies to the Reading, Listening and Use of English components in CPE and takes place *before* the exams are administered.

These papers are also analysed *after* each 'live' administration, prior to the grading. This allows for additional checks to be made on comparability where alternative forms of a component may have been used, e.g., for the Listening test. If necessary, further adjustments can be made at this time, for example, by scaling both versions of the paper to the same mean and standard deviation.

Weir (2003: 50) notes that, for the Speaking and Writing components in CPE, the issue of multiple topics raises different concerns, and other procedures have been developed to deal with the threat to reliability. The element of choice has been retained and is seen as an important consideration in relation to the validity and impact of the examination. However, the choice is carefully controlled and efforts are made to ensure that the tasks are of comparable difficulty, administered under standardized conditions and can be marked effectively by trained raters using task-specific and general rating criteria.

Quote 4.5   Weir on the steps now taken to ensure comparability in Cambridge ESOL productive tasks

All tasks for the Speaking and Writing components are tried out in advance on candidates representing the target range of ability. This allows for problems with the rubric to be adjusted to ensure that candidates understand what they have to do. In the case of the Writing component samples of language produced by candidates can be analysed and fed into the production of materials used to standardize examiners.

- In the case of Writing, the candidates complete two writing tasks, the first of which is obligatory, the second is chosen from 4 other possibilities representing a fixed set of 'genres'. The obligatory task acts as an anchor and helps to ensure that the positive feature of choice does not impact negatively on reliability.
- In the case of the Speaking test, the examination conditions themselves provide a threat to the reliability of the assessment made. The conditions need to be standardized to ensure that appropriate samples of speech are elicited which can be accurately rated. The use of an interlocutor framework helps standardize the language and in particular the questions and prompts used by examiners.
- The introduction of the pair format for all main suite exams, together with a tighter control of the testing format, has addressed many of the problems noted by Bachman and Spolsky. It is now routine practice to collect data in order to estimate rater agreement and to investigate the possibility of differential performance as a result of other features of the procedure, such as the tasks used.
- In order to monitor the relative difficulty of the task-based materials used in each administration of the Speaking tests, data are routinely analysed and, from time to time, experimental studies have also been carried out using G-theory and multi-faceted Rasch studies. These techniques allow the researcher to investigate the influence of tasks compared with other facets of the testing procedure, such as the rater and the rating scale. The evidence suggests that the tasks used randomly on large number of candidates are of comparable difficulty (e.g., in terms of the mean and standard deviation of ratings) and that attention should be concentrated on the assessment conditions and the conduct of the raters.

(2003: 50–1)

Internal consistency coefficients

Concept 4.5   Internal consistency; split-half reliability

Because of the problems associated with parallel forms and test–retest reliability, other measures may be called for. Another form of reliability, known as *internal consistency*, focuses on the consistency with each other of a test's internal elements, i.e., the homogeneity of its test items.

Where the test consists of a number of dichotomous items (0/1 scores), all of which are intended to test the same ability, the performance of the learners on one half of the items can be compared statistically with their performance on the other half. As the items are all intended to test the same ability, both halves should rank the students in the same way. Split-half reliability offers a measure of consistency with regard to content sampling but obviously has nothing to say about the temporal stability of the scores as they result from a single administration of the test.

If the items are administered in order of difficulty, for example beginning with the easiest items and ending with the most difficult, then one half of the test is taken to be items 1, 3, 5, 7, etc. while the other half is taken to consist of items 2, 4, 6, 8, etc. In theory, the learners' scores should be approximately the same on the two halves. Where items relate to the same source, e.g., questions on the same reading passage, the whole group of items should be placed in one of the two halves for as Anastasi points out (1988: 21), if they are placed in the different halves 'the similarity of the half scores would be spuriously inflated, since any single error in understanding the problem might affect items in both halves'.

The scores on the two halves can be correlated. A perfect match in the scores on the two halves results in a correlation of 1.0, while a correlation of 0.7 indicates approximately 50 per cent agreement between the two sets of scores. A reliability estimate of 0.8 is normally considered the minimum acceptable level but we would normally expect something in excess of 0.9 in tests of importance (see Nitko 2001).

Concept 4.6   KR20 and Cronbach alpha

A flaw in the split-half reliability method is that the items in one half may not be equivalent to the items in the other half. It might be possible to split the test into two halves in other ways than that suggested above, but whichever way is chosen may suffer from this or that lack of equivalence between the two halves. The solution to the problem of lack of equivalence between the two halves is to determine the mean of all possible split-half correlations. In this way, the biases of any individual split-halves are substantially ironed out. A simple formula for estimating the mean of all

> **Concept 4.6   (Continued)**
>
> possible split halves is known as *Kuder-Richardson 20*, or simply *KR20*. KR20 estimates of reliability are very widely used. An equivalent formula is known as *Cronbach alpha*. Whereas KR20 may be used where items are simply right or wrong and are scored 1 or 0, Cronbach's alpha may be used where items may be awarded scores on a range, e.g., 0, 1 or 2.
>
> N.B. The procedure for calculating KR20 and other reliability statistics is given in Chapter 9.

Of the three methods for estimating reliability discussed so far, the use of internal consistency coefficients to estimate the reliability of objective formats is most common and to some extent this is taken as 'the industry standard' (e.g., use of Cronbach's alpha or KR20). The fact that these coefficients are relatively easy to calculate means that other estimates are not used as commonly.

Quote 4.6   Hughes on the effects of test size

Other things being equal, the more items that you have on a test, the more reliable a test will be. This seems intuitively right. If we wanted to know how good an archer somebody was, we wouldn't rely on the evidence of a single shot at the target. That one shot could be quite unrepresentative of their ability. To be satisfied that we had a really reliable measure of the ability we would want to see a large number of shots at the target.... The same is true for language testing. It has been demonstrated empirically that the addition of further (independent) items will make a test more reliable.

... Jephthah used the pronunciation of the word 'shibboleth' as a test to distinguish his own men from Ephraimites, who could not pronounce *sh*. Those who failed the test were executed. Any of Jephthah's own men killed in error might have wished for a longer, more reliable test.

(2003: 44)

Cambridge ESOL regularly estimates the internal consistency of the separate components of the examinations using Cronbach's alpha – e.g., for the Reading, Listening and Use of English papers of CPE. However, the use of such *reliability coefficients* as evidence of test quality can be problematic to the extent that the estimated reliability is not a feature of the *test*, but rather of a particular *administration of the test* to a given group of examinees. This means that reliability indices of tests should not be compared simplistically.

Until recently, there was something of a fetish with internal consistency among the professional testing fraternity. In the 1990 Cambridge ESOL FCE/TOEFL comparison study, Spolsky (1995: 340), referring to Bachman *et al.* (1988: 61–2), describes how:

> One of the first questions tackled by Bachman and his colleagues concerned the statistical characteristics of the two test batteries.... There were three potential sources of measurement error. For the objective, discrete-point tests in the reading comprehension paper and for parts of the use of English and listening comprehension papers, the appropriate question was internal consistency. In listening comprehension, classical internal consistency estimates... were very low, so that over half the variance in scores resulted from measurement error. Even for the objective reading comprehension paper the internal consistency was around 0.73.

Does this lowish correlation mean that the exams set by Cambridge ESOL produce less reliable results than, say, those set by ETS, who regularly quote higher internal consistency figures for TOEFL? The answer – as always – is not that simple and statistics may be distorted by a number of factors. Given the restricted ability range of candidates taking each examination in the Cambridge main suite, they are not likely to get the high internal consistency figures that one gets for examinations such as TOEFL or IELTS where the whole range of ability takes a test.

Quote 4.7   Anastasi on problems with correlations

Like all correlation coefficients, reliability coefficients depend on the variability of the sample within which they are found.
(1988: 132)

Quote 4.8   Wood on the sampling problem

[B]ecause the wider ability range of GCSE entries should, *ceteris paribus*, conduce to higher reliability estimates, although that is strictly an artefactual effect since reliability being a correlation, is always influenced by range... with a greater proportion of the ability distribution entering for GCSE than for GCE and CSE combined, higher reliability estimates may be expected.
(1993: 133, 138)

N.B. The GCSE is an examination taken across many subjects by most UK schoolchildren at about age 16.

Candidates of widely ranging ability are easier to rank reliably, and so will produce higher reliability indices than groups that are more equal in level where all the scores tend to bunch together (lower standard deviations and lower variance). As with other Cambridge main suite examinations, the candidates for any particular examination represent a narrow range of ability and this effectively limits estimates of internal consistency reliability. TOEFL and IELTS attract a much wider ability range. CPE is sat by a truncated sample of candidates.

There is a further serious question which might be asked of internal consistency estimates and which takes us back to the earlier reliability/validity debate. Would we want a high internal consistency estimate in all cases? Though one might be expected for a multiple-choice test of knowledge of structure or discrete lexical items in the 5,000-word list it might be rather naïve to assume that skills/strategies such as listening and reading are as unitary (see Urquhart and Weir 1998, Grabe and Stoller 2002, who argue for a partially divisible view of reading). If they are divisible, then high internal consistencies presumably would not be expected in the papers testing these skills.

Quote 4.9   Wood on over-reliance on internal consistency

The plausibility of internal consistency estimates appears to be further compromised by the deliberate efforts made to introduce variety and heterogeneity into examinations. If the principle of inclusion in an examination is to mix modalities and skill requirements and contents so that individual opportunities to respond well are enhanced, why expect internal consistency?
(1993: 138)

It can be argued in the case of the Cambridge ESOL examinations, which employ a wide variety of task-based materials and item types, that very high internal consistency may *not* be an appropriate aim. Cambridge ESOL has always taken construct validity as the starting point, unlike other boards more influenced by the American psychometric tradition. It is interesting to note that TOEFL is now taking a much greater interest in context validity than has hitherto been the case. Whether this will mean an end to the hegemony of reliability (or at least the need to reconceptualize it) remains to be seen.

Task-based exercises, such as those now used in the Cambridge ESOL exams, have been replacing discrete-point multiple-choice items in order to provide far greater authenticity (both situational and interactional: see Bachman and Palmer 1996). However, a consequence of this is that the number of items in some papers may be limited to fit within practical time constraints. This may bring about a small reduction in the estimated reliability using an internal consistency estimate when compared with longer tests using discrete-point items (see Quote 4.6 above). While this estimate might be regarded as on the low side, it may be an unwarranted conclusion when the other qualities of the test are taken into account.

A further question relates to comparison between reported reliability figures on different tests. If the reliability figure for my reading test is 0.75 and my colleague in the same school reports a figure of 0.85 for hers, does that mean my test is bad?

Quote 4.10   Wood on false comparisons

Take a value such as 0.75 which we might regard as on the low side and therefore unsatisfactory. But that would be to jump to conclusions. Only after a coefficient has been compared to those of *equally valid* and equally practical and time consuming tests can such a judgment be made.
(1993: 139)

So far we have looked at the reliability of test scores in terms of the population who sat the test. What statistics can we use if we want to know the reliability of an individual student's score? In other words, how confident can we be in a reported score on the test?

Concept 4.7   Luoma on the use of the Standard Error of Measurement (SEM)

The SEM shows how far it is worth taking the reported score at face value. This can be important especially if individuals are compared on the basis of their scores. If one has a score of 28 and the other a score of 31, the SEM can indicate whether the difference between them is as clear as it may seem. This also applies to band scores, for example a range from 1 to 6. If the scoring is reliable, the SEM can be a fraction of a band score, for example .34. If it is more than one score band, the reliability of the scoring is in need of improvement, as it is only possible to say that the examinee's 'true score is two levels above or below a score that they received. On a scale of six levels, this amount of variation is too much.

It is relatively rare to see the SEM reported for speaking assessments. One explanation might be that reporting it breaks the illusion of accuracy that people have about test scores. At the same time, however, the SEM helps the assessment developers share the responsibility for score variation with score users, as they cannot say that they did not know. It is also a useful quality check for the assessment developers themselves. If the confidence band around the score is too broad, it serves as a cautionary flag that something should be done.
(2004: 183)

Quote 4.11   Anastasi on when to use each reliability measure

[B]eing reported in score units, the error of measurement will not be directly comparable from test to test.... Hence, if we want to compare the reliability of *different tests*, the reliability coefficient is the better measure. To interpret *individual scores* the standard error of measurement is more appropriate...
(1988: 134)

Marker reliability

As well as error variance arising from content sampling or change in conditions over time, there is a third type of error variance arising from the individual scorers involved in the process. If a colleague and I are marking the same writing scripts. I would want to know to what extent we are:

- in overall agreement;
- ranking a group of students in the same order;
- rating individuals at the same level of severity;
- consistent in our own judgements during the whole marking process.

Concept 4.8   Intra-rater and inter-rater reliability

When we are concerned with tests in which samples of writing or speaking are produced, it is the consistency of the markers which needs to be estimated. Markers need to be consistent in two ways: each marker needs to be consistent within himself (*intra-rater reliability*), i.e., given a particular quality of performance, he needs to award the same mark whenever this quality appears, and there needs to be consistency of marking between markers (*inter-rater reliability*), i.e., one marker will award the same mark as another when confronted with a performance of the same quality.

In many tests, two raters are used. In this case, inter-rater reliability is established via correlation, perfect agreement being indicated by a correlation of 1.0. A correlation of 0.9 or above is where we might start to feel comfortable that two markers are rating in a similar fashion (though their levels of marking would still need to be compared). The method for calculating this is explained in Chapter 9.

Quote 4.12   Saville on improving reliability in Cambridge ESOL speaking tests

In the 1990s Cambridge ESOL began a process of introducing the 'Pair format' as the standard format for the Speaking Tests in which an interlocutor and an examiner both assess the performance.... This approach enhances the reliability of the test as it means that the marks awarded to a candidate derive from two independent oral examiners; this increases fairness and allows the question of the accuracy and consistency of the ratings to be addressed, e.g., estimates of inter-rater reliability.

Traditional estimates of the accuracy and consistency are calculated using correlations, both inter- and intra-rater. These may be obtained operationally where double-ratings are used or by experimental methods. However, the interpretation of such correlations as estimates of reliability can be as problematic as other reliability coefficients. We know for example that correlations of this kind are affected by the nature of the rating scale used and by the range of ability of the candidates who are assessed. When the ability range is narrow, small differences between examiners can affect the correlations which are obtained; this may on first inspection make the test seem unreliable whereas in practice it may not truly reflect the accuracy of the *classification* which is made (an important consideration for criterion referenced tests). In other words, the accuracy and consistency of the classification may be acceptable even though the inter-rater correlation is not high.

(2003: 72–3)

In order to account for features affecting estimates of marker reliability in speaking and writing tests, it is now common to use sophisticated IRT statistical models. For example, Multifaceted Rasch (MFR) analysis may be applied. MFR has clear importance for detecting inconsistent individual marker behaviour both over time and in comparison with other markers (see Chapter 9 for a full description of MFR in practice).

Once steps have been taken to establish that reliabilities are achieved to an acceptable standard, there is the further area of grade awarding to be considered (see Chapter 9 for further discussion of this procedure).

Once scores and grades have been finalized, it is possible to evaluate the test along a range of *a posteriori* dimensions. It is to *criterion-related validity/reliability* and to issues of *consequential validity* and *impact* that we now turn.

4.2   Criterion-related validity

Concept 4.9   Validity evidence beyond the test itself

For theory-based and context validity, knowing what the test is measuring is crucial. There is a further type of validity which we might term criterion-related validity where knowing exactly what a test measures is not so crucial. This is a predominantly quantitative and *a posteriori* concept, concerned with the extent to which test scores correlate with a suitable external criterion of performance (see Anastasi 1988: 145, Messick 1989: 16) with established properties.

However, Moller (1982) points to the problems in establishing sufficiently valid criterion measures against which to correlate (see also Bachman 1990: 249–50, Oller 1979: 51).

> **Concept 4.9   (Continued)**
>
> There is a danger in a validation study of this type that one might be forced to place one's faith in a criterion measure which may in itself not be a valid measure of the construct in question. One cannot claim that a test has criterion-related validity because it correlates highly with another test, if the other test itself does not measure the criterion in question.

Criterion-related validity divides into two types: concurrent and predictive. *Concurrent validity* looks for 'a criterion which we believe is also an indicator of the ability being tested' (Bachman 1990: 248). Test scores could be correlated with another measure of performance, usually an older, longer, established test, taken at the same time or teachers' rankings of students, or even student self-assessment.

Teachers are often very familiar with their students and collect daily evidence of their language abilities in the classroom. They thus have a very broad frame of reference for estimating their relative performance levels. To the extent that one can depend on the reliability of the teachers' judgements and of the test, correlations between the two are potentially informative of the validity of the test. However, Alderson *et al.* (1995) and Weir (1983a) point to the low estimates that correlations with teacher and student assessments are likely to yield.

Criterion-related validity is also relevant for the Association of Language Testing in Europe (ALTE) foreign language (FL) examinations, but in this case the development of the five-level system, benchmarked to specific performance criteria at each level, provides the external criterion. It is this 'level' system, which provides the interpretative frame of reference for all the exams in the suite. In the case of performance, qualitative comparisons can be made between the criterion norms and samples of the output from the exam (e.g., in writing or speaking).

In the case of *predictive validity*, it may be that in certain circumstances the predictive power of the instrument is all that is of interest. If all one wants is to make certain predictions about future performance on the basis of results, this might entail a radically different test from that where the interest is in providing information to allow effective remedial action to be taken. However, it soon becomes clear that if we were to make judgements about the validity of a test for the purposes it was intended, notions of validity posited mainly on predictive and concurrent studies would not be enough, especially given the problematic nature of examining these. Establishing predictive validity through correlating language performance against later job/academic performance is often not possible, because of practical difficulties in mounting tracer studies and the problems associated with confounding intervening variables (see Banerjee 2003 for a review of predictive validity, and Davies 1990: 3–4).

4.3 Consequential validity

We have argued for a view of validity as unitary with theory-based, context- and criterion-related validation processes all having a part to play in contributing evidence in respect of the interpretation of test scores. Messick puts the case for a further component of the process of establishing validity.

Quote 4.13 Messick on consequential validity

The questions are whether the potential and actual social consequences of test inter-pretation and use are not only supportive of the intended testing purposes, but at the same time are consistent with other social values. Because the values served in the intended and unintended outcomes of test interpretations and test use both derive from and contribute to the meaning of test scores, the appraisal of social consequences of testing is also seen to be subsumed as an aspect of construct validity.... For a fully unified view of validity, it must also be recognized that the appropriateness, meaning-fulness, and usefulness of score based inferences depend as well on the social conse-quences of the testing. Therefore social values and social consequences cannot be ignored in considerations of validity.

(1989: 18)

Concept 4.10 Green on the nature of backwash in language testing

... Backwash is distinguished from test impact by Bachman and Palmer (1996) who, with McNamara (1996), Hamp-Lyons (1997) and Shohamy (2001) place it 'within the scope of impact' (ibid: 30). While impact may occur at a 'macro' or social and institutional level, backwash occurs only at the 'micro' level of the individual participant (primarily teachers and students)....

Backwash is considered a 'neutral' term (Alderson and Wall, 1993 and 1996) which may refer to both (intended) positive (Bachman and Palmer, 1996; Davies et al. 1999) or benefi-cial (Buck, 1988; Hughes, 2003) effects and to (unintended) harmful (Buck, 1988) or negative effects (Bachman and Palmer, 1996; Davies et al. 1999; Hughes, 1989).

Backwash is broadly defined as 'the effect of a test on teaching' (Richards, Platt and Platt, 1992) and often also on learning (Hughes, 2003; Shohamy, 2001). It has also been variously associated with effects on teachers, learners (Buck, 1988; Messick, 1994; Shohamy, 2001), parents (Pearson, 1988), administrators, textbook writers (Hughes, 2003), instruction (Bachman, 1990; Chapelle and Douglas, 1993; Weigle, 2002), the classroom (Buck, 1988), classroom practice (Berry, 1994), educational practices and beliefs (Cohen, 1994) and curricula (Cheng, 1997; Weigle, 2002), although for Hughes (2003) and Bailey (1999), the ultimate effects on learning outcomes are of primary concern.

(2003: 6–8)

Alderson and Wall (1993) caution that although the test may influence the content of teaching this may not be uniformly positive (see Green 2003) and, more critically, tests may have little impact on methodology – how teachers teach. Cheng (2004) found a similar situation following the exam reforms in Hong Kong, but her research clearly demonstrates that if new training is not provided, we should hardly find it surprising that old methodologies persist.

Messick (1996) further cautions that even if teacher behaviour is influenced by a test, this does not mean learners' behaviour is also influenced. It is the enhancement of learning itself that is true impact, the effects on teaching are only an intermediate stage towards this. For Bailey (1996: 228), it is the involvement of the learners in the process through self-assessment that is critical to achieving positive washback as well as transparency of assessment criteria.

Hamp-Lyons (1997) has argued for consideration of the effects of tests on society as a whole as well as on individuals and the education system. She sees washback as 'one form of impact' and sees impact as 'pervading every aspect of our instruments and scoring procedures' (p. 299). She suggests that 'we should evaluate our test instruments from the perspective not only of the test-setter but also of the other stakeholders', and identifies five categories of test stakeholders:

- Learners
- Teachers
- Parents
- Government and official bodies
- The marketplace

As well as the usefulness of test results for the principal stakeholders there is the question of ethics in eliciting and using such data.

Test impact and washback studies can play an important role in ensuring ethical language testing is achieved (cf. International Language Testing Association [ILTA] Code of Ethics) and in helping tests to meet some of the even stronger demands of the *critical language testing* view (Shohamy 2001). At its extreme, this view tends to see tests as instruments of power and control as, intentionally or not, biased, undemocratic, unethical and unfair; their main impact being the imposition of constraints, the restriction of curricula, providing disciplinary tools for implementing political agenda, and the possible encouragement of boring, mechanical teaching approaches.

Shohamy (1993: 37) argues that 'Testers must begin to examine the consequences of the tests they develop...often...they do not find it necessary to observe the actual use of the test.' Similarly, Messick (1996: 247) questioned whether 'the scores have utility for the proposed purposes in the applied settings. Are the short and long term consequences of score interpretation and use supportive of the general testing aims and are there any adverse side effects?'

Weir (2001) points out that in recent years there has been an unfortunate tendency to link language testing to summative evaluation; as a result, the important formative capacity of testing in the classroom has often been overshadowed. The increased expectation that providers of educational services should be made accountable to external bodies for the impact of their work has been a powerful driving force behind this. It has encouraged a swing from viewing tests as instruments for assisting in the development and improvement of student language ability to treating them as indicators of performance for outside agencies. The formative dimension of testing has been marginalized.

The formative focused types of tests they need for these purposes may differ radically from those available for summative assessment (see Weir 2001 for discussion of this point). The former needs to be structured in such a way that diagnostic profiling is readily available from test results. Informing teachers that student X achieved an 'A pass' but Y received a 'D fail' in terms of some vague, general overall proficiency does not even tell them about relative strengths and weaknesses in the four macro-skills. Moreover, teachers really need even more focused information than this. For example, in reading they need to know whether problems in reading occur in expeditious, or in careful, readings skills and strategies, and preferably at an even more precise level than this within each area.

Our concern in this book is to equip you with the knowledge you need to develop and evaluate such formative tests in the classroom and to critically scrutinise the summative instruments provided by examining boards. To this end you need a test validation framework to understand and operationalize validity in its various manifestations. In Part 2 of the book we map out such a framework.

Further reading

Cheng (2004) looks at the backwash effect of new English examinations in Hong Kong and contains useful methodological tools for doing this.

Green (2003) looks at the backwash effect of IELTS and provides an excellent review of the literature on backwash.

Hughes (1988a) provides a convincing example from Turkey of where an EAP test had a positive backwash effect on the teaching that preceded it.

Hughes (2003) provides informative and accessible introductions to validity, reliability and washback in language testing.

Kunnan (1998) is a useful collection of papers on validation particularly the paper by Hamp-Lyons and Lynch which looks for the emergence of new interpretive perspectives on validity that take language testing beyond the traditional modes of inquiry of the positivist/psychometric paradigm.

Nitko (2001) provides a useful and accessible discussion of reliability in education assessment.

Shohamy (2001) provides a stimulating, critical, if fairly one-sided, radical view of the power of tests.

Wall (2004) looks at the effects of backwash of the O level English examination in Sri Lanka.

Weir and Milanovic (2003) offer a detailed account of the exam practices adopted by Cambridge ESOL over the last century in respect of these aspects of validity.

Language Testing (Vol. 13, No. 3, 1996) is a special issue devoted to washback in language testing.

Language Testing (Vol. 14, No. 3, 1997) is a special issue devoted to ethics in language testing.

The International Language Testing Association has developed a code of ethics, which can be found at http://www.dundee.ac.uk/languagestudies/ltest/ilta/ilta.html.

Part 2

New Frameworks for Developing and Validating Tests of Reading, Listening, Speaking and Writing

Introduction

In Part 1 we discussed the key elements of a validation framework that test developers need to address to ensure fairness:

- Context validity
- Theory-based validity
- Scoring validity
- Consequential validity
- Criterion-related validity

In Part 2 we describe in detail the characteristics of each of these and, where appropriate, exemplify them in relation to actual test examples or practice. In this way we hope to enhance your competence in evaluating, and also designing, appropriate tests and test items.

First we present diagrammatic overviews of our framework in relation to the four macro-skills of reading, listening, speaking and writing (Figures 5.1–5.4). These are intended to provide a map for the more detailed descriptions of each characteristic in the frameworks that follow in Chapters 5–10. The intention is to show graphically how the pieces fit together temporally as well as conceptually. The arrows indicate the principal direction(s) of any hypothesized relationships: what has an effect on what. The timeline runs from top to bottom: before the test is finalized, then when it is administered, and finally what happens after the test event. We feel the temporal sequencing for thinking about validity is helpful as it provides you with a map of *what* should be happening in terms of validation and just as importantly *when*.

Thus as well as *a priori* (before-the-test event) validation components of context and theory-based validity we also include *a posteriori* (after-the-test event) components of scoring validity, consequential validity and criterion-related validity. The pictorial representation offers a view on how the different types of validity evidence fit together.

We no longer polarize reliability and validity (see Chapter 4) but see these as part of a unified approach to establishing the overall validity of a test. To locate reliability more centrally in the validation process we find it helpful to use the term *scoring validity* as the superordinate for the reliability and other statistical attributes listed in this box in the frameworks below.

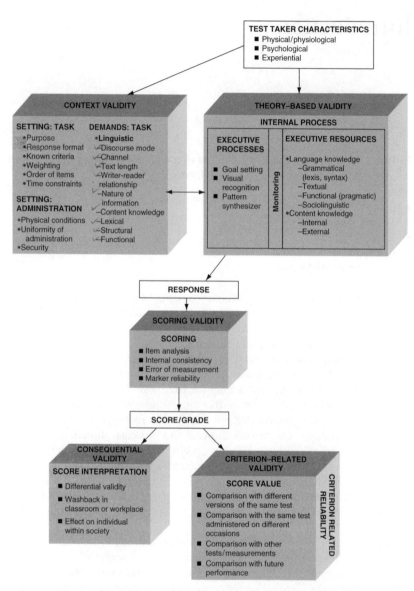

Figure 5.1:   A Socio-cognitive Framework for Validating Reading Tests

Scoring validity seems apt as an umbrella term as we are concerned with the validity considerations that arise at the point in time of the testing process where performances on test tasks are translated into scores. At the time of scoring we are primarily concerned with the reliability of marking.

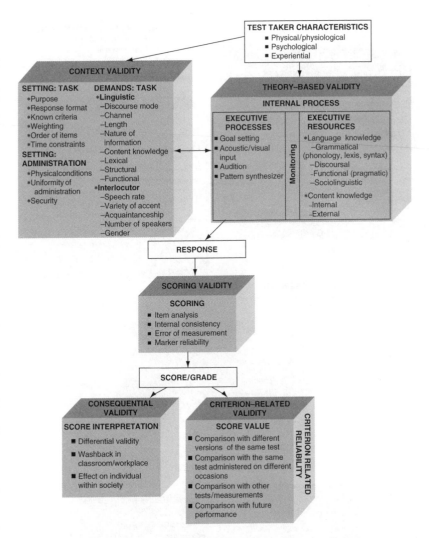

Figure 5.2: A Socio-cognitive Framework for Validating Listening Tests

In addition when dealing with reading and listening tests at the scoring stage we also consider internal consistency matters as well. Interestingly, this tells us retrospectively just as much about the construct we have measured as the scoring process itself. We include it here because it is only when the test is scored that we can consider the internal consistency elements of a test and explore its other important statistical attributes. Once the scores are finalized they can be used to examine *a posteriori* external issues of consequential and criterion-related validity.

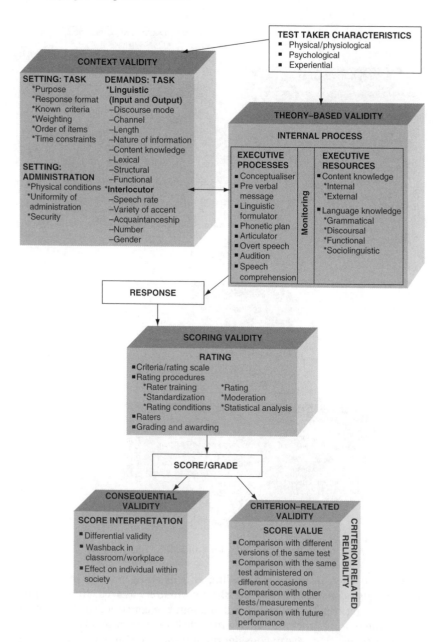

Figure 5.3:   A Socio-cognitive Framework for Validating Speaking Tests

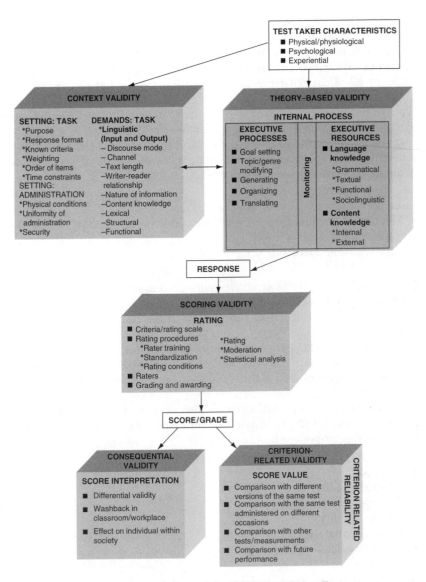

Figure 5.4: A Socio-cognitive Framework for Validating Writing Tests

The more comprehensive the approach to validation, the more evidence collected on each of the components of this framework, the more secure we can be in our claims for the validity of a test. The higher the stakes of the test the stricter the demands we might make in respect of all of these.

We have provided a separate framework for each macro-skill, but there is obviously a good deal of overlap between the four, particularly within the 'receptive or productive' skills. The contents of the boxes on test taker characteristics, consequential and criterion-related validity are generic, i.e., the same for all skills. What the individual brings to the test can be treated under the same descriptive categories. We need to consider the impact of all types of test on the individual within society and we also need to establish external criteria to shed further light on how fair our tests are.

Real differences emerge in the theory- and context-based elements in the different modes. However, even here there is obvious commonality in terms of a number of categories of description:

- Linguistic resources available to candidates
- Linguistic demands made on them: lexical/structural/functional/discoursal
- Task demands
- Administrative elements

In the scoring validity box the elements overlap because we can look at internal reliability/validity of items for listening and reading as well as the marker reliability which is crucial for evaluating the productive skills of writing and speaking.

This conceptual framework will be supplemented in Part 3 by a description of the activities and instruments that can be employed to provide empirical evidence in respect of each of the components of the frameworks in a variety of research studies.

In Chapters 5–7 and 9–10 below we discuss each of the elements of the four frameworks for test validation (listening, speaking, reading and writing) under the six component headings:

- Test taker
- Context validity
- Theory-based validity
- Scoring validity
- Consequential validity
- Criterion-related validity/reliability.

We argue that test developers or users need to address all the following general questions:

- How are the physical/physiological, psychological and experiential characteristics of candidates addressed by the test?
- Are the contextual characteristics of the test task and its administration situationally fair to the candidates?

- Are the cognitive processes required to complete the tasks interactionally authentic?
- How far can we depend on the scores on the test?
- What impact does the test have on its various stakeholders?
- What external evidence is there that the test is doing a good job?

The description of each element covered by these six areas is then followed by a specific question we should always ask of our own tests and those of any commercial test we enter students for. This may seem a demanding exercise but failure to do so may adversely affect the fairness of the tests students are exposed to. It is very much like the surveys one finds in consumer magazines such as *Which?* in the UK where the criterial attributes of, for example, television sets are listed and then a range of different televisions are presented and rated in terms of each criterion. The discerning shopper would do well to consult such reviews before purchasing a television. Commercial exams can likewise be considered as products for sale and should be subjected to similar scrutiny in terms of the criteria we discuss below.

You may be wondering why we have not included practicality in our model. Our heretical view (and certainly not one shared by Exam Boards) is that practicality is simply not a necessary condition for validity. Only when sufficient validity evidence is available to justify interpreting test scores as an acceptable indication of the control of an underlying construct should we concern ourselves with practicality. If practicality is allowed to intrude before such evidence is available we run the risk of not assessing what we want to. The convenience of the method should not be allowed to subvert the measurement of the construct. As in all research we need to know what we are looking for first before we select the most appropriate methods for doing the evaluation. We should not consider method before trait. Practicality considerations are often allowed to intrude at too early a stage and validity is often threatened rather than enhanced as a consequence.

5
Test Takers

The test taker box in the frameworks above is directly connected to the theory-based validity box because these individual characteristics will directly impact on the way individuals process the test task set up by the context validity box. Obviously, the tasks themselves will also be constructed with the overall test population and the target use situation clearly in mind as well as with concern for their theory-based validity.

In Chapter 10 we will consider consequential validity where one of the criterial areas we are concerned with is test bias. When we are considering test results we need to be clear that no group bias has been occasioned by the test in respect of these test taker characteristics. Methods of investigating this are discussed in Case study 5 in Part 3, for example, by using personal data collected at the same time as test administration and comparing this with test results. Test takers' characteristics may prove to be important moderator variables in so far as they affect test performance significantly.

O'Sullivan (2000) provides a useful synthesis of a fairly disparate literature on test taker characteristics that have the potential to affect test performance. His overview is detailed in Concept 5.1.

Concept 5.1   O'Sullivan on test taker characteristics

Physical/Physiological	Psychological	Experiential
Short-term ailments *Toothache, cold, etc.* Longer-term disabilities Speaking, hearing, vision *(e.g., dyslexia)* Age Sex	Personality Memory Cognitive style Affective schemata Concentration Motivation Emotional state	Education Examination preparedness Examination experience Communication experience TL country residence

Characteristics of the Test Taker

In this table, Physical/Physiological characteristics can be seen in terms of:

Concept 5.1   (Continued)

- Short-term ailments, such as a toothache or earache, a cold or 'flu, etc. – by their nature these illnesses are unpredictable and are not normally relevant to the construct, and
- Longer-term illnesses or disabilities, such as problems with hearing, vision e.g., dyslexia, or speaking – either speech defects such as a stammer or lisp, or a deformity of the mouth or throat which affects production; or by other attributes such as age or sex.

The characteristics listed under 'Psychological' are ordered to suggest that there will be some that are unlikely to change to any great extent with time; while others will be more or less likely to change within particular individuals (this list represents an admittedly anecdotally derived continuum).

Experiential characteristics are seen as being comprised of all those influences that have essentially come from outside of test takers, and refer to:

- Their education.
- Their experience of the examination in question – in terms of having prepared through a course of study for example, or having taken the examination on a previous occasion.
- Their experience in communicating with others, particularly in the target language, but may also refer to L1 communication – this would be of particular concern where, for example, younger learners are expected to interact in the TL with a partner who is unknown to them, something they may rarely have done in their own language.
- The final characteristic referred to may be connected to this idea of communication, in that it is more likely that a learner will experience reduced anxiety having lived for some period of time in the TL country or culture.

(2000: 82–3)

O'Sullivan argues that it is important that we are aware of characteristics of test takers, such as age, sex and education so that test tasks can be framed in this knowledge and bias for or against a particular group can be avoided.

5.1   Physical/physiological characteristics: making accommodations

Individuals may present special needs that have to be catered for, e.g., they may be partially sighted candidates or dyslexic. It is now a legal requirement in some countries, e.g., in the USA, that such candidates are accommodated. In the UK, exam boards such as UCLES attempt to make appropriate special provisions once decisions have been made on the acceptability of a request for an accommodation.

Quote 5.1   Taylor on special arrangements at Cambridge ESOL

Major categories of special arrangements across the Cambridge ESOL tests are:

- Braille Versions
- Enlarged Print Versions
- Hearing-impaired (lip-reading) Versions
- Special Needs Listening Test Versions
- Separate marking for candidates with Specific Learning Difficulties
- Exemption from Listening or Speaking components

Other categories include: extra time, a reader/amanuensis, blue paper/overlay for dyslexic candidates.

An application from just one learner with a disability may lead to provision of several different special arrangements. For example, a visually impaired candidate is likely to require not only a specially modified test paper – Braille or enlarged print – but also:

- separate facilities for taking the test or test battery;
- an individual invigilator as well as a reader/amanuensis on the day;
- permission for extra time to complete their papers.

(2003: 2)

A question must remain for end-users of the results: if the conditions for the performance of a task are altered too much, can one generalize to performance in the real world in the same way as if the conditions had not been altered, i.e., to what extent has the construct been altered?

Does the test make suitable accommodations for candidates with special needs?

5.2   Psychological characteristics: affective schemata

Quote 5.2   Alderson on motivation in reading tests

Reading might be tested within a content-focused battery: texts that carry meaning for readers, that interest them, that relate to their academic background, leisure interests, intellectual level and so on, might motivate a deeper reading than the traditional, relatively anodyne or even contentless texts.
(2000: 29)

A test taker's interest or motivation may affect the way a task is dealt with. Affect can help or hinder performance. Given that we wish in most cases to 'test for best', steps must be taken to make test events as positive as we can in the full knowledge that some stress is perhaps unavoidable.

Quote 5.3   Fulcher on psychological effects in speaking tests

Berry... has undertaken extensive research into the interaction of introvert and extrovert students, and found that discourse varies according to the pairing. She has found that both introverts and extroverts performed better when placed in homogeneous pairs. Whereas in mixed pairs introverts did not perform as well as extroverts. Further, the performance of introverts is affected more depending on the degree of extroversion of the partner. Nevertheless, both introverts and extroverts performed better in a paired test than they did in a one to one interview.
(2003: 188–9, referring to Berry 1993)

Factors such as preferred learning styles or personality type may have an influence on performance. Extroversion/introversion might be addressed in the pairing of candidates. The Royal Society of Arts Communicative Use of English as a Foreign Language (CUEFL) examination allowed candidates to choose the person they would like to interact with in the spoken language examination (see Hawkey 2004). Beyond this, most exam boards take the view that a candidate's psychological characteristics will affect their real-life performances in similar ways so such variables are left well alone. However, it seems unlikely that in the test event much can be done to cater for individual differences in these respects except to put the candidates at their ease as far as is possible.

In what ways does the test put candidates at their ease?

5.3   Experiential characteristics: familiarity

Every attempt should be made to ensure that candidates are familiar with the task type and other environment features before sitting the test proper. The degree of a test taker's familiarity with the demands of a particular test may affect the way the task is dealt with. Specimen past papers and clear specifications should help alleviate any differences in this respect. Handbooks for candidates with exemplification of tasks and procedures should be readily available (for downloadable examples see Cambridge EFL Examinations http://www.cambridge-efl.org.uk/exam/index.cfm. and TOEFL homepage http://www.toefl.org/).

With the onset of computerization it might, where appropriate, be useful to establish that differences in performance are not occasioned by an individual's familiarity with and competence in using the computer. Taylor *et al.* (1998) carried out an extensive study for ETS on candidate's familiarity with IT equipment and effects on performance in preparation for the new computerized version of TOEFL (see Part 3, Case study 2 for further discussion on how this might be investigated).

Test preparation courses may also have an effect. To the extent that candidates are prepared for the linguistic and meta-linguistic demands of the test this is positive, but if the test lends itself to test taking strategies that enhance performance without a concomitant rise in the ability being tested then there must be some concern (see Green 2003 for an extended discussion of this in relation to the writing component of the IELTS).

As well as the candidate, we need to consider carefully the test tasks themselves and we now turn to this in Chapter 6.

Are the candidates sufficiently familiar with what they have to do in the test?

Further reading

No single book deals with the issues of test taker characteristics covered in this chapter.

Alderson and Urquhart (1985) look at the effect of background academic discipline on performance in a reading test.

Angoff (1989) deals with investigation for context bias in TOEFL.

Berry (1993) looked at personality characteristics as a potential source of test bias.

Chapelle (1988) looks at field independence as source of variation in test performance.

Chihara *et al*. (1989) deal with background and culture in EFL reading comprehension.

Clapham (1996) deals with effects of background knowledge on reading test performance.

Green (2003) surveys background variables and their effect on performance in IELTS.

Kunnan (1995) looks at test taker characteristics and effects on performance.

Ryan and Bachman (1992) use DIF to investigate bias in proficiency tests.

Swinton and Powers (1980) look at the effect of L1 on performance.

6
Context Validity in Action

The last decade of the twentieth century saw a general decline in the prestige of psychometric, statistically-driven approaches to testing. In its place there has been a growing interest in the importance of *context*, in defining domain of use *performance* conditions and *operations*.

Quote 6.1 Weir on context

The important role of context as a determinant of communicative language ability is paramount. The context must be acceptable to the candidates and expert judges as a suitable milieu for assessing particular language abilities. The conditions under which tasks are normally performed should obtain as far as is possible in a test of these abilities. A conscious effort should be made to build into tests as many real-life conditions as are feasible and considered criterial by the test writers and their peers.

If the test tasks reflect real-life tasks in terms of important contextually appropriate conditions and operations it is easier to state what a student can do through the medium of English. . . . unless steps are taken to identify and incorporate such features it would seem imprudent to make statements about a candidate's ability to function in normal conditions in his or her future target situation.

(1993: 28–9)

Every attempt should be made within the constraints of the test situation to approximate to situational authenticity (see Douglas 2000, O'Sullivan 2004). Full authenticity of setting is obviously not attainable in the classroom or the language test, but the settings selected for testing and teaching should be made as realistic as possible in terms of as many criterial contextual features as possible. Most teachers are teaching language for eventual use for real-life purposes under real-life conditions. We should attempt to maximize the involvement of these use domain features.

We first look at the setting under which the test activity takes place, starting with those elements normally to be found in the task rubric.

6.1 Task setting

Rubric

The instructions given to candidates will determine their responses to a particular test. The test tasks should be unambiguous, giving a clear indication of what the examiner is asking. No candidate should be able to misinterpret the task. The test rubric should be candidate-friendly, intelligible, comprehensive, explicit, brief, simple and accessible. The rubric should not be more difficult than the text or task. In monolingual situations where complex instructions are involved it is preferable to give them in the candidates' first language though there may be strong views against this in some countries. It would be difficult, however, to argue that a test should aim to test comprehension of a rubric. With computerization it is now often possible to select the language you wish the instructions to be in (see DIALANG at: http://www.dialang.org/).

Example Item 1

Unscramble the jumbled letters below to form English words:
MEAX
GMAEUZ
TAC
ALAVGI

Here the instructions are potentially more difficult than the items. In addition they are ambiguous as the candidate may infer that he or she is to form as many words as he or she can from each set of jumbled letters. Khalifa (2003: 73) suggests a number of questions which might be asked of a rubric:

- Is the rubric clear on what students have to do?
- Is the rubric written in as short as possible, simple sentences?
- Is the rubric grammatically correct?
- Is the rubric spelled correctly?
- Is the rubric in the First Language (L1) or the Target Language (TL)?
- Is the rubric familiar to the students?
- Is the rubric clear about the amount of time to spend on each part of the task?
- Will the task require different types of response? If so, it may be necessary to provide separate specific instructions for each type of response required.

Is the rubric accurate and accessible?

Purpose

Test takers should be given a clear unequivocal idea in the rubric of what the requirements of the task are so that they can choose the most appropriate strategies and determine what information they are to target in the text in comprehension activities and to activate in productive tasks. Having a clear purpose will facilitate *goal-setting* and *monitoring*, two key meta-cognitive strategies in language processing which we will discuss under theory-based validity. For example, if the students see the questions before a reading/ listening task the activity becomes more purposeful and planning and execution is likely to be enhanced (see 'theory-based validity' in Chapter 7 below; and Brindley 1998 and Buck 1990, for support for this view). There is a symbiotic relationship between the choices we make in relation to purpose and the processing that results in task completion.

Quote 6.2   Weigle on designing appropriate tests

[It] is clear . . . that the writing needs of different groups of second language learners are quite varied in terms of both cognitive demands and communicative function. In developing appropriate writing tests for these different populations then, it will be important to keep these differences in mind.
(2002: 12)

Writing tasks in tests can be referential (intended to inform) or conative (meant to convince or persuade) and, less frequently, emotive (intended to convey emotions or feelings) or phatic (to keep in touch) (see Weigle 2002 for a discussion of these types). Weigle also details how writing for these purposes can be further categorized according to three different levels of cognitive processing: reproduction, organizing known information and generation of new ideas and information. We will return to these in Chapter 7 on theory-based validity when we deal with the cognitive processing involved in knowledge telling and knowledge transformation in writing.

In a writing task, the rubrics are the directions to the reader of what is required by the task. The way the prompt is worded can influence significantly what the candidate does, i.e., what s/he perceives the purpose of the task to be. An ambiguous term like 'discuss' is open to multiple interpretations without further categorization (see Evans 1988 for an interesting study on this). The test writer has to make it clear which version of 'discuss' is intended. A further problem arising from the wording of the prompt occurs in the following example of an IELTS-type writing task from IELTS specimen materials quoted in Moore and Morton (1999):

> Present a written argument or case to an educated non-specialist audience on the following topic.

'The first car appeared on British roads in 1888. By the year 2000 there may be as many as 29 million vehicles on British roads.

Should alternative forms of transport be encouraged and international laws introduced to control car ownership and use?'

Moore and Morton (1999) found in their research on the current IELTS writing task that the way the prompt is worded, e.g., words such as *should* in the rubric, encourages candidates to adopt a hortatory style, relatively rare in university writing. It prompted candidates to comment on the desirability of a given course of action or state of affairs rather than offer the balanced argument normally expected by the target academic discourse community. They observed a restricted range of functions resulting from the IELTS Writing Task 2 compared with the diversity of functions in university academic writing tasks. In university tasks, summarization and description, comparison, explanation and recommendation are often required as knowledge is transformed from external sources into an assignment. In the essay test above it is more a case of knowledge telling. It may be the case that:

> writing in a hortatory mode, of its nature, may not require the same amount of background knowledge that is needed to deal with topics of an epistemic nature.... The prominence given to hortation in IELTS Task 2 items is probably attributable to certain test specific exigencies, this feature nevertheless represents a substantial difference in the nature of writing in the two domains... (Moore and Morton 1999: 95)

So decisions taken in terms of purpose in the task design and also in terms of input will have serious effects, not only on the processing in writing, in this case between knowledge telling and knowledge transformation but also will affect the functional resources that will be stimulated in executive processing (see the section on writing in Chapter 7 below). The work of Hamp-Lyons (1991) clearly demonstrates that we need to be extremely careful in the selection and wording of the prompts we use in our writing tasks, not only in general, but also in relation to the needs and background knowledge of the candidates.

In the case of reading we may often read something just because it looks as though it might interest us – for example, an article about a country or a place we have visited or intend to visit; conversely, we may choose not to read something because it does not appeal to us. At other times it may not be interest that is the deciding criterion but rather the assumed usefulness of the text. If we buy something that comes in kit form, we often read the accompanying instructions on the reasonable (though usually misguided) assumption that they will help us to put the thing together. These categories of interest and usefulness are not mutually exclusive and we may read things that we need to read that are also interesting in themselves.

Most people process written text for a purpose; this may be for pleasure in the case of a novel or to find out how something works, as in a car instructions manual. Reading for a purpose provides motivation, in itself an important aspect of being a good reader.

Quote 6.3   Grabe and Stoller on motivation

These results provide a strong argument for the importance of motivation. Motivation directly impacts the amount of reading done.... Amount of reading in turn, influences reading comprehension activities. Perhaps more importantly, motivation also strongly predicted reading comprehension abilities as students become more fluent readers. (Grabe and Stoller 2002: 121)

In reading tests we need to match purposes to appropriate text types and vice versa. Here is a list of some text types and possible reasons for reading them:

ADVERTISEMENT	to see if something is worth buying
ARTICLES	to find information for an assignment
BIBLIOGRAPHY	to find a reference to an article or book
BOOKS FICTION	to gain pleasure
BOOKS NON-FICTION	to extract specific details or main ideas
BROCHURE	to find out specifications of a product
FORM	to find out what information is wanted
GUIDE	to find out where something is
INDEX	to find a page reference
INSTRUCTIONS	to find out how to put an object together
LEAFLET	to find out how to make something
LETTER	to see whom it's from and what it's about
MAP/PLAN	to find your way
NEWSPAPER	to find out what's happening in the world
POSTCARD	to find out whom it is from
TEXT MESSAGE	to find out who wants to contact you
TIMETABLE	to find out the time of departure

The purpose of a reading activity will determine the operations performed on it. If the purpose is to go quickly through a passage to extract dates and figures, or through an index to find a page reference, then scanning is likely to be the type of reading called for. To establish the author's attitude to a topic might demand closer careful reading. To get information for a university assignment might involve expeditious search reading of several articles and/ or books with careful reading kicking in when appropriate information is located. To establish the general gist of an article to decide if it is worth reading you might skim it quickly. The cognitive processing underlying these different types of reading is discussed in Chapter 7.

In constructing tests it is important to include texts and activities that mirror as closely as possible those that students have been exposed to and/or are likely to meet in their future target situations. The purposes for reading them in the test should, wherever possible, match the purpose(s) for reading those texts in real life. The purposes for reading involved in our tasks should be as appropriate as we can make them. We recognize the difficulty in achieving full authenticity of purpose in the test situation but would nevertheless wish to make our test tasks as realistic as possible.

In a spoken language test the purpose of the speakers will help to define the structure and focus of the interaction, as well as some outcome towards which the participants will be required to work. It is highly unlikely, however, that any one test can accommodate the wide variety of conditions and operations that different situations might demand. It may be that appropriately differentiated tests where feasible might need to be made available for evaluating different groups of candidates with different target situation needs. Air traffic controllers may require a different test from doctors. It might be easier to give them both the same tests but the consequences might be disastrous.

The test writer needs to make it clear to candidates why they are doing the task (beyond demonstrating ability in a variety of features of spoken language). A good example of this was found in the test for overseas doctors administered by the General Medical Council in Britain (the PLAB test). Candidates might have to give a correct diagnosis on the basis of information provided by another doctor, or elicit crucial symptoms from a patient before suggesting a particular course of action. In every sense there is a real purpose for these activities that matches very closely what they will have to do in real-life interaction.

Achieving such realism in tests for general English students may not be so easy, but the emphasis must still be on giving the interlocutors as realistic, and as needs-based a purpose as possible. Full authenticity of task may not be achievable, but we need to make our tests as valid as possible if we are to measure anything of value. The more we compromise the more difficult it will be to make meaningful statements about what candidates can or cannot do on the basis of test results.

Is the purpose of the test made unequivocally clear for the candidate?
Is it an appropriate purpose?

Response format

Quote 6.4   Alderson *et al.* on response technique

The response format [test method] used for testing language ability may itself affect the student's score.... Since the effects of the response format tend to be unpredictable, it can be a potential source of construct-irrelevant variance. The best advice that can be offered is ensure that more than one response format for testing any ability is used. (1995: 44–5)

The effects of different formats on processing need to be investigated. When we look at the assessment formats we might select on the basis of context- and theory-based validity in Chapter 8 we will examine a number of appropriate formats in more detail. Here we merely wish to make the point that the choice you make about format will critically affect the cognitive processing that the task will elicit, i.e., it will affect theory-based validity. You have to be certain that the technique you choose does not adversely affect the cognitive processing you would want to occur to answer the tasks you set. We will look at a format whose shortcomings in terms of method effect are well documented and we will leave those techniques that are less susceptible to creating a method effect until Chapter 8.

There are obviously differences occasioned by using Multiple-Choice Questions (MCQ) as opposed to short-answer questions (SAQ) (see Weir 1990). A multiple-choice test item is usually set out in such a way that the candidate is required to select an answer from a number of given options, only *one* of which is correct. Despite their earlier pre-eminence in the psychometric–structuralist era (see Chapter 1), there is now considerable doubt about the validity of MCQ items as measures of language ability. Hughes (2003: 75–8) lists the following problems associated with MCQ:

- The technique tests only recognition knowledge.
- Guessing may have a considerable but unknowable effect on test scores.
- The technique severely restricts what can be tested.
- It is very difficult to write successful items.
- Backwash may be harmful.
- Cheating may be facilitated.

The scores gained in MCQ tests, as in true–false tests, may be suspect because the candidate has guessed some or all of the answers. A candidate might get an item right by eliminating wrong answers – a different skill from being able to choose the right answer in the first place. If the answers are provided in this format, we can *never* say whether a candidate would have got the item right without this assistance. The distracters present choices that otherwise might not have been thought of. It would seem likely that the cognitive processing involved in determining an answer in this format bears little resemblance to the way we process texts for information in real life, and to the extent that this is the case, they may be considered deficient in terms of theory-based validity. When we look at theory-based validity in action in Chapter 7, we need to consider whether the cognitive processing occasioned by the use of such tests is too far removed from real-life processing (see Nevo 1989, Wu Yi'an 1998, Farr *et al.* 1990 for interesting research studies on the process of taking MCQ tests, and Part 3, Case study 2 for ways you might investigate whether response format makes a difference).

Is there any evidence that the test response format is likely to affect the test performances?

Known criteria

As well as having a clear idea of what they are expected to do in the task and how to set about it, candidates should be given a clear idea of how they will be judged. The criteria by which their answers will be judged also need to be made apparent, for example, if accuracy is important in answering comprehension questions, this must be made clear. This information should be available to candidates and their teachers prior to the examination.

Published information about how the tasks are scored, including criteria for correctness, steps used for scoring and how the item scores are combined into the test score, should be readily available. If certain criteria are not to be used in the marking, this will have an effect on both *planning* and *execution* mechanisms in the cognitive processing involved in task completion. If mechanical accuracy is not counted in a writing task, you would be wasting your time worrying about this in planning and *monitoring* your output with regard to this.

There seems little justification for penalizing candidates in constructed response reading and listening tests (e.g., short-answer questions) for errors in their answers of a mechanical nature (punctuation, spelling) in so far as these errors are not interpretable as a semantically incorrect answer. This is even more the case when candidates are not warned of such punitive marking schemes and cannot set the monitor accordingly.

Are the criteria to be used in the marking of the test explicit for the candidates and the markers?

Weighting

Weighting is concerned with the assignment of a different number of maximum points to a test item, task or component in order to change its relative contribution in relation to other parts of the same test. If different parts of the test are weighted differently, then the timing or marks to be awarded should reflect this and be evident to the test takers so that they can allocate their time accordingly in the goal-setting phase of processing (see Chapter 7 for discussion of this). Candidates would be well advised to allocate their time and attention in accordance with the weighting of a particular task. Similarly, if any of the marking criteria are to receive differential weighting (see the discussion of Test of English for Academic Purposes in Weir 1983a, 1988c), then candidates need to know this and allocate time and attention for monitoring their output accordingly.

While it might be easier to determine a differential weighting at the task level (writing an essay is perhaps more important than writing a postcard) it is less so for individual items on more discrete point tests, say of vocabulary and grammar. In what way is an item testing the present continuous more or less important than one testing the present perfect?

Are any weightings for different test components adequately justified?

Order of items

We need to consider closely the order the questions should come in. In the past many reading tests were a hotchpotch of items testing different skills and strategies requiring recourse to different parts of the text in a seemingly random fashion. As we shall see in Chapter 7, careful reading is normally carried out in a linear, incremental fashion as a picture of the whole text, and its macro-propositions are built up serially through an understanding of the micro-propositions in the first sentence, then the next, and so on. So in a test of careful reading, it is usual for questions in a text to follow a serial order as the evidence suggests that this is the way we construct meaning, i.e., incrementally (see Kintsch 1998, Urquhart and Weir 1998).

Furthermore, we shall argue in Chapter 7 that in a reading test it may be beneficial to separate into distinct 'testlets' those items focusing on expeditious, quick and efficient reading strategies from those catering for more intensive careful reading skills. Within the expeditious reading section (see Urquhart and Weir 1998) we might also wish to separate surveying for gist from scanning for specific information. The order of items in each section must reflect the way such skills and strategies are deployed in normal processing for the particular reading purpose. Careful reading requires a linear sequencing of questions whereas scanning (expeditious local) permits of random access into the text. In a search reading or scanning test we want candidates to look for semantic or exact word equivalents in a whole text. Serial ordering of questions would progressively reduce the difficulty level of the exercise. If you know the questions are in order you would naturally not go back over what you had covered for the previous questions. There is an argument for randomizing the items in tests of these strategies.

In the case of a listening test, the items should ask for information in the same order in which it occurs in the passage; if not, it may confuse test takers, which could lead to unreliable performance (see Buck 2001: 119, 138). In a speaking or writing test there may be logical or affective reasons for the order in which tasks occur.

Are the items and tasks in a test in a justifiable order?

Time constraints

> **Quote 6.5 Alderson on speed**
>
> Timed readings, especially in computer-based test settings, might provide useful diagnoses of developing automaticity, and thought needs to be given to measuring the rate at which readers read, as well as to their comprehension of the text. Speed should not be measured without reference to comprehension, but at present comprehension is all too often measured without reference to speed.
> (2000: 30)

In testing reading and listening it is important to consider the time constraints for the processing of text and answering the items set on it. The test developer has to sequence the texts and tasks, and ensure there is enough time allowed for all activities; if time allotment is not carefully planned, it may result in unpredictable performance. In a listening test there needs to be sufficient time between questions to allow for processing and writing of answers. If too much time is given in a reading test or is not strictly controlled per section, candidates may simply read a passage intensively, and questions designed to test ability to process text expeditiously (i.e., selectively and quickly) to elicit specified information may no longer activate such operations (see Weir *et al.* 2000 for an example of a research project where this happened). If time is more than sufficient in an expeditious reading task then careful cumulative, linear processing rather than quick selective processing will result. Decisions relating to timing clearly impact on the processing and hence on the theory-based validity of our test tasks. With computerization it will be easier to control the amount of time spent on each task in a reading test by preventing candidates going back to earlier tasks or spending more than the suggested time on any one activity. This should facilitate the testing of expeditious reading.

Can the tasks be answered satisfactorily in the time allowed? In non-speeded tests, a reasonable amount of time must be provided for the majority of the test takers to be able to complete the task. If too little time is made available, stress will result and we will not be eliciting the student's best performance. It must be clear to candidates how much time should be spent on each part of a test. The amount of time should also reflect the importance of this ement in the part of the course or the domain being tested. Where feasible, setting appropriate time limits is best done empirically. In other words, you should trial a test on a small similar group to get a reasonable estimate, or relate to similar tasks that have been taught during a course.

The time to be spent on each task should be clearly indicated on the test paper and the invigilators should encourage students to comply with the instructions.

In writing we are also concerned with time available: the speed at which processing must take place, the length of time available to write, normal time constraints, whether it is an exam or an assignment to hand in, and the number of revisions or drafts allowed, i.e., the process element. Outside of examination essays, in the real world, writing tasks would not be timed at all and students would be allowed maximum opportunity and access to resources for demonstrating their writing abilities. There are, as we know, many difficulties in fully replicating reality. Considerations such as time constraints, scoring validity and test security requirements make longer, process-oriented tests impractical in most situations (see Chapter 7 for discussion of this in relation to portfolio assessment).

The texts we get candidates to produce obviously have to be long enough for them to be marked reliably. If we want to establish whether a student can organize a written product into a coherent whole, length is obviously a key factor. As regards an appropriate time for completion of product-oriented writing tasks in an actual examination setting, Jacobs *et al.* (1981: 19), in their research on the Michigan Composition Test, found that a time allowance of 30 minutes probably gave most students enough time to produce an adequate sample of their writing ability.

It had been thought in the past that time-restricted test tasks are only a limited representation of what writers usually do in creating written discourse and that it could not lead to work that was representative of anyone's best capabilities. Interestingly, Kroll (1990: 140–54) reports on research comparing the essays written in class under pressure of time and essays written at home over a 10–14-day period. Her results suggest that in general, time does not buy very much for students in either their control over syntax – the distribution of specific language errors being remarkably similar in both – or in their organizational skills. However, no process data were collected on the take-home tasks and there remains the possibility that these were left to the last minute and completed hurriedly.

In tests of speaking, different issues relating to time also present themselves. Normal speech takes place under time pressure. In England, only a relatively limited amount of silence is tolerated (in other countries, e.g., Finland, there may be far greater tolerance of silence between turns) and smoothness of execution is often seen as evidence of fluency in the language. If it took an inordinate amount of time for a customer at a ticket sales counter to say what he or she wanted, the other customers in a long queue behind might

well feel that the condition of normal processing was not being met,
react accordingly. Giving prominence to normal time processing in language
tests might encourage more practice in operating under this important condition in the language classroom.

It will also make a difference to what is said if the speaker has time to
prepare in detail, as against having to speak spontaneously. It is possible to
distinguish between long and short speaking turns. Short turns are more
common; usually more spontaneous, loosely strung together phrases, rather
than neat sentences. Long turns, e.g., oral presentations or lectures, by definition require more planning decisions, and thus often tend to be more
prepared. In tests where long turns are a feature, a decision has to be made
as to how much planning time candidates should be allowed: three months,
30 minutes, two minutes, etc. In the Institute of Linguists English examinations, candidates were given a period of months to prepare for the oral
presentation and invariably this was the part of the speaking test they did
best on.

Foster and Skehan (1996) explored the effect on learners' performance (in
accuracy, complexity and fluency) of a series of tasks (personal, narrative
and decision-making) performed under three different planning conditions
(no planning, unguided planning and guided planning). This research illustrates the effects due to different planning conditions with no planning in
most cases proving the least helpful to candidate performance. Different
types of planning also had variable effects.

Planners produced more accurate performance than the non-planners,
and the most accurate performers of all were the *unguided* planners. Foster
and Skehan interpret their results to suggest that the guided planners did
indeed make the task they were doing more complex, in contrast to the
unguided planners, who were hypothesized to have used preparation time
to rehearse language. The guided planners, then faced with a more complex
task, could not achieve the same degree of accuracy as the unguided planners, who had given themselves an easier task to do.

Response level

Quote 6.6   Norris *et al.* characterize time conditions as response level

Response level addresses the extent to which an examinee must interact with input in
an *on-line* or real-time sense. In order for response level to be considered as playing a
central role in the difficulty of a given task, successful task performance must require
the examinee to process task-essential information in a relatively immediate manner.
Thus, tasks that involve a substantial amount of planning time for the central communicative act would be considered less difficult according to this variable (and would
therefore receive a minus). However, any task that requires relatively immediate
production in response to any form of input or stimulus would be considered more

difficult according to the response level variable. Although such difficulty could be authentically reduced in certain tasks (e.g., where repeated listening is a possibility), the reality of most listening tasks is that they require *on-linedness* from the listener. Listening comprehension in authentic communicative situation often poses an immediate demand.
(1998: 81–2)

Is the timing for each part of the test e.g., preparation and completion appropriate?

6.2   Task demands

Discourse mode: writing

This includes the categories of genre, rhetorical task and patterns of exposition.

Quote 6.7   Weigle on genre, rhetorical task and patterns of exposition in writing

The genre refers to the expected form and communicative function of the written product; for example, a letter, an essay, or a laboratory report. The rhetorical task is broadly defined as one of the traditional discourse models of narration, description, exposition, and argument/persuasion, as specified in the prompt, while the pattern of exposition...refers to subcategories of exposition or specific instructions to test takers to make comparisons, outline causes and effects, and so on.
(2002: 63)

In writing tests, increasing the number of samples of a student's work that are taken can help reduce the variation in performance that might occur from task to task. We know that student performance will vary even on very similar tasks as well as when writing in different discourse modes. This argues for sampling students' writing ability over a number of tasks, typical and appropriate to their discourse community. This will give them the best chance of showing what they can do. Setting candidates more than one task has obvious implications for test practicality, particularly in terms of time.

Obviously, there can be more than one task in a test and validity judgements will relate to the whole test rather than an individual task. Validity has been found to increase by sampling more than one composition from each candidate, and there is a widespread feeling that the performance on one writing task is not representative of a candidate's general writing ability (see Hamp-Lyons 1991). In general it is felt advisable to take at least two samples (see Jacobs *et al.* 1981: 15).

The more samples of a student's writing in a test, the more reliable the assessment is likely to be and the more confidently we can generalize from performance on the test tasks. As in comprehension tests, the validity of a test score tends to increase as the number of items in the test is increased, provided each sample gives a reasonable estimate of the ability. We obviously cannot elicit samples of all the operations that candidates may have to perform, even in a closely specified EAP situation. Therefore, we must make every effort to ensure that the tasks we set and the conditions we build in to our tests are as representative and as criterial as possible in the practical context obtaining. We certainly cannot rely on one sample if important decisions are going to be made on the basis of evidence provided by the test.

Discourse mode: reading

Quote 6.8   Urquhart and Weir on choosing appropriate discourse modes

Test developers decide what text types are appropriate for a particular test population through needs analysis of the students' target situations, and careful examination of the texts (and tasks) used in other tests and teaching materials aimed at the target population. The texts should be reasonably authentic. In other words, they should either be taken from the target-language use situation, or possess salient characteristics of target-language use texts.

The relationship between text type and operations being assessed is important. In reading tests for example, if scanning is the focus then collection of description texts containing lots of factual detail are likely to be more suitable than argumentative. Conversely if main ideas are the focus then argumentative texts are likely to contain more macro-propositions than texts full of specific details, i.e., descriptive.

(1998: 141 *et seq.*)

Quote 6.9   Alderson on text features of different genres

Knowing how texts are organized – what sort of information to expect in what place, as well as knowing how information is signalled and how changes of content might be marked – has long been thought to be of importance in facilitating reading. For example, knowing where to look for the main idea in a paragraph, and being able to identify how subsidiary ideas are marked, ought in principle to help a reader process information. However, there has been surprisingly little empirical research into readers' knowledge of the text features of particular genres, and its relationship to reading process or product.

(2000: 39)

Depending on the purpose of the test and the intended target audience, criteria for text selection will vary:

- In achievement reading tests you will have a number of parameters already established, i.e., the text types you have used with the students.
- If you are writing a proficiency test such as an English for Academic Purposes (EAP) reading test, then you will need to identify what is appropriate for the audience in their future target situation and select texts accordingly.
- If you are looking for an article for science students, you might wish to find one that has an introduction, a methods section, a results section, an analysis section and a discussion section as these would seem to be salient features of much scientific article discourse.
- If you were writing a test for arts, humanities and social science students you might select texts which expound a conventional view and then suggest modifications, criticisms of, or challenges to this established view and end with a clear conclusion.

Whatever type of text you need to select, there are a number of organizational features that should be taken account of:

- The way a text is structured would seem to affect the ease with which it is processed (see Williams and Moran 1989: 220). Coherent text is easier to understand at the main ideas level than incoherent text, as any teacher marking essays will attest to (see also Kintsch and Yarborough 1982 for evidence of how organization aids global processing). One would ideally like texts in tests to be clearly sequenced or have a clear line of argument running through it. We appreciate that real life does not always meet these demands but feel, that in tests, the failure of the writer shouldn't mean the reader is held to account.
- One would perhaps also look for texts which are *clearly organized* into sections as this will enhance the writing of test items on surveying for gist and understanding the main ideas where these are the focus.
- Other organizational features at the levels of grammar, cohesion and rhetorical structure need to be suitable for the intended candidature (see Williams and Moran 1989: 218–20 for an extended discussion of these; also Alderson and Urquhart (eds.) 1984).

The bottom line is whether the reading text is appropriate for the specific operation(s) you want to test

- Has the text got sufficient and varied specific details where this is the focus of the test, e.g., a scanning test?
- Has the text got enough main ideas (important points), where this is the focus of the test, e.g., a careful reading test?
- Does it have pieces of information that can be linked together, where inferencing is the focus of the test?

- Does the text have a very clear, organized structure (key words, obvious topic sentence) for testing skimming and search reading? Text should have surface-level information. Ideas should be explicit. Students should not have to read between the lines.

Examples of different texts for reading are provided in Chapter 8 and these illustrate clearly that different text types lend themselves more readily to testing different skills and strategies.

Discourse mode: speaking

Quote 6.10   Johnson and Tyler on difference between conversation and interview

The analysis of this model OPI interview shows the salient features of natural conversation involved in turn taking and negotiation of topic are not present.
(1998: 47)

In spoken discourse there are important differences between the more formal interview between a student and the examiner and a conversation between peers (see van Lier 1989 for an extended discussion of this and Chapter 8 for examples of these techniques). The functional range elicited may differ markedly between the two, as well as features such as *reciprocity* in taking the responsibility for the interaction, and in the interview examiners may respond to the interviewee in ways which would not be deemed acceptable in natural conversation – for example, challenging the candidate's point of view.

Concept 6.1   Reciprocity in spoken interaction

Reciprocity conditions are concerned with the dimension of interpersonal interaction, the relation between speaker and listener. The concern here is with who has speaking rights and with the sharing of responsibility in the maintenance of an interaction. The degree of reciprocity/participation in a developing interaction varies, depending on whether it is a lecture, interview, conversation, etc. In some situations, such as a formal lecture, only the speaker normally has speaking rights and takes on almost total responsibility for keeping the speech going. In a conversation, normally both speaker and hearer have speaking rights, rather than the speaker alone. In an interview situation in a test, we normally find that the examiner dominates the conversation at least in terms of agenda management: initiation of discussion, continuance and completion.

In a reciprocal exchange the speaker must adjust vocabulary and message to take the listener's reactions into account. This process affects all participants involved in an interaction in that they share the responsibility for making communication work, with the consequence that each participant may be required to be flexible in communication.

In most speaking situations, the person we are speaking to is in front of us and able to put us right if we make a mistake. He or she can also generally show agreement and understanding – or incomprehension and disagreement. Speakers have to pay attention to their listeners and adapt their messages according to their listeners' reaction. If the listener signals that they have perfectly well understood, it would be odd if the speaker persisted in explaining.

Clearly, if we wish to test spoken interaction, a valid test must include reciprocity conditions. This contrasts with the traditional interview format in which the interviewer asks the questions and the interviewee answers. So if we are interested in the candidate's capacity to take part in spoken interaction, there should be reciprocal exchanges where both interlocutor and candidate have to adjust vocabulary and message and take each other's contributions into account. This means that the candidate must be involved in the interaction to a greater extent than that of merely answering questions. It is worth noting that there may well be cultural problems here with some candidates, as what might be appropriate in terms of this condition may well vary from culture to culture. The co-constructed nature of the discourse in conversation, as against interview, may in itself be a variable that we must start to address in evaluating such joint performances.

Is the discourse mode appropriate for the skills or strategies being tested?

Channel of communication

The channel for the communication can have an obvious impact on the performance in a speaking test. For example, it may place greater burdens on candidates if they have to simulate a telephone conversation with an interlocutor in a different room, as against carrying out a face-to-face conversation in the same room. It may be crucially important – say, for air traffic controllers or business people – that they can cope with spoken interaction whilst being denied face-to-face contact.

In the input to a writing task graphs or charts are sometimes employed in an attempt to equalize the knowledge base required to complete the task and also to save time as compared to processing verbal input. It may be that the additional difficulty for processing that such multi-tasking involves explains the negative attitude some candidates have to this type of input especially among arts and humanities students at tertiary level. Work on the effect of multiple input on performance in speaking tasks indicates that increasing the types and number of written inputs is likely to add to code complexity and make processing the task more difficult. It may be that this also helps to explain why students perform better on listening tests based on simple audio input than on video-based tests.

Again, one has to resort to the demands that will be placed on candidates in the future target situation to inform judgements on the condition that should obtain. This information is usually available from the tester's own experience of the target situation, but should always be checked out with reliable informants, or failing that, through some limited form of empirical needs analysis.

Decisions would have to be made on the nature and amount of *non-verbal information* that is desirable, e.g., graphs, charts, diagrams, etc. In addition, the layout or even the typeface may merit careful consideration.

Is the channel appropriate for the target situation requirements of the students being tested?

Text length

Johnston (1984: 151) noted that the texts employed in reading comprehension tests tended to be many and brief and this trend has continued to this day. A simple comparison of texts on the old ELTS test with its replacement IELTS illustrates the point. TOEFL to date has focused on even shorter multiple texts but this situation is designed to change when the revised TOEFL appears in 2005. An interesting comparison can be made with the Test of English for Educational Purposes (TEEP) (Weir 1983a) designed to test academic English, where texts of over 1,000 words were used to test expeditious reading skills on the grounds that this was more representative of real-life demands than the length of texts (relatively speaking) used in many exams for similar purposes (e.g., ELTS and TOEFL). Engineer (1977) had found that by using texts greater than 1,000 words in length you can measure different abilities, for example, discoursal rather than syntactic or lexical. The Language Training and Testing Centre (LTTC) examinations from Taiwan (see Chapter 8 for examples of these) are also noteworthy in their use of longer texts, necessary because of their desire to test expeditious as well as the conventional careful reading.

The trade-off is between incurring potential topic bias from using single longer texts as against multiple short texts, and an obvious gain in both situational and interactional authenticity from using the longer text.

Crucially, we want to know in comprehension tests whether the text allows you to write the number and type of questions you need. This includes a number of considerations: if texts are too short in reading tests, you may not be able to test skimming or search reading strategies, you may only be able to test intensive careful reading.

Quote 6.11   Buck on texts for listening

[I]n listening longer texts tend to require discourse skills, whereas shorter texts tend to focus more on localized grammatical characteristics.
(2001: 123).

Weir *et al.* (2000) surveyed the various lengths of texts undergraduate students were exposed to in China, and found 'Clear evidence emerges from the needs analysis that a variety of text types are met by the majority of students. Almost all are exposed to extensive as well as intensive reading. Most have to read at least chapters from books which can be up to 3000 words in length.'

As well as the type of skills and strategies, the length of texts enables you to test, there must be a serious question mark whether a few items on a number of small texts (c. 250 words) enable us to generalize to a student's ability to cope with the amount of reading, say in academic study. Coping with the vast volume of reading was clearly established by Weir (1983a) as a major difficulty for students in tertiary level study in the UK. Recent illuminative work by Banerjee (2003) in this area suggests that the situation may have altered little in twenty years on. It is clear that many Exam Boards (with the notable exceptions of LTTC in Taiwan and Test for English Majors, TEM, in China) still choose to ignore this fact.

Text length potentially has an additional effect in terms of the executive resources that will be called into play in cognitive processing. In general, the longer the text candidates are presented with, the greater the language knowledge that might be required to process it. If short texts are not making the demands on these resources that will occur in normal cognitive processing, theory-based validity is compromised.

Is the text length appropriate for the target situation requirements of the students being tested?

Nature of information in the text

Whether the information in the text is abstract (ethics, love, etc.) or concrete (the objects in a room, for example) is relevant to the appropriateness of the test. Both types may of course be present in the same text. Abstract information may in itself be cognitively as well as linguistically more complex and more difficult to process.

Is the type of information appropriate for the target situation requirements of the students being tested?

Content knowledge required

The content knowledge required for completing a particular task will affect the way it is dealt with. The relationship between the content of the text and the candidate's *background knowledge* (general knowledge which may or may not be relevant to content of a particular text which includes cultural knowledge) and *subject matter knowledge* (specific knowledge directly relevant to text topic and content) needs to be considered (see Douglas 2000). It is this interaction between the executive resources of the candidate and those demanded by the task, which once again emphasizes the symbiotic nature of context- and theory-based validity.

Concept 6.2   Douglas's definition of a test of specific purposes

One in which test content and methods are derived from an analysis of a specific purpose target language use situation, so that test tasks and content are authentically representative of tasks in the target situation, allowing for an interaction between the test taker's language ability and specific purpose content knowledge, on one hand, and the test tasks on the other. Such a test allows us to make inferences about a test taker's capacity to use language in the specific purpose domain.
(2000: 19)

Quote 6.12   Urquhart and Weir on background and content knowledge

There is a considerable amount of experimental evidence in L2 reading that background knowledge can play the part envisioned for it in (reading) theory. Bernhardt (1991) gives an extensive list of studies.... The majority of studies she cites were successful in showing the reader's familiarity with content had a significant effect on their performance.
(1998: 63)

The text should be suitable in terms of genre, rhetorical task(s) and pattern(s) of exposition and at an appropriate level of specificity, and should not be biased or favour one section of the test population. In those situations where we are writing tests for heterogeneous groups of students, we are by necessity forced to select texts with a wider appeal than is the case when we have a more homogeneous group. In EAP testing this leads us to areas such as health education, study skills and habits, ecology, etc.

The content of a text should be sufficiently familiar to candidates so that candidates of a requisite level of ability have sufficient existing schemata to enable them to deploy appropriate skills and strategies to understand the text (see Urquhart and Weir 1998: 143). A text should not be so arcane or so unfamiliar as to make it incapable of being mapped onto the reader's existing schemata. As Alderson (2000: 29) argues: 'every attempt should be made to allow background knowledge to facilitate performance rather than allowing its absence to inhibit performance'. Neither should a text be *too* familiar as then there is a danger that the candidate will be able to supply some or all of the answers from his existing knowledge store. Candidates should not be able to answer questions without recourse to the text – what Buck (2001: 126–7) labels for listening testers as the need for 'passage dependency'. This should be checked, whichever of the formats for testing reading are employed.

In writing, choosing topics is the teacher's most responsible activity. This applies to testers as well. It is necessary to ensure that students are able to write something on the topic(s) they are presented with. The task we set candidates should be seen by these writers as realistic, appropriate and feasible if they are to attend to the topic as intended (see Hamp-Lyons 1990: 53). If a task is seen as unrealistic, inappropriate or impossible, then candidates will not perform to the best of their abilities and may challenge or ignore the task. There is clear evidence (Read 1990) that different topics elicit responses that are *measurably* different. This raises the further issue of whether to allow a choice of topics, for it too could affect the validity of the test.

According to Jacobs *et al.* (1981: 1), it is generally advisable for all students to write on the same topics because allowing a choice of topics introduces too much uncontrolled variance into the test. Their research raised the issue of whether observed differences in scores are due to real differences in writing proficiency or occur as a result of the different topics. They conclude that there is no completely reliable basis for comparison of scores on a test unless all of the students have performed the same writing task(s). Moreover, reader consistency in evaluating the test may be reduced if all the papers read at a single scoring session are not on the same topic.

By basing writing tasks on written and/or spoken text supplied to the candidates or on non-verbal stimuli, it is possible to ensure that in terms of subject knowledge all start equally, at least in terms of the information available to them. In addition, Campbell (1990) suggested that practice in reading-into-writing tasks is beneficial later in academic writing, but refers to difficulties this integration may cause when done under time pressure.

In general, then, all students should write on the same topic and preferably more than one sample of their ability should be measured. Where possible they should all be in possession of common information. So we need to ask:

- Is the topic within the students' likely age group experience and level?
- Is the topic suitable for every student? The topic should not be biased in any way (in terms of urban/rural, boy/girl, cultural, etc.).
- Are there any unsuitable topics such as war, death, politics and religious beliefs that may offend or distress some students? These should be avoided.

- Is there too great an assumption of cultural knowledge in the topic? There should *not* be.
- The topic of the text should be unseen but familiar, though not too familiar to the students, i.e., the text should be unseen but students have an existing schema (organized mental framework) for the topic.
- Is the style of dialogue/passage familiar to the students? Type of the text should be similar to those in the textbook, e.g., description, narrative, argument.

Is the topic content appropriate for the target situation requirements of the students being tested?

Input/output

Material may be provided in a test task for the candidate to use in order to produce an appropriate response, for example a reading text on which to base a written performance. Such input may be verbal, non-verbal or a combination of these:

- text illustrations or photographs (e.g., a picture of a room with people in it);
- spoken (audio, video, live);
- written text or written symbols.

The evidence for the effects of reading into writing is mixed and this demands further research (see Lewkowicz 1997, Weigle 2002: 68).

If provision of stimulus texts reflects the real-life situation and ensures a balance of content knowledge across candidates, then there is a strong case for providing such input in writing tests though there is emerging evidence that it does present problems for markers in making decisions about what level of borrowing from these texts is permissible; the issue of plagiarism. Weigle (2002: 68) refers to research showing evidence of heavy reliance on the language of the source text and also notes a concern that the provision of a text results in less developed ideas than when none is provided.

As well as the task demands discussed so far in this chapter, candidates may have to process input text/discourse in both receptive and productive tasks, as well as produce it as output in the latter. We have now to consider a further set of linguistic variables, which are applicable to both task input and task output where appropriate.

Lexical

Texts with more high-frequency vocabulary tend to be easier than texts with more low-frequency vocabulary. In listening, low-frequency lexical items are less likely to be recognized or more likely to be misheard (see Bond and Garnes 1980).

For lower-level general English students we need to look at the *range of language forms* candidates can be expected to handle. Does the input or output text require knowledge of too many unknown lexical items? For higher-level English for Specified Purposes (ESP) students we need to examine whether the lexical range is appropriate in terms of common core, technical and sub-technical vocabulary.

Are the lexical items in the test both in input text and required as output appropriate for the level of the candidates?

Structural

Listener familiarity with a speaker's preferred syntactic patterns may influence understanding at a global level. A speaker's use of long, complex syntactic constructions, more characteristic of written style, may prevent the listener from using 'normal' syntactic expectations for understanding spoken language (see Rost 1990: 49–50).

Alderson (2000: 37) refers to the 'importance of a knowledge of particular syntactic structures, or the ability to process them, to some aspects of second language reading.... The ability to parse sentences into their correct syntactic structure appears to be an important element in understanding text.' Recent work by Shiotsu (2003) evidences the importance of syntactic knowledge in explaining variance in tests of reading administered to Japanese undergraduates.

Texts with less complex grammar tend to be easier than texts with more complex grammar. Berman (1984) considers how opacity and heaviness of sentence structures sometimes may lead to increased difficulty in processing.

Are the grammatical items in the text both in input text and required as output appropriate for the level of the candidates?

Functional

Function is a term used to describe the illocutionary force of what is said. Examples of communicative functions might be where a speaker has to persuade, advise, describe, etc. (see O'Sullivan *et al.* 2002). As well as the organizational and propositional facets of a text, the test writer needs to take into account its functional purpose, the effect intended by the writer of the text. Do we need to include a variety of texts with different functional purposes? One normally improves the validity of a test by increasing the number of passages and items, but this obviously conflicts with the concern of practicality.

Are the functions in the test both in input text and required as output appropriate for the level of the candidate?

Quote 6.13 Alderson on the interaction among these linguistic variables

[T]he language of texts would seem, *prima facie*, highly relevant to the testing and assessment of reading. The interesting thing about much of the research is that a common-sense assumption proves too simplistic, and that identifying text variables which consistently cause difficulty is a complex task. Clearly at some level the syntax and lexis of texts will contribute to text and thus difficulty, but the interaction among syntactic, lexical, discourse and topic variables is such that no one variable can be shown to be paramount.
(2000: 70–1)

Alderson's caveat is well taken and the dearth of multivariate L2 componential studies of reading comprehension is highlighted by Shiotsu (2003). His study confirms the important contribution both syntax and vocabulary knowledge make to reading comprehension along with the speed of lexical semantic access.

However, if we recognize the need to consider these factors even in isolation from each other in text selection then a start has been made.

Interlocutor variables in written language: addressee

The purpose for writing, and genre, will obviously impact on writing, but the person to whom the writing is addressed will affect the content and the nature of the text as well.

Quote 6.14 Hyland on expressing social relationships

[A]ny act of writing, whether personal, academic or workplace, is embedded in wider social and discursive practices which carry assumptions about participant relationships and how these should be structured and negotiated. Electricity bills, personal letters and school essays all have conventional ways of expressing content and addressing readers which draw on culturally and institutionally legitimate ways of framing relationships. Whether we decide to establish an equal or hierarchical affiliation, adopt an involved or remote stance, or choose a convivial or indifferent interpersonal tenor, we are at least partially constrained by the dominant ideologies of our institutions. These ideologies help establish cohesion and coordinate understanding through mutual expectations but in so doing they also represent particular representations of power and authority.... Managing social relationships, then, is crucial in writing as a text communicates effectively only when the writer has correctly assessed both the resources for interpreting it and likely response to it.
(2002: 69)

For example, a 'thank you letter' a child writes to his or her friend will probably differ from one written to an older relation who is not well known to the writer, in terms of 'personal disclosure, informality, deference, inter-actional involvement and the amount of topic elaboration needed to establish common ground' (Hyland 2002: 72). The consequences of not specifying an addressee in a writing task or in a reading test including a text meant for a different discourse community than the test takers are obvious.

Quote 6.15   Alderson on the hidden participant in reading

The reader's relationship with the writer and their degree of familiarity with their opinions, past intentions and so on, is clearly an important part of the reader's background knowledge, which we have seen many times already is demonstrably an important variable in reading.

Interestingly, in testing conditions, texts to be read are often anonymous, with no author attributed, or source from which a writer might be inferred . . . . Such conditions might be expected to influence performance and to reduce the correspondence between test task and Target Language Use (TLU).

(2000: 144)

Interlocutor variables in spoken language: input dimensions

This is perhaps the least definable part of our framework and it may be problematic to put it into operation unless an interlocutor frame is employed as in Cambridge ESOL examinations (see Weir and Milanovic (eds.) 2003). We are concerned here less with the candidate's contribution to the interaction than with the speech of the interlocutor, which the candidate has to process.

What is said to the candidate by the other participant(s) will influence his or her own performance. We need to take into account potential sources of variance in performance caused by features of the language used by the interlocutor, e.g., rate of utterance, accent of the examiner, clarity of articulation of the examiner, length of discourse (long turns by one interviewer may be more difficult to process than shorter turns by another).

To give candidates an equal chance to demonstrate their ability, it would seem that we should at least address the issue of how we might ensure that the size, complexity, referential and functional range of the other participant's contribution to the interaction should not be widely dissimilar from candidate to candidate. In other words, *the examiner/interlocutor's contribution to the interaction must be standardized as far as is possible.* In peer–peer interaction we must try to balance the contribution of both participants in terms of the relative contributions.

The following are the dimensions we should be concerned with.

Speech rate

A level of speed with which the speaker is delivering speech; the most common measure of speech rate is words per minute (wpm), while syllables are a much better unit of measurement whenever precision is necessary. Buck (2001: 38) argues that research results generally support the commonsense belief that the faster the speech, the more difficult it is to comprehend.

Quote 6.16   Buck on speech rate

[R]esearch has shown speech rate to be clearly an important variable in listening comprehension. Comprehension declines as the listener talks faster, and the weight of the evidence suggests that the decline in comprehension is rather slow until a threshold level is reached, at which time an increased speech rate leads to a much more rapid decline in comprehension. As for the particular speech rate at which this rapid decline takes place, the weight of evidence suggests that this varies from one listener to another and is affected by a variety of factors. There is strong evidence to suggest that the language ability of the listener is important – non-native speakers seem to have a lower threshold – and that the accent of the speaker is also important. Based on this, we can probably assume that other text variables, such as vocabulary, syntax or topic, would also interact with speech rate.
(2001: 40)

Variety of accent

Different groups of language users pronounce language in characteristic ways. It is sometimes suggested that the stronger the accent, the lower the listeners' comprehension. An unfamiliar accent can make comprehension difficult for the listener. Professionals who make audio recordings for a living usually have rich, authoritative voices, with clear enunciation. However, they speak quite differently from how most people generally speak. The best speakers for any test are speakers typical of the target-language use situation (Buck 2001). The bottom line is that they have clear accessible pronunciation and intonation.

Acquaintanceship

The degree to which the listeners are familiar with the voice of the speaker is relevant, e.g., they would know their teachers' voices but not those of strangers on tapes they had never heard before. It may well be easier for a candidate to speak to people he or she is *familiar* with. It may be easier to speak to a single peer rather an unknown authority figure such as an unfamiliar examiner. The more relaxed the candidate is, the greater the sample of language that may be elicited. The tester needs to consider who the candidates will be using English with in their future target situations (see Brown and Yule 1983).

Number

The number of participants in an interaction or the number of things being referred to in a picture description or discussed has an effect (Brown *et al.*

1984) and the distinguishability of these is also important. A male and a female voice in an interaction are easier to distinguish in a listening test than two voices of the same gender. It is easier to describe what a boy and a girl are doing in a picture than to describe what two boys or two girls are doing, because the latter requires more language to distinguish between the participants.

The number of people involved in the interaction in the test should accord wherever possible with the situation in real life that one wishes to make statements about. Should it be a dialogue or a group discussion? Complexity of task can be related in part to the number of people involved in an interaction and to the *status* of those involved, because of the demands this may make on formality.

Gender

There is some evidence that the interaction between the gender of the interlocutor and the gender of the candidate can affect performance (O'Sullivan 2000) and this would need to be dealt with in the specification. Some students seem to interact more easily with a female examiner. Women are likely to be better at keeping a conversation going, whereas men are more prone to interrupt. The sex of the participants should perhaps also correspond with people candidates are likely to have to interact with in real life. Obviously, in certain contexts some of these features may be difficult to operationalize.

Are the interlocutor variables – speech rate, accent, acquaintanceship, gender and number – appropriate for the test?

6.3   Setting and test administration

Primary considerations affecting validity are the circumstances under which the test takes place. These conditions need to be similar across sites or the processing will differ. If the test is not well administered, unreliable results may occur. Precise steps should be laid down to ensure that the test is administered in exactly the same efficient way whoever is in charge or wherever it takes place. This requires that exam invigilators are provided with a clear and precise set of instructions and are familiar and comfortable with all aspects of the test before administering it: test conditions, especially rooms in listening tests, should be of equivalent standards and suitably equipped (chairs, desks, clock, etc.); test materials and equipment should be carefully screened for any problems before the test is administered; procedures for dealing with candidates' cheating should have been sorted out in advance with the invigilators. All administrative details should have been clearly worked out prior to the exam, in particular, ground rules for late arrivals, the giving of clear test instructions, ensuring candidates have properly recorded names and other necessary details (see *SATD Manual Egypt*, ed. Khalifa, 2003, for a comprehensive approach to this aspect of test validity).

Physical conditions

Here we are concerned with actual place, background noise, live or recorded materials, lighting, air-conditioning and power sources, all of which are of great importance especially in listening tests. It is necessary to ensure good acoustics and minimal background noise so test takers can hear clearly and comfortably in a listening test. Buck (2001: Chapter 6) provides a valuable and comprehensive overview of how we might go about providing and delivering suitable texts for listening comprehension. Critically, recordings and equipment should be of a uniform, acceptable standard. Listening in a noisy environment or through inferior equipment will alter the performance conditions under which listening operations are performed and the cognitive processing will be seriously affected in terms of audition at the very least. As Buck (2001: 193) points out: 'without good texts we cannot make good listening tests'.

In general, we should aim at providing non-distressing or adverse physical conditions so that we bias for best in our tests.

Were the physical conditions of the test administration satisfactory?

Uniformity of administration

A constant testing environment where the test is conducted according to detailed rules and specifications so that testing conditions are the same for all test takers is essential. If the uniformity rule is broken, say by one centre giving extra time for planning, producing or monitoring a task, then the theory-based validity of the test is compromised because executive processing may as a result differ markedly across testing sites.

Was the test administered in the same manner across sites?

Security

This involves limiting access to the specific content of a test to those who need to know it for test development, test scoring, and test evaluation. In particular, test items of secure tests are not published; unauthorized copying is forbidden by any test taker or anyone otherwise associated with the test. If tests are not secure, then some candidates may know the answers in advance and their processing will be of an entirely different nature, i.e., solely reliant on memory.

Was the test secure?

This brings us to the end of the elements relating to the context validity of test tasks and it is perhaps worth reiterating that it is these conditions that the test developer/user in the classroom can do most about. Suggestions for researching the context validity of tasks will be examined in Part 3, Case study 1.

We have made frequent references in this chapter to the effects that context validity choices have on theory-based validity and emphasized the reciprocal nature of their relationship. We next look in more detail at theory-based validity where we are concerned with what actually happens when a candidate processes the task that we have attempted to construct and administer in a context valid fashion. We would argue that just as the classroom tester can do something about context validity, s/he can also directly address theory-based validity, despite the scant attention previously paid to this in the testing literature.

Further reading

General
Bachman *et al*. **(1988, 1995)** use task and ability analysis to compare two EFL proficiency batteries.

Reading
Alderson (2000) deals with many of these elements at various stages in his book.
Urquhart and Weir (1998) deal with many of the issues raised in this chapter.
Weir *et al*. **(2000)** describe the development of a national reading test for China.

Listening
Buck (2001) is a comprehensive and useful study of the testing of listening.
Shohamy and Inbar (1991) look at the effect of text type and question type on listening comprehension tests.

Writing
Weigle (2002) is a comprehensive study of the testing of writing, with much useful exemplification.

Speaking
Luoma (2004) deals solely with the testing of speaking, with a lot of useful exemplification.

7
Theory-based Validity in Action

In Part 1 we argued that approximation to the construct in a measurement instrument is essentially the result of the interactions between its context and theory-based elements. In Chapter 6 we looked at the elements of the validity framework that need to be considered under context validity. We now turn to the theory-based elements. In our present state of knowledge it is easier to treat context- and theory-based aspects of validity separately for descriptive purposes but we recognize that it is the interaction between them and the scoring criteria that lies at the heart of construct validity; see Chapter 11, Case studies 1–3 for ways we might start to address these relationships. Establishing the nature of these interactions is what will take forward our understanding of language testing and the constructs it attempts to measure (see Chaloub Deville 2003 for a programmatic discussion of the 'abilities-in language users-in contexts' participant metaphor perspective).

Bachman's Communicative Language Ability (CLA) model is particularly valuable for its explanation of the cognitive components of an individual's language competence and strategic competence. These components are subsumed within executive resources and executive processing in the theory-based aspect of our validity framework presented at the start of this Part.

Concept 7.1   Bachman's description of communicative language ability

Communicative language ability consists of language competence, strategic competence and psycho-physiological mechanisms. Language competence includes organizational competence, which consists of grammatical and textual competence, and pragmatic competence, which consists of illocutionary and sociolinguistic competence. Strategic competence is seen as the capacity that relates language competence or knowledge of language, to the language user's knowledge structures and the features of the context in which communication takes place. Strategic competence performs assessment, planning

Concept 7.1 (Continued)

and execution functions in determining the most effective means of achieving a communicative goal. Psycho-physiological mechanisms involved in language use characterize the channel (auditory, visual) and mode (receptive, productive) in which competence is implemented.
(1990: 107–8)

The area of processing that will probably lend itself most to investigation is that of *metacognitive strategies* or 'strategic competence' as Bachman termed it.

Quote 7.1 Bachman and Palmer on strategic competence

[A] set of metacognitive components, or strategies, which can be thought of as higher order executive processes that provide a cognitive management function in language use, as well as in other cognitive activities.
(1996: 70)

Bachman and Palmer (1996) detail some basic metacognitive strategies in writing:

- Goal-setting for the task: what do I have to accomplish?
- Assessment of what is needed to achieve purpose (e.g., linguistic resources required, audience, etc.).
- Planning how to do it.
- Monitoring effectiveness.
- Organization of the required elements of language and topic knowledge to carry out the planned activity (added by Douglas 2002).

A valid writing task from a theory-based perspective would involve the candidate's competence in all of these areas. In testing writing the differences in metacognitive processing between selecting the part of a sentence that contains an error from four options, as against writing an argumentative essay based on input in the form of a number of academic articles are obvious. To the extent that a test does not result in these metacognitive activities it might be considered deficient in this mediational aspect of theory-based validity and raise concern about any attempt to generalize from the test task to the real-life language in use domain.

Chapelle similarly recognizes the importance of these metacognitive strategies as the mechanisms which initiate access to executive resources in response to the recognized contextual demands established by the test task.

Quote 7.2   Chapelle's interactionalist view of language performance

Performance is viewed as a sign of underlying traits, and is influenced by the context in which it occurs, and is therefore a sample of performance in similar contexts. Moreover, to incorporate a dimension of interaction between trait and context, an interactionalist definition must include metacognitive strategies responsible for mediating between the two.
(1998: 43)

You may feel that the actual cognitive operations involved in accessing executive resources are not susceptible to direct investigation, but this in itself does not invalidate a concern with theory-based validity. In tests of speaking and writing the development of corpora of exam scripts or discourse collected at different proficiency levels is beginning to offer us interesting insights into the results of this cognitive processing, e.g., of accessing the lexicon and/or syntactic parser, differences in levels of grammatical competence are emerging for each level of proficiency. Preliminary studies of the relationship between perceptions of metacognitive strategies employed in writing tasks and levels of performance in terms of specified analytic criteria are also suggesting a close connection between what happens in terms of executive processing in completing a writing task and the scores that result. Again, we find further evidence of the interconnectedness between theory-based and scoring aspects of validity.

Though there is obvious overlap in the executive processing and the executive resources between the four skills, for ease of use we will present a separate description for reading, listening, speaking and writing.

7.1   Reading

The argument as to whether reading is divisible into component skills or operations that can be identified clearly, or whether it is an indivisible, unitary process, continues. Proponents of the unidimensional/indivisible view of reading would argue that by testing enabling skills we are not getting a true measurement of the construct. Following their argument, if we wanted to test English for Academic Purposes (EAP) reading ability in a British academic context, we might indeed be happy with a reading-into-writing task and not be worried overmuch about muddying the reading measurement by having a writing output to the integrated task (see Chapter 8, Example W7).

Quote 7.3   Grabe and Stoller on reading and writing

Reading to integrate information requires additional decisions about the relative importance of complementarity, mutually supporting or conflicting information and the likely restructuring of a rhetorical frame to accommodate information from multiple sources. These skills inevitably require critical evaluation of the information being read so that the reader can decide what to integrate and how to integrate it for the reader's goal. In this respect, both reading to write and reading to critique texts may be task variants of reading to integrate information. Both require abilities to compose, select, and critique information from a text. Both purposes represent common academic tasks that call upon the reading abilities needed to integrate information.
(2002: 14)

However, given that in many places in the world employers, admissions officers, teachers and other end-users of test information want to know only about a candidate's reading ability *per se*, then we must where appropriate address the problems in testing this and try to avoid other constructs, such as writing ability, interfering with its measurement. In our present state of knowledge, if we wish to report on students' proficiency in reading as distinct, say, from writing ability, then we are forced to break reading down into what we hypothesize are its constituent parts.

Quote 7.4   Grabe concluded

A 'reading components' perspective is an appropriate research direction to the extent that such an approach leads to important insights into the reading process. In this respect, it . . . is indeed a useful approach.
(1991: 382)

It is accepted pedagogical practice to break the reading process down in this way and to address the component skills and strategies to a certain extent separately. So, to that extent, it should be possible to focus on these components for testing purposes. If we can identify skills and strategies that appear to make an important contribution to the reading process, it should be possible to test these and use the composite results for reporting on reading proficiency (see Urquhart and Weir 1998, Weir *et al.* 2000, Shiotsu 2003 for a further discussion of these issues).

This does not remove from us the obligation to explore further our uncertainty about the skills that might be involved in various types of reading, nor when we have developed items in the light of this, to check that they actually test what we think they are testing. These issues will be addressed more substantially in Part 3, Case study 3, where we deal with research intended to generate evidence on the theory-based validity of a quadripartite reading skills and strategy test (for those interested in the debate on sub-skills in reading, see Weir *et al.* 1990, Weir and Porter 1996, Alderson 1990a and b, Lumley 1993).

This does not mean that we believe that this is a fully valid model of what reading comprehension is. We admit to the possibility that the sum of the parts may not necessarily equate fully with what readers would normally take away from a text. Whatever theoretical position we take, we inevitably measure reading skills/strategies (individually or in combination) as soon as individual items are written on a passage. The debate would seem to be more a question of the strength of any claims concerning which skills/strategies are being tested by which items (see Alderson 1990a and b, Weir *et al.* 2000), than a strong claim for treating reading as a unified skill.

Their review of the background literature led Weir *et al.* (2000) to make the following distinctions:

- Skills and strategies: The process of reading involves the use of different skills and strategies. The term 'strategies' is used for conscious problem-solving activities and that of 'skills' for automaticized abilities performed largely subconsciously (Cohen 1998, Urquhart and Weir 1998), though, as Grabe and Stoller (2002: 15–17) caution, the distinction may sometimes become blurred as strategies become automatized in fluent readers and they argue that 'strategies for definitional purposes are best defined as abilities that are potentially open to conscious reflection and use ...'

Quote 7.5 Cohen on the 'conscious' nature of strategy use

[S]trategies are either within the *focal attention* of the learners or within their *peripheral attention*, in that learners can identify them if asked about what they have just done or thought.... For example, learners may skim a portion of text in order to avoid a lengthy illustration. If the learners are at all conscious (even if peripherally) as to why the skip is taking place, then it would be termed a strategy.
(1998: 11)

- Reading at the global and local level: Reading can be at the global and local level. Global comprehension refers to the understanding of propositions beyond the level of microstructure, that is, any macro-propositions in the macrostructure, including main ideas and important details. Local comprehension refers to the understanding of propositions at the level of microstructure, i.e., the meaning of lexical items, pronominal reference, etc.

Urquhart and Weir (1998: 123) provide a four-part matrix of careful and expeditious reading skills and strategies at the global and local levels:

Concept 7.2   Types of reading

	Global Level	Local Level
Careful Reading	Establishing accurate comprehension of explicitly stated main ideas and supporting details Making propositional inferences	Identifying lexis Understanding syntax
Expeditious Reading	Skimming quickly to establish: discourse topic and main ideas, or structure of text, or relevance to needs. Search reading to locate quickly and understand information relevant to predetermined needs.	Scanning to locate specific points of information.

Concept 7.3   Skills and strategies

Urquhart and Weir (1998) offer the following descriptions of their skills and strategies:
Skimming – reading for gist. The reader asks: 'What is this text as a whole about?' while avoiding anything that looks like detail.

Reading schemes like SQ3R recommend starting the reading to learn process with skimming, so that the reader has a framework to accommodate the whole text. The defining characteristics are (a) the reading is selective, with sections of the text either omitted or given very little attention; (b) an attempt is made to build up a macro-structure (the gist) on the basis of as few details from the text as possible.
Search reading – locating information on predetermined topics. The reader wants information to answer set questions or to provide data for example in completing assignments. It differs from skimming in that the search for information is guided by predetermined topics so the reader does not necessarily have to establish a macro-propositional structure for the whole text.

Unlike careful reading, in expeditious reading, the linearity of the text is not necessarily followed. The reader is sampling the text, which can be words, topic sentences or important paragraphs, to extract information on a predetermined topic in search reading or to develop a macro-structure of the whole text as in skimming. The process can be top-down when the reader is deciding how to sample the text and which part(s) of the text to be sampled. It can also be bottom-up w hen the reader's attention is on the sampled part(s) of the text.
Scanning – reading selectively, to achieve very specific reading goals, e.g., finding the number in a directory, finding the capital of Bavaria. The main feature of scanning is that any part of the text which does not contain the pre-selected symbol(s) is dismissed. It may involve looking for specific words/phrases, figures/percentages, names, dates of particular events or specific items in an index.
Careful reading – this is the kind of reading favoured by many educationalists and psychologists to the exclusion of all other types. It is associated with reading to learn, hence with the reading of textbooks. The defining features are that the reader attempts to handle the majority of information in the text, that is, the process is not

> selective; that the reader adopts a submissive role and accepts the writer's organization, including what the writer appears to consider the important parts; and that the reader attempts to build up a macro-structure on the basis of the majority of the information in the text.
>
> In careful reading, the process can be sequentially bottom-up, from letters to words and from words to sentences and finally to texts. It can also be top-down, a process of confirming and correcting predictions by sampling the visual input. Most likely, the process is interactive involving both bottom-up and top-down reading by interactively using all sources of information and background knowledge.
> (Urquhart and Weir 1998: 102-3)

These enabling skills or strategies are obviously still theoretical constructs, with only a hypothesized existence. Their separate nature or the extent to which they interact with other reading skills needs to be empirically investigated. One way the teacher might do this in the classroom is to get students to *introspect* (through think-aloud protocols or verbal retrospection) about the processes they are using to solve questions set on the various skills (see Chapter 11 for discussion of different methods for investigating strategy use). In this way we can investigate whether we are in fact testing what we set out to test. In addition, it may be possible to determine whether there are different routes, for example to working out the main idea(s) in a passage. It may show us what differentiates good and poor readers.

It may eventually be possible to determine what the interactional relationships might be between the skills or strategies which we have allowed a hypothetical separate existence. At present we have little idea about the relationship between these skills or whether some skills are superordinate to others. A number of critical questions remain unanswered:

- Does possession of one skill imply the possession of other skills in some sort of hierarchical arrangement?
- Is the ability to carry out certain activities dependent on the prior possession of other skills? It would seem improbable that students would be able to work out the main ideas of a text without some baseline competence in the micro-linguistic skills (see Alderson and Urquhart 1984, Grabe 1991: 391).
- Do students find greater difficulty with some of the more specifically linguistic skills than they do in the more global comprehension areas?
- Can students transfer the more global comprehension skills across from their L1? If this can be shown to be the case, then this has important

implications for the assessment of reading skills in English for Academic Purposes.

Urquhart and Weir (1998) expanded Just and Carpenter's (1980, 1987) model using two additional components from Kintsch and van Dijk (1978, 1983): *Goalsetter* and *Monitor*. In the expanded model, the *Goalsetter* determines the overall goal of the reading, and also selects the type of reading which is likely to achieve that goal, and the *Monitor* provides the reader with feedback about the success of the particular reading process (Urquhart and Weir 1998: 105). The monitoring procedure is contingent on the type of reading, and therefore the *Monitor* is activated in accordance with the *Goalsetter*. The relationships among different components in the expanded model are illustrated in Figure 7.1 and the glossary below explains the component parts.

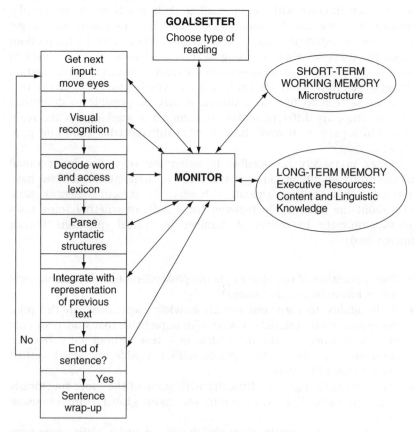

Figure 7.1   Adapted from Urquhart and Weir (1998: 106)

Concept 7.4   Reading process glossary (Urquhart and Weir 1998)

Executive processing

Goal-setting
Once the test takers have a clear idea of what they will be reading for, they can choose the most appropriate strategies and determine what information they are to target in the text.
Monitoring
The test takers check the effectiveness of their performance while engaged in a reading task.
Visual recognition
Character/word recognition; lexical decoding.
Pattern synthesizer
Parse syntactic structure. Integrate with representation of previous text. Building up macrostructure (see Concept 7.6 below).

Executive resources

Linguistic knowledge (Bachman 1990)
– Grammatical knowledge (lexis, syntax)
Access to the lexicon and syntactic parser (see Urquhart and Weir 1998)
– Textual knowledge
Understanding longer texts includes knowledge of textual features, such as cohesion, and coherence. It includes what is often referred to as 'formal knowledge' of how written text is structured.
– Functional (pragmatic) knowledge
Understanding the function or illocutionary force of a statement or longer text, and interpreting the intended meaning in terms of that.
– Sociolinguistic knowledge
Understanding the language of particular socio-cultural settings, and interpreting texts in terms of the context of situation. This includes knowledge of appropriate linguistic forms and conventions characteristic of particular sociolinguistic groups, and the implications of their use, or non-use.

Content knowledge

Internal
The test taker's prior knowledge of topical or cultural content (background knowledge)
External
Knowledge provided in the task in the rubrics or text

As shown in Figure 7.1, the components of *Goalsetter* and *Monitor* can be viewed as *metacognitive mechanisms* that mediate among different processing skills and knowledge sources available to a reader. Urquhart and Weir (1998) provided detailed explanations about how these metacognitive mechanisms enable a reader to activate different levels of strategies and skills to cope with different reading purposes. The reader may choose to skim, search read, scan, read carefully, in response to the perceived demands of the test task. For example, when in-depth comprehension is required, perhaps for a study purpose, the *Goalsetter* will be set to *careful reading*. Then, the reader will go through the majority of the information in the text, following all components of the model in use, i.e., extracting features, encoding words, parsing syntactic structures, processing microstructures, building up a macro-structure, etc. Meanwhile, the *Monitor* will be in full operation and mediate among all components of the model.

If scanning is the purpose of the task, fewer components of the model are involved. When the reader needs to process a large amount of reading material quickly in order to locate specific information, he/she will focus on the parts of the text relevant to his/her goal and skip the irrelevant parts. For example, we may search a text for a reference to a particular author or look for details of when something happened or how many people were involved. The reading process for scanning might just involve a limited amount of word encoding and lexical access, with little or no syntactic processing required, no checking of coherence and no attempt to build up a macrostructure. The monitor is set at a simple yes/no level to see if the word being scanned fits the search description. If it does then the scan is over.

Obviously, there may well be individual differences in the way texts are processed. What we are interested in is whether there are any general procedures that we should try to incorporate into our tests which would bring the process of doing the test closer to what we might generally agree on as 'reading a text' in its different manifestations as laid out above. It is important that the formats we adopt reflect as adequately as possible what we believe reading to be even if we accept that the test does not imply a *fully* valid model of what reading comprehension is. The bottom line is whether the tasks students have to carry out in the test reflect realistic discourse processing in relation to the theoretical model of reading displayed above.

In tests of the various types/purposes of reading we would expect the successful candidate (see Weir *et al.* 2000 for exemplification of why sampling in this way is crucial here) to mirror the processes we have described above and not to use skills and/or strategies associated with other types of reading. If we checked we had succeeded in testing what we intended to test through verbal protocol studies or survey studies (see Part 3, Case study 3), neither would we expect *test taking strategies* such as the following to appear:

- Matching words in the question with the same words in the passage.
- Using clues appearing in other questions to answer the question under consideration.
- Using one's existing knowledge or experience to answer the questions.
- 'Blind' guessing not based on any particular rationale.

Rather, we hope candidates would identify only the components of the process of reading appropriate to the skill or strategies that were identified above. In a test of scanning, we would expect the candidate only to encode lexical items and to access the mental lexicon. Our tests would possess theory-based validity to the extent that each item utilized processing in terms of skills and strategies that were appropriate to the particular type or purpose for reading under review.

7.2 Listening

Rost (2002) offers a comprehensive account of the listening process, describing in detail the neurological, linguistic, pragmatic and psycholinguistic processes involved in the comprehension of speech. His description of the processing involved in comprehension is of particular relevance to the language tester, as one would hope, if claims are to be made for the theory-related validity of such tasks, that candidates would be involved in such processing as they take test tasks.

Concept 7.5 Rost on comprehension

(Listening) Comprehension is the process of relating language to concepts in one's memory and to references in the real world. Comprehension is the sense of understanding what the language used refers to in one's experience or in the outside world... Complete comprehension then refers to the listener having a clear concept in memory for every referent used by the speaker...the most fundamental aspect of comprehension is the integration of the information conveyed by the text with information and concepts already known by the listener. Comprehension occurs as an internal model of the discourse by the listener, in which information in the text only plays one part...while attending to speech over a period of several intonation units, the listener has to store a mental representation of the discourse and continuously update the representation with new information. The listener's representation of text is stored as sets of interrelated propositions. Propositions may be seen as units in memory which are used both in encoding and retrieval of comprehended information.
(2002: 59–61)

The componential model for listening presented below includes both linguistic and psycholinguistic elements and has much in common with reading except for phonology (e.g., assimilation, elision), accented speech, prosodic features (stress and intonation), speech rate, hesitation phenomena, discourse structure and some grammatical features (see Bae and Bachman 1998, Freedle and Kostin 1994, 1999). With these exceptions, there is considerable overlap between the processing in each.

Concept 7.6   The listening comprehension process

Executive processing: strategic competence

Goal-setting
Buck (2001: 104) describes this as 'assessing the situation taking stock of conditions surrounding a language task by assessing one's own knowledge, one's available internal and external resources and the constraints of the situation before engaging in the task'.

Acoustic/visual input
The external input into the listening comprehension process is an acoustic signal representing the phonemes, the meaningful sounds of the language (Buck 2001).

Audition
The act of hearing and identifying sounds. Rost (2002: 8) describes how 'perception creates knowledge of these distal objects (sounds) by detecting and differentiating properties in the energy field . . . the air surrounding the listener. Neural activity takes place in what are called excitation patterns . . . the output of the hearing mechanism. These sounds are held briefly in echoic memory and then pass to working memory.'

Pattern synthesizer
Rost (2002: 61) describes how the pattern synthesizer focuses attention on and then processes acoustic/visual input in short-term memory (STM; or 'working memory') and stores a representation of the discourse as either linguistic propositions or more likely as mental images of the content described in the discourse which are continuously updated by new information (Van Dijk and Kintsch 1983). The mental model provides the context for the interpretation of the next part of the text (Buck 2001: 28).
  Rost (2002: 63) details how Schank and Abelson (1977) suggested that if the input contains previously processed chunks of information, these parts may be *automatically processed* by activating the existing files containing the relevant linguistic knowledge or propositions and schemata in what Rost later calls 'activation spaces' in the long-term memory (LTM). Activating the relevant schema 'allows the listener to make the inductions that are essential to comprehending the text'. Buck (2001: 7, 26–7) states that 'if the input is not familiar in terms of linguistic content and/or real world knowledge, then it is more likely to go through a *controlled processing* stage, which involves a sequence of cognitive activities under active control and which the listener must pay attention to, as it leaves the STM and enters the LTM where things are stored for a much longer duration. In LTM the input is reconciled with other existing knowledge linguistic or background. A feedback loop then relays the results back to the executive processor in working memory where appropriate use can be made of it.'

Monitoring
The test takers check the effectiveness of their performance while engaged in a task.

Executive resources: language knowledge

Grammatical knowledge (phonology, lexis, syntax)
'Understanding short utterances on a literal semantic level. This includes phonology, stress, intonation, spoken vocabulary, spoken syntax' (Buck 2001: 104). Rost (2002: 20, 26) argues that 'recognising words in fluent speech is the basis of spoken language comprehension...under normal speech conditions listeners need only draw upon a set of grammatical cues to assist them as needed in interpretation of form-function mappings.' (See Kintsch 1998 for a thorough discussion of comprehension.)

Discoursal knowledge
'Understanding longer utterances or interactive discourse between two or more speakers. This includes knowledge of discourse features, such as cohesion foregrounding, rhetorical schemata and story grammars and knowledge of the structure of unplanned discourse' (Buck 2001: 104). It includes what is often referred to as 'formal' knowledge of how discourse is structured.

Functional (pragmatic) knowledge
'Understanding the function or illocutionary force of an utterance or longer text, and interpreting the intended meaning in terms of that. This includes understanding whether utterances are intended to convey ideas, manipulate, learn or are for creative expression, as well as understanding indirect speech acts and pragmatic implications' (Buck 2001: 104). Rost (2002: 26) argues that 'because the listener has limited processing resources, he will attend primarily to communicative function of the communication and only secondarily to the formal (i.e., grammatical) manifestations of that function.'

Sociolinguistic knowledge
'Understanding the language of particular socio-cultural settings, and interpreting utterances in terms of the context of situation. This includes knowledge of appropriate linguistic forms and conventions characteristic of particular sociolinguistic groups, and the implications of their use, or non-use, such as slang, idiomatic expressions, dialects, cultural references, figures of speech, levels of formality and registers' (Buck 2001: 104).

Content knowledge
Internal: the test taker's prior knowledge of topical or cultural content (background knowledge)
External: knowledge provided in the task

Quote 7.6   Buck on the interactive nature of the listening process

Listening comprehension is a top-down process in the sense that the various types of knowledge involved in understanding language are not applied in any fixed order – they can be used in any order, or even simultaneously, and they are all capable of

interacting and influencing each other ... Meaning is not something in the text that the listener has to extract, but is constructed by the listener in an active process of inferencing and hypothesis building.
(2001: 3, 29)

Rost (2002: Chapter 3) also highlights the importance of pragmatic as well as linguistic and psycholinguistic processing.

Quote 7.7   Rost on pragmatic processing

From a pragmatic perspective, listening is an intention to complete a communication process. In order for this completion to occur, there must be engagement, in which a listener switches from becoming a mere 'presence' to an interpreter.... The implicit assumption in a pragmatic view of communication is that language resources – the listener's knowledge of phonology, morphology, syntax, lexis – cannot be activated until he takes on a pragmatic perspective. Such a perspective includes the degree of coordination and collaboration between speaker and listener on the goals of the interaction and the rules for conducting the interaction ... There are four key pragmatic notions that contribute to an understanding of listening: (1) deixis; (2) intention; (3) strategic use; and (4) conversational meaning ...
(2002: 40)

To test listening we must understand the processing that takes place in real-life situations and attempt to see that communication in our tests is anchored in the real world as far as possible. Rost's pragmatic notions listed above (see Rost 2002: 40–58 for full exemplification of these) will help us to do that. The *deictic* elements of an utterance (time, space, objects, persons and status) can only be interpreted in the context in which they are uttered, i.e., listening occurs in a context, as we discussed in Chapter 6, and elements of addressor, addressee, topic, code, channel, purpose, etc. will all impact the interaction. The *intention* of the speaker, the locutionary and illocutionary force of an utterance, is related to the functional knowledge of language in our model above. Rost (202: 42–3) describes *strategic use* as taking place when 'speakers create meaning in part through their use of language conventions and norms, or conversational maxims. Listeners understand speakers' meanings by evaluating speakers' utterances in the light of the cooperative principles of conversation'. He also points out that specific nuances of meaning can be created by deliberately flouting or violating these maxims through uninformative or false contributions. (p. 43). Rost argues (p. 45) that '[conversation] *meaning* emerges from the context and is not determined in advance. Meaning expressed in conversation is mutually built incrementally and through an interactional structure created by both the speaker and the listener'.

As we argued above, theory-based validity is a major contributor to the overall validity of our tests and so fidelity in terms of the construct we are measuring is vital. Buck (1990) and Rost point out that if we are to measure listening ability rather than general comprehension ability we must ensure we include 'those aspects of proficiency and comprehension that are unique to listening.' In Quote 7.8, Rost describes a set of characteristics representative of oral English (see also Carter and McCarthy 1997).

Quote 7.8   Rost on textual and psychological aspects unique to listening

1. All **physical features** of spoken language that are *not* reflected in written language

   - pause units (short 2–3-second bursts of speech)
   - hesitations
   - intonation
   - stress
   - variable speeds
   - variable accents
   - background sounds

2. **Linguistic features** that are more common in spoken language

   - colloquial vocabulary and expressions
   - shorter, paratactically (additive) organized speech units
   - false starts
   - frequent use of ellipsis
   - frequent use of unstated topics
   - more indexical expressions (keyed to visible environmental features)
   - more two-party negotiation of meaning (less original clarity)

3. **Psychological features** unique to listening

   - negotiative mode: the possibility for (and sometimes the necessity of) interacting with speaker to clarify and expand meaning
   - constructive mode: the possibility of working out a meaning that fits the context, and is relevant to the listener and to the situation, incorporating visible contextual features
   - transformative mode: the possibility of interacting with, 'connecting' with, and
   - influencing the speaker's ideas.

If we wish to test listening ability and listening ability only we need to be sure that the input to test takers and the activities of test takers include these features – as many as are feasible in the testing situation. If we do include these features, we can be *more* comfortable with the construct validity of the listening test than if we do not include them . . . (2002: 31, 171–2)

Buck (2001: 112) argues unequivocally that 'listening tests ought to require fast, automatic, on-line processing of texts that have the linguistic characteristics of typical spoken language'.

In many situations the testing of listening is handled as part of the testing of spoken interaction. In the real world, however, there are a number of occasions when listening is not the precursor of speech; for example, listening to lectures, railway announcements, recorded messages or television and radio programmes. It is essential in these cases to decide on the context- and theory-based criteria on which to base decisions on what to include in a test of listening comprehension. To determine what is a satisfactory performance one needs to specify in some detail what it is the candidate can do (*operations*), under what circumstances (*conditions*) and to what *level*.

In the past, emphasis was placed on the candidate's ability to discriminate phonemes, to recognize stress and intonation patterns and to record through a written (usually multiple-choice) product, what had been heard. The sum of a candidate's appropriate responses in these 'discrete' sub-tests was equated with proficiency in listening comprehension (the listening component of the UK General Medical Council's PLAB test is an example of this discrete point approach which until recently was still in use).

We saw in Chapter 1 how an emphasis on phonology in language testing had disappeared from Cambridge tests by the 1950s. Few people would now maintain that an ability to discriminate between phonemes implies a capacity to comprehend verbal messages. The emphasis has shifted to contextualized tests of listening comprehension, incorporating all the additional redundant features that facilitate comprehension. The concern now is with testing the communication of meaning as against structural understanding. (For further discussion of the shift, see Brindley and Nunan 1992, Buck 1991, Rost 1990, 2002, Weir 1990: 51–4.)

Much of the current thinking on the nature of listening comprehension is based on earlier work on reading comprehension (see Dunkel 1991, Brindley and Nunan 1992). Both are receptive skills and the testing of listening has many similarities with the testing of reading, not least in its invisible, cognitive nature, which makes it difficult to describe and to assess. The elements for consideration in the operations part of our framework for testing listening were covered above in our discussion of reading (see Concepts 7.2–7.4). It is important to repeat that such taxonomies have the status of hypotheses only, premised on what experience and opinion suggest are important (see Buck 1990). The operations identified all need extensive validation before their status is raised and, according to Buck, this may be problematic.

Quote 7.9　Buck on the problems of identifying listening skills

[B]ecause: 'listening comprehension is a massively parallel interactive process taking advantage of information from a large number of sources, both linguistic and non-linguistic', it may not be possible to separate out individual variables.
(1990: 5)

In most contemporary approaches to the testing of listening, the texts are no longer broken down into small chunks, and as far as possible they retain their integrity. This situational authenticity contributes to their validity as tests of listening. Although it is now usual to provide long, uninterrupted texts as stimuli in a test battery, in terms of the tasks and scoring, it might still be desirable to focus on individual operations, rather than testing a global understanding of the passage through written summary.

The items set on these texts tend to focus on 'discrete skills' of the type listed for reading. However, as with reading, the strength of the claims for the discreteness of these skills has still to be established, and it is likely that different candidates might arrive at acceptable answers to test items by different routes, depending on individual processing – whether top-down, bottom-up or interactive-compensatory processing (see Brindley and Nunan 1992: 3–40, Dunkel 1991: 438–51, for a thorough discussion of these skills).

Validity is, however, likely to be enhanced by having a larger number of individually focused items, rather than testing understanding of a spoken passage through an integrated writing task such as a selective summary of the discourse. In the latter case the danger of muddied measurement cannot be ignored, i.e., are we testing listening and/or writing?

If we wish to make test tasks more like those in real life, the unbroken, sequential nature of extended spoken discourse precludes items that focus on the more specifically linguistic skills such as understanding lexis from context or recognizing the meaning value of specific features of stress or intonation. Candidates would find it extremely difficult to backtrack and focus on specific features of discourse while listening to and attempting to understand a continuing discourse. If we wish to preserve the authentic nature of the listening material, we have to focus questions on the more global processing skills, which enable us to extract meaning from a spoken text (for example, gist, main ideas, speaker attitude/intention). These questions would reflect the sequence in which information occurred in a text and there would need to be sufficient time between them in order not to make undue demands on a candidate's processing capacity.

Where the purpose of the task is transactional (to understand the main ideas and important details in a piece of discourse), it should be possible to establish a reasonable consensus on what students could take away from texts through text map exercises with colleagues (see Sarig 1989). It can then be established through trialling that candidates who we would pass can extract this information. As with reading it may well be that non-native speakers can extract this global information, but might not do as well on tests focusing on the more specifically linguistic items. If non-native speakers do not know the meaning of a particular lexical item or connector, this should not trouble us unduly. We can be reasonably sure that to cope with global processing in terms of global comprehension skills candidates will, in any case, need a minimally adequate competence in micro-linguistic skills.

One of the main differences from reading comprehension is the effect of speaker-related conditions on these operations, for example, stress, intonation, pausing, rhythm, propositional density and an amount of built-in redundancy. Another difference arises from the transient nature of spoken language. Normally, the listener is not able to backtrack over what has been said, in the way that a reader can when faced with a permanent written text. Processing has to take place in real time.

In designing listening tests we noted above that the test writer has to make additional decisions on *speaker-related* variables, such as speed of utterance, degree of sympathetic adjustment (see Rost 1990, 2002), accent and pronunciation, familiarity, status, gender and on the nature of the text types to be selected (see Chapter 6). The number of speakers the candidate has to understand in audio tests will also have an important influence on performance (see Brown and Yule 1983). The sound quality of the input, particularly if audio-recorded, and the acoustic environment may also require close attention if validity is not to be affected adversely.

The decisions taken on these conditions are important because of the added load they can place on processing, especially given the serial nature of the listening experience, where we normally only have an opportunity to listen to something *once* as we process it under normal time constraints. It bears repeating that the effect of decisions taken with regard to context validity will impact on the processing that will take place.

We need to investigate systematically the context- and theory-based elements in our proposed frameworks in order to determine which are criterial and how they relate to each other. In our present state of knowledge, the safest approach for teachers is to try and make test tasks approximate as closely as possible to the real-life abilities they wish to say something about, in terms of both situational and interactional authenticity. Through careful sampling of listening tasks which demonstrably approximate to desired performances, in terms of likely operations and specified conditions, we can be reasonably confident that we are doing the best we can in attempting to describe candidates' language abilities. We need through empirical research to determine the types of task (identified operations performed under specified conditions) that can be carried out at various ability levels. In Part 3 we will return to some of these issues when we look at the ways research can help establish the validity of tests.

7.3   Speaking

Hughes (2002: 119–30) draws our attention to the growing realization that processing in speech may differ from processing in writing in terms of cognitive functioning and cites work from speech pathology and memory in support. She offers evidence for the independence of orthography and phonology and for a separation of the lexicon for the two forms.

Quote 7.10   Hughes on mode-based research

The status of speech in applied linguistics is a little problematic....Much of the theory underpinning language teaching is a-modal, yet in other academic disciplines there is growing evidence that language is organized and processed quite differently according to mode...

These kinds of study suggest a clear distinction between the attentional demands of the two forms, the output and processing of them and the coding and representation of them in the brain...

There is a growing body of evidence that spoken and written forms of the language are processed differently internally, and have different cognitive effects (particularly in relation to memory) when regarded as external modalities.
(2002: 120, 124, 129)

Unfortunately, to date the dominant a-modal approach has resulted in limited research into the nature of speech processing and production with primacy, perhaps mistakenly, being given by linguists and many 'applied linguists' to the written form. Hughes signals the need for a change in this predisposition.

As regards executive processes, in order to be able to speak a foreign language it is obviously necessary to encode syntactically and phonologically and to access lexical form (i.e., operate at the grammatical level in terms of phonology, lexis and syntax). However, to determine whether learners can communicate orally, it is necessary to get them to take part in direct spoken language activities. We are no longer interested in testing whether candidates merely know how to assemble sentences in the abstract: we want candidates to perform relevant language tasks and adapt their speech to the circumstances, making decisions under time pressure, implementing them fluently, and making any necessary adjustments as unexpected problems arise.

The dependence on 'fill in the blanks' in written dialogues as a measure of spoken competences in many high-stakes examinations around the world (e.g., Thanawiyama school leaving examinations in Egypt) has obvious limitations in this respect. When oral examinations are addressed in national examinations in countries like China in the College English Test (CET) with a candidature of over ten million it is clearly a question of allocation of resources and effort rather than logistics that is the issue.

In terms of validity there is a strong case for testing spoken language performance directly, in realistic situations, rather than testing hypothetical knowledge of what might be said. If we wish to make statements about capacity for spoken interaction we are no longer interested in multiple-choice, pencil-and-paper tests, that is, indirect tests of speaking where spoken language is conspicuously absent. To test speaking ability we should require candidates to demonstrate their ability to use language in ways which are characteristic of interactive speech, i.e., to process the language in the way described in the model below over an adequate sampling of the routines detailed by Bygate (1987). Obviously, for certain contexts we are also interested in their ability to perform extended monologues where informational routines are likely to predominate.

Concept 7.7   The speaking process

Executive process (based on Levelt 1993)

Conceptualizer: conceiving an intention, selecting relevant information to be expressed to realise this purpose, ordering information for expression, keeping track of what was said before; paying constant attention to what is heard and own production, drawing on procedural and declarative knowledge.
   The speaker will monitor messages before they are sent into the formulator.
Pre-verbal message: product of the conceptualization.
Linguistic formulator: includes grammatical encoding and phonological encoding which accesses lexical form.
Phonetic plan: an internal representation of how the planned utterance should be articulated; internal speech.
Articulator: the execution of the phonetic plan by the musculature of the respiratory, the laryngeal and the supra-laryngeal systems.

Overt speech

Audition: understand what is being said by others or self, i.e., interpret speech sounds as meaningful words and sentences.
Speech comprehension: involves access to various executive resources, e.g., lexicon, syntactic parser, and background knowledge. A representation is formed of the speech in terms of its phonological, morphological, syntactic and semantic composition. The process is applicable to both internal and external overt speech.
Monitoring both of internal and external speech can be constantly in operation, though sometimes this filter is switched off.
Executive resources are the same as for Listening, Concept 7.6 above.

The earlier discussion under 'listening' concerning the linguistic, psycholinguistic and pragmatic aspects of processing is obviously in large part applicable to our discussion of the theory-based aspects of the testing of spoken interaction and the reader is referred back to that for information on the receptive part of the processing that takes place in interaction.

Despite the universal importance of spoken language, it is evident from the literature that little attention has been paid to the speaking process *per se* and even Levelt's work outlined in the executive process part of the table above is largely focused on the utterance rather than interaction (Hughes 2002: 31). O'Loughlin's (2001) observations of candidates performing in direct and indirect speaking tests provide one of the few examples of research into the response processes of candidates.

In making decisions about what operations we wish to be called into play by test tasks, it is useful to refer to Bygate (1987), who offers a description of how speakers organize in *routines* what they have to communicate. Construct definition is related to the particular types of activity that the examinees are asked to perform in specified contexts. This procedural view of how spoken interaction takes place is a useful complement to the componential view described above.

According to Bygate, learners have a repertoire of both *informational* and *interactional* routines which reflect their familiarity with certain kinds of communication. Routines are normally recurring patterns of organization of communication, and can be found, first, in the organization of *information*, and second, in the organization of *interaction*. As well as these, Bygate argues, we need to be aware of *improvisational skills* which are brought into play when an interaction falters. In specifying what is to be tested either for achievement or proficiency purposes, the test developer can usefully identify what are the salient routines for the audience in question and what improvisational skills might be expected of them. An outline of these is provided below, based on Bygate (1987). In making decisions on what activities to test, it would be necessary to refer to a listing of what has been taught or is criterial in the target situation.

Routine skills

Informational routines

These routines are conventional ways of presenting information, and are best seen as frequently recurring ways of structuring speech. Brown and Yule (1983) distinguish between four different types of informational talk: description (Bygate 1987 adds comparison here), instruction, storytelling and opinion-expressing/justification. They can be either *expository routines* – which involve factual information, typically concerned with questions of sequencing or identity of subject, or *evaluative routines* – which involve drawing of conclusions, usually requiring expression of reasoning; explanations, predictions, justifications, preferences and decisions. These are normally made in connection with expository routines. Both types of informational routines can be catered for in test tasks such as oral presentations which cater for long turns, but they may also form part of *interactional routines* and may be tested through information gap tasks, role play or interview.

Interactional routines

This kind of routine can be found in interactions such as buying goods in a shop, or telephone conversations, interviews, meetings, discussions, decision making; etc., which on the whole tend to be organized in characteristic ways.

Message planning skills draw upon the underlying knowledge of routines to predict what may happen and pre-plan turns, assisted by interaction management skills involving content-focused agenda management and interaction-focused turn-taking. At the selection stage linguistic choices are made and negotiation of meaning takes place. In the light of our developed/developing knowledge of the other speaker a level of explicitness is selected and procedural skills facilitate the communication, for example, through repetition or requests for clarification.

The routines described above, if sufficiently grounded through previous experience, are normally available to us at the conceptualization stage when we take part in a spoken interaction and allow us to select from a known repertoire at the planning stage. Hughes (2002: 81) refers to additional skills indicative of a learner's strategic and discoursal competence that one might expect in 'coherent fluent turn-taking and in successful negotiation of meaning in the case of potential communication breakdown'. The strategic competence elements of the latter are similar to Bygate's conceptualization of procedural and production 'improvisational' skills, which come into play if the communication falters.

Quote 7.11   Riggenbach on discourse and strategic competences in conversation

Conversation micro-skills

- The ability to claim turns of talk
- The ability to maintain turns of talk, once claimed
- The ability to yield turns of talk
- The ability to back-channel
- The ability to self-repair
- The ability to ensure comprehension on the part of the listener (e.g., comprehension checks such as Does that make sense? Are you with me? Get it?)
- The ability to initiate repair when there is a potential breakdown (e.g., clarification requests)
- The ability to employ compensatory strategies (e.g., avoidance of structures or vocabulary beyond the learner's proficiency, word coinage, circumlocution and even shifting topics or asking questions that stimulate the other interlocutor to share the responsibility for maintaining the conversation flow)

(1998: 57; quoted in Hughes 2002: 81)

Also of interest here is the work of Ron Carter and Mike McCarthy on the processes of talk (1997) and on spoken grammar (1995), which provides valuable insights into why speakers use the language they do in a variety of generic and social contexts. In particular, there is the exciting possibility of a spoken corpus such as their CANCODE providing a principled basis for language testing, in that it might help indicate the elements of discourse or strategic competence that a variety of tasks/situations might result in. In

Exploring Spoken English (1997) Carter and McCarthy illustrate a variety of speech genres based on the Cambridge-Nottingham Corpus of Discourse in English (CANCODE is part of the Cambridge International Corpus). They provide examples and analyses of storytelling, narrative description, informal conversation, language in action conversations, service encounters, transactional discourse, radio phone-ins (debate, argument, comment-elaboration), symmetrical/asymmetrical discussion and seminar/tutorial discussion.

In providing such exemplification through corpora development of what is actually said in real life, it also means that we might be able to avoid creating *unrealistic* criteria for assessing performance on tasks, through enhanced awareness of what native speakers actually say in these contexts – a point of concern for Hughes (2002: 76–8) in assessing spoken language.

Hughes, with reference to naturally occurring spontaneous speech, rightly cautions about focusing too heavily in spoken language tests on language proficiency as against speaking proficiency, and emphasizes the frequent inattention to the mechanics of the language as against the content (ideas/emotions/information) in normal spoken interaction. We need to bear this in mind in developing criteria for use in our language tests.

Quote 7.12   Hughes on language proficiency vis-à-vis speaking proficiency

[S]pontaneous interactive speech will be full of hesitations, false starts, grammatical inaccuracies, have a limited vocabulary, tend towards repetition and be structured around short thought units or quasi-clauses based on the constraints of breath and of spoken language processing. It takes a considerable change in preconceptions about language proficiency for, for example, single word answers to be regarded as 'good' . . . it takes a change of mind set to realize that hesitancy, short clauses (or even single word turns), ellipsis, repetitions, self repair and simple or inexplicit vocabulary may be the essence of excellent speech production in certain conversational genres. In contrast, long turns, explicit phrasing and densely structured talk may be found in spoken narrative. This is why the issue of speech genre would need to be taken into account in relation to 'authentic' oral testing.
(2002: 77, 82–3)

Ongoing work at Cambridge ESOL in attempting to develop a common assessment scale for writing (see Hawkey and Barker 2004) demonstrates clearly the value of corpora in establishing assessment criteria which relate directly to the texts they are applied to. Corpora can clarify what criteria are necessary, as well as setting benchmarks for the differing levels of proficiency that can be supported by the empirical data (see also Fulcher 1993, 1996a).

It is increasingly recognized that test interaction really is co-constructed (Lumley and Brown 1997, Brown and Hill 1998, Brown 2003), but ratings are invariably given to individuals. We will return to issues of scoring spoken language test performance in Chapter 9.

The test tasks we employ need to reflect the target situation in terms of the functional *operations* described above. In addition we need to try and ensure that the *conditions* under which the operations are performed (described in Chapter 6) similarly accord with that target situation as far as is possible within the logistics of the testing situation. In this way, the test score resulting from the task may be premised on tasks that exhibit both theory and context-based validity. In Chapter 8 we will look at a number of spoken language tasks and discuss how they relate to these *a priori* aspects of task validity.

7.4 Writing

There are various ways to approach writing: textual, cognitive and contextual. Hyland (2002) advocates looking beyond the more traditional applied linguistics view of texts as autonomous objects; i.e., not restricting ourselves to the 'surface structures to see texts as attempts to communicate with readers'. In Chapter 6 we argued that appropriate contextualization of test tasks along a number of dimensions was essential if claims for context validity were to be made for a test. Though we are treating theory-based validity separately for descriptive purposes in this chapter; it is very much affected by the context of situation the cognitive processing takes place in. Writing is a social and a cultural act and is not limited to the individual space of the writer. The model we are advocating for test development is essentially socio-cognitive.

Quote 7.13   Hyland on texts as discourse

Discourse refers to language as use, and to the purposes and functions linguistic forms serve in texts. Here the linguistic patterns of finished texts point to contexts beyond the page, implying a range of social constraints and choices which operate on writers in any context. The writer, then, has certain goals and intentions, certain relationships to his or her readers, and certain information to convey, and the forms of a text are resources used to accomplish these. These factors draw the analyst into a wider paradigm which locates texts in a world of communicative purposes and social action, identifying the way texts actually work as communication.
(2002: 11)

In this section we are primarily interested in what competent writers do when they are confronted with a writing task, and will focus on writing as a cognitive activity; but inevitably we will be referring back to the context of writing, the performance conditions discussed above in Chapter 6.

Hayes and Flower (1980) were among the early theorists concerned with developing explanatory models of writing ability. Their model detailed a hierarchical but essentially interactive organization of the writing process.

Quote 7.14   Hyland on Flowers and Hayes' model of the writing process

[It] suggested that the process of writing is influenced by the task environment and the writer's long-term memory. Its main features are that:

- writers have goals;
- they plan extensively;
- planning involves defining a rhetorical problem, placing it in a context, then making it operational by exploring its parts, arriving at solutions and finally translating ideas onto the page;
- all work can be reviewed, evaluated and revised, even before any text has been produced;
- planning, drafting, revising and editing are recursive, interactive and potentially simultaneous;
- plans and text are constantly evaluated in a feed back loop;
- the whole process is overseen by an executive control called a monitor.

(2002: 25)

Though of value as a general indication of processing, their original model was too imprecise to predict what real writers might do (Hyland 2002: 27). What was needed was a way of capturing differences in ability levels between writers.

Bereiter and Scardamalia (1987) provided two models of *knowledge telling* and *knowledge transforming* to demonstrate the different composing processes of good and bad first-language writers, which were better able to account for the various research findings.

Quote 7.15   Hyland on knowledge-telling and knowledge-transforming models

A *knowledge-telling model* addresses the fact that novice writers plan less often than experts, revise less often and less extensively, and are primarily concerned with generating content from their internal resources. Their main goal is simply to tell what they can remember based on the assignment, the topic, or the genre.

A *knowledge-transforming model* suggests how skilled writers use the writing task to analyse problems and set goals. These writers are able to reflect on the complexities of the task and resolve problems of content, form, audience, style, organization, and so on within a content space and a rhetorical space, so that there is a continuous interaction between developing knowledge and text. Knowledge transforming thus involves actively

> reworking thoughts so that in the process not only the text, but also ideas, may be changed (Bereiter and Scardamalia 1987).
> (2002: 28, quoting Bereiter and Scardamalia 1987)

Though the cognitive approach marks a definite improvement on an earlier view of writing dominated by a concern with product, these process models might be considered deficient to the extent that they largely neglected the *contextual* factors that affect the writing process (see Grabe and Kaplan 1996 for a full critique of these earlier attempts to explain writing, and Hyland 2002 for a clear and readable conceptual overview of writing). The focus was very much on the cognitive processing side and no account was taken of the performance conditions the tasks were affected by and the potential effect of these on the theory-based elements.

Grabe and Kaplan (1996) were among the first to offer a socio-cognitive model of *writing as communicative language use*, taking into account both internal processing and contextual factors in writing (see Hyland 2002: 30–3). The reader is referred to the contextual factors outlined in Chapter 6, which provide a comprehensive account of elements in the task environment that we need to consider if we view writing as a social act taking place in a specifiable context. In particular attention needs to be paid to:

- The writer's understanding of the knowledge, interests and expectations of a potential audience (Hyland 2002: 34–6) and the conventions of the appropriate discourse community as far as this can be specified (for example, each university in Britain clearly spells out the requirements for PhD dissertations). In English as a subject of study this also involves the writer taking the responsibility for making explicit the connections between the propositions and ideas they are conveying and hierarchically organizing their writing (Weigle 2002: 21).
- The purpose of the writing (Nystrand *et al.* 1993).
- The text type or perhaps more accurately its intertextuality: the conventions relating to the text type or genre you are involved with for example the IMRAD (introduction, methods, results, analysis, discussion) structure of many scientific articles.
- The importance of the demands the task makes in terms of language knowledge: linguistic, discourse and sociolinguistic (see Bachman 1990 and the discussion in Chapter 6).

Establishing theory-based validity in writing is concerned with evaluating the activation of *executive resources* and *executive processes* prompted by the task. 'Executive resources' involve *linguistic resources* and *content knowledge* (see the description of these above). Content knowledge may already be possessed by the candidate through developed schemata or might be available in information supplied in task input. The 'executive process' refers to cognitive processing and includes the procedures of *goal-setting, topic and genre modifying, generating, organizing, translating* and *reviewing*. These processing procedures are described in detail by Hayes and Flower (1980), Bereiter and Scardamalia (1987) and Grabe and Kaplan (1996) and are glossed in Concept 7.8. This executive process is similar to the 'strategic competence' elements of Bachman's model of language ability (1990: 98–107). The *contextual* features of writing are described above in Chapter 6.

Concept 7.8   Writing (see Grabe and Kaplan 1996)

Executive process

Goal-setting refers to setting goals and purposes, offering initial draft of the task representation, connecting 'context' with 'verbal working memory' (see Grabe and Kaplan 1996: 226).

- *Topic and genre modifying* is used to provide topic relevance (or topic cues) and genre relevance (or genre cues) to the composition.
- *Generating* refers to producing the ideas or the retrieved content from memory and/or from input provided.
- *Organizing* involves grouping, categorizing ideas, establishing new concepts and putting ideas in suitable order.
- *Translating* is putting ideas into appropriate, cohesive and coherent language.
- *Monitoring* covers evaluating and revising both text development and content development, both written and unwritten thoughts and statements.

Executive resources are the same as for Concept 7.6 above

Linguistic knowledge

Content knowledge

Acknowledgements to my PhD students Xiu Xudong and Tony Green for their valued contribution to the development of this model.

Process writing

Quote 7.16   Weigle on inadequacies of the single timed essay

Two of the most serious limitations are: (1) the fact that writing under timed conditions on an unfamiliar topic does not accurately reflect the conditions under which most writing is done in non-testing situations or writing as it is taught and practiced in the classroom, and (2) the fact that it is difficult to generalize from a single writing sample to a much broader universe of writing in different genres and for different purposes and audiences.
(2002: 197)

Of course, writing in the classroom does not have to be constrained by time limits or single shot tasks rather than a series of recursive drafts, so the first of these criticisms can be easily mitigated. To deal with the second limitation, the growing interest in portfolio assessment in the United States is worth noting (see Hamp-Lyons 1991: 261–3, Hamp-Lyons and Condon 2002, Weigle 2002: Chapter 9) because it offers the potential to meet the criterion of theory-based validity better than almost all other forms of assessment, for example, MCQ tests or essays. Hyland (2002: 138) argues that a clear advantage of portfolios is that 'multiple samples will increase validity even further and at the same time make evaluation more congruent with teaching programmes'.

In this system, a collection of texts a writer has produced over a period of time in line with the specifications of a particular context is used to assess competence on exiting a programme. This has some similarity with the continuous assessment mode familiar from the former externally moderated Mode 3 examinations, administered by the General Certificate of Education Boards (GCE) in the United Kingdom in the 1970s and 1980s.

The Council of Europe's European Language Portfolio (http//culture2.coe. int/portfolio/) is an example of a recent adoption for assessment in foreign languages where member states have developed their own models for portfolios but with the common thread of their being tied to the Common European Framework of Reference: learning, teaching assessment (Council of Europe 2001).

The portfolio approach sees writing as an exploratory, generative, collaborative, recursive process rather than as a linear route to a predetermined product, as in the case of an examination essay. From this viewpoint, writers rarely adhere to a preconceived plan or model, and in attempting to approximate meaning, writers discover and reformulate their ideas. The *monitoring* element of the above model figures largely in this approach and *input* to this process may be provided additionally by peers or tutors, as well as from written information from appropriate texts which the writer transforms to make the meaning his/her own. What is represented as a linear sequence of events in our model might be repeated in a lengthy iterative process, as happens in real life when writing an assignment, a paper for publication, or a book.

Concept 7.9   Hamp-Lyons and Condon define the portfolio

[B]efore everything else a portfolio is a collection...a portfolio must consist of a collection of writing that contains a multiplicity of texts and that incorporates information about the writing context, not merely the writing itself.

...without reflection all we have is simply a pile, or a large folder – a collection of texts. Reflection starts the deliberative process, recognizes strength and need, places pieces together mentally, relates them to each other, engages in a host of mental processes; This can happen with just a collection, but a collection is not a portfolio until the reflection is there...For a writer to learn from the work she or he has produced and collected, reflection is necessary.

...What shape the collection takes...depends on the quality of the reflection the writer engages in, and on the selection of texts that follow logically from the reflection ....Without selection ... the writer would be unable to shape the portfolio as a conscious exhibit of what has been done, what has been learned.
(2000: 118–21)

It is easy to see how this format might take account of redrafting and other developmental aspects in writing to match our theory-based framework for writing more closely. Their claims to greater content coverage than in essay-based assessment are also compelling. Weigle (2002: 203–4) emphasizes the authenticity and interactiveness of portfolios.

Quote 7.17   Weigle on the authenticity and interactiveness of portfolios

[F]or school-based writing in particular, portfolios are clearly superior to timed writing tests in terms of authenticity...they can be designed to include writing samples that were written for some authentic purpose other than the evaluation of writing *per se* – for example, papers that were written for other academic courses...

...compared to timed writing tests, portfolio assessment is clearly on the high end of interactiveness (the extent and type of involvement of the test taker's individual characteristics in accomplishing a task. Specifically, an interactive task engages a test taker's language ability, metacognitive strategies, topical knowledge and affective schemata). In particular, the act of collecting, selecting and arranging the portfolio contents engages the metacognitive strategies to a considerable extent and, ideally, involves personal investment on the part of the student/portfolio author.
(2002: 203–4)

Quote 7.18   Hamp-Lyons and Condon caution

As portfolios become more widely known and used, the questions will become more focused, and the audiences will demand more solid proof of effectiveness rather than being content to rely on potential, on what portfolios might do, or could provide.
(2000: 195)

The *practical* constraints on language testing, particularly as regards the time available, have resulted in the main in test tasks in which the candidate is asked to display his or her ability to produce a piece of written work composed under restricted time conditions. The usually means the ubiquitous exam essay format where knowledge telling rather than knowledge transformation is invoked.

Quote 7.19   Hyland on the validity of portfolios

In fact issues of reliability and validity are actually more complex when considering the multiple entries of a portfolio than when grading a single timed essay. These difficulties relate both to the need to ensure reliability across raters and rating occasions, and to the heterogeneous nature of what is assessed. Standardizing a single score in order to express adequately a student's ability from a variety of genres, tasks, drafts and different subject discipline material can be extremely difficult.
(2002: 142)

The theory-based validity argument for portfolio assessment to include writing tasks completed by students at home is also subject to reservations about the amount of help individuals have received and the extent to which we can be certain the portfolios are the students' own work. This is a serious problem for assignments anywhere; for example, how much help do parents give their offspring in completing work done at home even at undergraduate level? The major disadvantages for portfolios may well lie in the scoring validity aspect of our framework. As a result, little interest has been shown by Examinations Boards in tasks which focus on the composing process itself, where a number of drafts might be involved and a number of people might provide feedback to the writer *en route* to a finished product. This stems from a desire for the written product to be assessed as the work of a particular candidate alone, who may differ in proficiency from her contemporaries. However, compare Gollin (in Candlin and Hyland (eds.) 1999) on the growth of interest in collaborative writing in specific circumstances.

Quote 7.20   Weigle on agendas and movements in writing assessment

[T]hree main movements to writing assessment in the C20th – the use of so-called indirect tests of writing (i.e., multiple-choice tests of usage), the renewed acceptability of the timed impromptu writing test, and now the movement towards portfolio assessment- can be seen as directly tied to the agenda of groups . . .

Indirect test of writing represented the domination of the agenda of testing firms and their clients, who wanted fast, reliable, and inexpensive ways of sorting students according to the status quo of existing social patterns.

The first major challenge to this state of affairs was led by teachers who felt that these tests did not meet their needs or those of their students. The impromptu essay test subsequently became the standard approach to testing writing . . . a compromise between the views of teachers who see writing as a complex multifaceted process and assessment as something which must be closely integrated with instruction, and the view of psychometricians, whose equally valid concerns for reliability lead them to a preference for tasks that break writing down into writing ability as the sum of discrete, measurable component parts.

The move towards portfolio assessment represents a further stage in this tension, with teachers again leading the effort to have their perspectives on writing influence the way writing is assessed.

(2002: 239–40)

We have discussed portfolio assessment at length in this chapter as its major strengths are in its claims to context and theory-based validity. However, serious doubts concerning its scoring validity mean that we will only consider further the two other approaches for assessing writing ability in high-stakes tests. We will briefly survey these here and consider them more closely in the section on writing in Chapter 8 when we will critically examine test techniques along the indirect–direct continuum.

First, writing was sometimes divided into more specific, 'discrete' micro-linguistic elements, e.g., grammar, vocabulary, spelling, punctuation and orthography, and attempts were made to test these formal elements separately by the use of objective tests. These tests would be indirect in that they would only be measuring parts of what we take to be the construct of writing ability.

Quote 7.21   Hyland on indirect tasks

Hyland describes the Test of Standard Written English (TSWE) and Test of English as a Foreign Language (TOEFL) as exemplars of this indirect approach:

Often, *summative*, emphasizing the product rather than writing development, and *indirect*, typically drawing on test measures which produce strong statistical reliability . . . they clearly have little to do with the fact that communication and not absolute accuracy, is the purpose of writing.

(2002: 9)

Indirect tasks suffer from a number of major drawbacks:

- They involve few of the elements we have listed under 'executive processing' or 'executive resources' above and to this extent they can not be said to meet the demands of theory-based validity.
- What they test may be related to proficient writing, as statistical studies have demonstrated, but they cannot represent what proficient writers can do (Hamp-Lyons 1990).

- It would be difficult to generalize from these types of test to how candidates might perform on more productive tasks which required construction of a complete text and involved all or most of the elements in the executive processing and executive resources parts of our model.
- It would be difficult from these discrete item tests to make direct statements about how good a writer is or what he or she can do in writing.

Such indirect tests might also have an extremely negative washback effect on the teaching that precedes them. Having said this, at a very elementary level micro-linguistic features may be all the candidates are capable of being tested on. In any case, at higher levels of ability these micro-linguistic elements are likely to be subsumed by the informational and interactional operations involved in more authentic tasks.

Direct extended writing tasks of various types, such as the Test of Written English (TWE) which, since 1986, can be taken with TOEFL and the IELTS writing test involving extended informational and/or interactional routines, now offer a more construct-valid approach. Because these tasks can approximate more closely to the operations and conditions involved in writing academic, social and service texts in the real world, they are likely to have greater context- and theory-based validity. Producing such texts is also likely to involve most of the elements of executive processing and resources we have described above. Directness is, of course, a relative concept as all tests are at best only 'indirect' indictors of the underlying ability. However, the distinction is common and useful for categorizing tests.

Quote 7.22   Hyland on direct writing essays

Many direct tests also have problems with contextual validity however. While students may actually produce some writing in direct tests such as TWE and IELTS, this is often based on a brief, timed response to one or two topics. Although there is some attempt to create a genuine context, these samples provide little information about students' abilities to provide a sustained piece of writing for different audiences or purposes. In addition, the holistic scoring procedures generally used to mark this work often conceal a lack of consensus on writing quality and can disguise the influence of local errors on raters' scores...

In fact there is little evidence to show that syntactic complexity or grammatical accuracy are either the principal features of writing development or the best measures of good writing. Many students can construct syntactically accurate sentences and yet are unable to produce appropriate written texts...focusing exclusively on formal features of text as a measure of writing competence ignores how texts are the writer's response to a particular communicative setting...students don't just need to know

how to write a grammatically correct text, but how to apply this knowledge for particular purposes and contexts.
(2002: 8–10)

Concept 7.10 Weigle on rating scales

As McNamara (1996) notes, the scale that is used in assessing performance tasks such as writing tests represents, implicitly or explicitly, the theoretical basis upon which the test is founded: that is, it embodies the test (or scale) developer's notion of what skills or abilities are being measured by the test. For this reason the development of a scale (or set of scales) and the descriptors for each scale level are of critical importance for the validity of the assessment.
(2002: 109)

We will return to this issue of marking in Chapter 9, where we consider the scoring validity elements of our validation framework. Before that, it seems sensible in the next chapter to look at a number of examples of language tests along a direct–indirect continuum in the various skills areas and to examine how they relate to the context and theory-based elements we have raised in Chapters 6 and 7.

Further reading

Speaking
Bygate (1987) is an early, but still useful, view of the speaking process, focusing on procedural aspects as against the componential approach adopted by many other writers.
Levelt (1993) is one of the few researchers to address the process of speaking compared to the decidedly a-modal mindset of other applied linguists preoccupied with the written mode.
Hughes (2002) sets the record straight about the importance of researching speaking in its own right with its own grammar and its own theory.
Fulcher (2003) addresses the need to include empirical and theoretical analyses of response processes as part of developing a validity argument for a test.

Reading
Alderson (2000) provides a comprehensive account of reading research and theory.
Grabe and Stoller (2002) offer a comprehensive and readable account of reading theory, research and practice.
Urquhart and Weir (1998) provide further detail on the conceptualization of reading adopted in this chapter. A thoughtful, if occasionally irreverent, overview of practice, process and product in reading.

Listening

Rost (2002) provides an excellent overview of teaching and researching listening and
   provides a thorough treatment of the linguistic and pragmatic processes involved
   in listening.

Writing

Hyland (2002) offers a wide review of writing research and teaching.

8
Response Formats

8.1 Techniques for testing reading comprehension

Quote 8.1   Alderson on the need for diversity in techniques for testing reading

It is now generally accepted that it is inadequate to measure the understanding of text by only one method, and that objective methods can usefully be supplemented by more subjectively evaluated techniques. Good reading tests are likely to employ a number of different techniques, possibly even on the same text, but certainly across the range of texts tested. This makes good sense since in real-life reading, readers typically respond to texts in a variety of different ways.
(2000: 206)

What follows are test examples that have been constructed for specific students in specific contexts around the world requiring a variety of abilities in reading. They are taken from a variety of levels from elementary to advanced. It may well be that particular techniques and what they test are inappropriate as they stand for your own students. Do not worry about this. Try to establish whether they might usefully be customized for the students in your particular context.

The examples represent some of the more valid options for testing reading ability along an indirect/direct continuum. Read the texts and complete the test items set on each. While you are completing the items, think hard about the skills/strategies we discussed in Chapter 7 that you are using to answer them. For each technique consider:

- What can you say about their context-based validity?
- What can you say about their theory-based validity?

It will be helpful here if you could refer back to Chapters 6 and 7 and in particular look at the model of the reading process (Chapter 7) and the context validity part of the sociocognitive framework (Chapter 6).

Indirect task types

Example R1 selective deletion gap filling

Read the passage below and find where words are missing. Choose **one** word from the list of words provided to fill in each gap. Write the word opposite the corresponding question number on the answer sheet.
Example: **Choose from the following words: down, morning, is, not, hello.**
Good morning everybody. Good (1), sir.
Sit (2) everybody. My name (3) Mr Hunt.

Answer sheet

1. morning
2. down
3. is

Now look at the passage below and do the same. You have **10 minutes** to finish this task.

Words: **Freetown, likes, they, her, them, sings, years, works, is, she, go, doesn't, live, a, never, their, sister, but, lives, town, dog, does, plays, on, brother**

Yemi is in the eleventh grade and (1) seventeen years old. She does not (2) in Bamako. (3) lives in a small (4) nearby. (5) father (6) in a factory in Bamako, and her mother works in (7) hospital in the town. She has four brothers and one (8). Her sister (9) not live in Bamako. She (10) in Freetown and works in an office. Yemi's brothers live with (11) parents and (12) to school in Bamako. Yemi (13) basketball at school. She (14) English but she (15) like Mathematics.

Answers

(1) _____
(2) _____
. . .

Comment on Example R1

In this variation on traditional random-deletion cloze procedure, content words are deleted from the text on a principled basis and candidates have to provide an accurate and appropriate word for each blank from a list provided.

Example R1 is made more of a test of reading than writing by providing the answers for the candidates to select from, rather than requiring candidates to supply them. In some versions, where the number of options is equal to the number of gaps, this might create problems of its own. If a student gets one item wrong, then it means s/he is penalized twice, and guessing is encouraged towards the end of the task. The way round this is to provide a number of additional distracters within the list of correct answers. Even where answers are not provided, with careful consideration at the moderation stage, marking should be relatively straightforward, and items can be selected which have a restricted number of possible answers. You should not penalize for spelling unless it cannot be understood or the spelling could be taken as another word.

In line with developments in both TOEFL and Cambridge examinations, vocabulary testing has become more embedded and context-dependent over the last 50 years (see Read 2000: 139, and Weir and Milanovic 2003: 137–41, for evidence of this). In fact, the vocabulary sections of tests in both organizations are located in the reading sections of their tests and no separate scores for vocabulary are provided. As such tests involve comprehending most of the words in the passage in order to provide the context for selecting the appropriate answer, this seems a reasonable decision.

Quote 8.2   Read refers to an important study by Henning (1991), which found:

[V]ocabulary test formats that encouraged the test takers to make use of contextual information had not only greater face validity but also very desirable psychometric qualities. It seemed that Oller's faith in the value of context was justified . . .

Later he adds:

. . . A whole passage offers greater opportunities to assess aspects of word knowledge in addition to meaning, for example, the grammar of the word, its inflectional and derivational forms, collocational possibilities, stylistic appropriateness to the context and so on . . .
(2000: 144, 164)

Items are relatively easy to construct for this technique. Selective deletion enables the test constructor to determine where deletions are to be made and to focus on those items which have been selected *a priori* as being important to a particular target audience. It is also easy for the test writer to make any alterations shown to be necessary after item analysis and to maintain the required number of items. This might involve eliminating items that have not performed satisfactorily in terms of discrimination and facility value (see Chapter 9).

Texts can be selected to satisfy appropriateness in terms of all the contextual variables identified in Chapter 6, for example: discourse type, length, topic, lexical and structural range. There is, however, some debate on what is being tested where only single lexical items are deleted. Is it testing the ability to recognize which form of the word is required and/or lexical knowledge? Read (2000: 106–7) in his comprehensive review of research on vocabulary assessment notes: 'there has only been a small amount of research that has investigated the rational cloze in a systematic way with second language learners'. Such investigation may be difficult to progress as, apart from the subconscious and interrelated nature of these aspects of processing, individuals may vary in the way they process deleted items.

Alderson's research (1978) on random-deletion cloze suggested that readers rely on the immediate constituents surrounding the gap to fill it in, so to the extent that this is the case, text level processing is often limited. It is unclear whether any demand is placed on discoursal, or sociolinguistic knowledge and the monitor only serves to check the suitability for each gap of the lexical item and does not play the central and wide ranging role outlined in the model of the reading process presented in Figure 7.1 above, p. 92.

The technique is indirect, as normally it measures a limited part of what might constitute reading proficiency, namely lexical and syntactic contributory skills, and it does not seem to provide any evidence of a candidate's ability in other important skills and strategies normally involved in text level reading, such as those brought into play by extracting information quickly by search reading or reading carefully to understand main ideas and important information (see, however, Bensoussan and Ramraz 1984 for attempts to test at the macro-level using this technique, with items aimed at testing functions of sentences and the structure of the text as a whole but with short phrases). Anecdotal evidence suggests that after many candidates take gap-filling tests they are often unable to say what the passage was about.

The more indirect tasks are, the more difficult it is to generalize from scores on the test to statements about students' reading ability. How many would the student have to score to be deemed to have met the pass grade in reading, to be deemed a competent reader? This is difficult to say because such tests normally only tell us about micro-linguistic skills/knowledge. We have no data on other skills and strategies on which we might premise an inference. The wider the base for the inference the more grounded it would be. On its own, therefore, it is likely to be an insufficient indicator of a candidate's reading ability because of limited content coverage and the restricted processing involved. If the purpose of a test is to sample the range of our hypothesized components of reading, including strategies such as skimming, search reading and scanning, then an additional technique to gap filling is essential.

There might be some concern over the purpose of completing such a test task. The technique does not have a positive washback effect on learning as it is not in itself a direct measure of the reading construct. It is difficult to see how this test relates to a normal reading process. Would the time spent on practising this particular technique not be better spent on processing real texts in a more natural fashion?

As a technique it has many of the advantages to SAQ (described below) but because it controls the insertions that can be made more closely, it lessens further the need for the candidate to use productive skills. High marker reliability is likely with a carefully constructed answer key that accounts for all the possible acceptable answers; Hughes (2003: 80–1) provides useful advice on grammar and vocabulary items the technique does *not* work well on.

Tests of this type may be more happily described as tests of general proficiency rather than tests of reading, although there is some evidence from statistical analysis that a reading factor is quite strong in determining test results (Weir 1983). There is also growing evidence (Shiotsu 2003) from TESOL research done with Japanese undergraduates that tests of syntactic knowledge and tests of lexical knowledge may, in that order, be crude but efficient indicators of careful reading ability, particularly for lower-level students. Shiotsu administered a battery of tests to the same group of students and carried out a number of sophisticated statistical analyses between the results on the indirect tests of syntax and vocabulary breadth with performance on traditional MCQ tests of careful reading ability. His results show that syntactic knowledge rather than lexical knowledge was a better predictor of performance on the reading tests.

In tests of single lexical items real issues of content coverage emerge and raise the question of the extent to which we can generalize from the results on this task to how candidates might cope with broader demands on their lexical knowledge. A 20-item test of any vocabulary would only sample one word in 500 from a 10,000-word vocabulary. Read (2000: 247) does point out, however, that 'computer corpus software allows us to calculate the frequency and range of particular lexical items in large sets of texts more efficiently than was possible in the past. Concordance programs can rapidly assemble multiple examples of a particular word or phrase, each in its linguistic context, so that we can see its typical meaning(s), its grammatical function(s), the other words it collocates with and so on'. Such developments will improve the basis on which items can be selected but the generalizability issue still remains.

Norbert Schmitt (personal communication) argues that: 'Perhaps the best and most valid type of vocabulary test is a reading passage with comprehension questions, but with the items requiring a full understanding of particular words of phrases in the text. This would mimic the real world task of reading for comprehension and also the loss of comprehension when key vocabulary is not known.'

Direct task types

Example R2 SAQ careful reading

Look at the following questions and then read the text below.

Questions

1. According to the passage, give **two** advantages of TV.

A _____

B _____

2. According to the passage, give **two** reasons why TV is sometimes considered a bad thing.

A _____

B _____

3. What does **double-edged sword** mean?

_____

Television is an important technological development but, as with many other popular inventions, it has advantages and disadvantages and its advocates and its critics. It presents a variety of programmes, films, and other shows that give pleasure to different tastes and ages. However, watching it too often may not always be the best use of time especially for children, because they need to study and engage in sports and hobbies. TV does provide educational programmes for all stages in the school system and also for adults who can watch these programmes when they are not working. It makes a positive contribution to life long learning. On the other hand, it sometimes shows programs that contain a high level of violence which may lead to unacceptable behaviour in society. TV is thus a **double-edged sword** with obvious benefits but also some definite drawbacks.

Comment on short-answer questions (SAQs) R2

Short-answer questions are generically those that require the candidates to write down answers in spaces provided on the question paper. These answers are normally limited in length either by the space made available to candidates, by carefully worded questions or by controlling the amount that can be written by deleting words in an answer that is provided for the candidate.

With careful formulation of the questions, a candidate's response can be brief and thus a large number of questions may be set in this technique, enabling a wide coverage. In addition to careful reading this technique lends itself to testing skimming for gist, search reading for main ideas, scanning for specific information – the expeditious strategies we identified as important in Chapter 7 (see Examples R3 and R4). Testing these strategies is not normally possible in indirect techniques such as gap filling.

Given that translation of questions into an L1 may prove problematic (Shohamy 1984), it is obviously sensible to ensure that questions are phrased in simple language or at least language simpler than the text itself.

In skills and strategy testing it is important that students should understand the purpose of the questions before they actually read the text, in order to maximize the effectiveness and efficiency of the goal-setter and monitor. Thus, if the questions only demand specific pieces of information, the answers can be sought by quickly scanning the text for these specifics rather than by reading it through very carefully, line by line. In this way a clearer purpose for reading is apparent.

Activities such as inference, recognition of a sequence, comparison and establishing the main idea of a text require the relating of sentences in a text with other items which may be some distance away in the text. This can be done effectively through short-answer questions where the answer has to be sought rather than being one of those provided. Answers are not provided for the student as in multiple-choice task: therefore if a student gets the answer right, one is more certain that this has not occurred for reasons other than comprehension of the text.

All of the performance conditions identified in Chapter 6 as suitable for consideration by the test writer can be addressed through this technique. A strong case can be made in appropriate contexts, such as EAP tests, for the use of long texts with short-answer techniques on the grounds that these are more representative of required reading in the target situation, at least in terms of length and discourse type. The beneficial washback effect of this type of technique on the teaching that precedes it cannot be ignored. The drawback of course is that including longer texts may mean fewer texts can be included and the range of topics is diminished. TOEFL uses a number of short passages for this reason, preferring to lessen potential bias from fewer topics even if situational authenticity is thereby reduced.

Answers should have to be worked out from the passage, and not already known because of world knowledge or easily arrived at by matching wording from question with wording in the text (Buck 2001: 153).

If the number of acceptable answers to a question is limited, it is possible to give fairly precise instructions to the examiners who mark them. Trialling the items should ensure questions are unambiguous and sufficiently focused but will also help determine the range of alternative answers. Mechanical accuracy criteria (grammar, spelling, punctuation) should not feature in the scoring system as this affects the accuracy of the measurement of the reading construct.

The main disadvantage to this response format is that it involves the candidate in writing, and there is some concern, largely anecdotal, that this interferes with the measurement of the intended construct. In testing both reading and listening comprehension we must be alert to the problem of the measurement being 'muddied' by having to employ writing to record answers. Care is needed in the setting of items to limit the range of possible acceptable responses and the extent of writing required. In those cases where there is more debate over the acceptability of an answer, in questions requiring inferencing skills, for example, there is a possibility that the variability of answers might lead to marker unreliability. However, careful moderation and standardization of examiners should help reduce this.

Information transfer

In an attempt to avoid this contamination of scores, Exam Boards have included tasks where the information transmitted verbally is transferred to a non-verbal form, e.g., by labelling a diagram, completing a chart, numbering a sequence of events or by multiple-matching of numbered paragraphs to key information. These are known as *information transfer tasks* and are best seen as part of the short-answer question (SAQ) family.

Example R3 Language Training and Testing Centre (LTTC) General English Proficiency Test (GEPT): Advanced Level

Expeditious search reading

In the following article, each paragraph has a heading which expresses the main idea of that paragraph. Six of the headings have not been filled in. For questions 27–32, choose one of the headings from the list (A–K) for each paragraph that lacks a heading. Note that you will not use all the headings in the list. One of the missing headings has been filled in for you as an example (E for paragraph 1). Mark the appropriate letters for questions 27–32 on your answer sheet.

You have **5 minutes** to complete these questions.

Questions 27–32

Headings for 'The First Greenlanders'

A.	A New Culture	G.	Invaders from the West
B.	Communities Are Established	H.	Life on the Land
C.	Crops Flourish	I.	Difficult Times
D.	Natives Resist Icelanders	J.	A Pioneer Attracts Followers
E.	Early Stories May Be True	K.	Ties with North America Strengthen
F.	Greater Dependence on the Sea		

The First Greenlanders

E

About a millennium ago, legends tell us, a Viking named Leif Eriksson sailed to the shores of North America, arriving hundreds of years ahead of Christopher Columbus.

Even though archaeologists have yet to uncover any physical evidence of Eriksson's visit, the presumption that a Viking band travelled that far has gained credibility in recent years. Excavations in Greenland indicate that Vikings flourished there for hundreds of years, trading with the European continent and probably Native American tribes, before disappearing.

27.

A central figure in this story was Eriksson's father, Erik the Red, who grew up in Iceland. In 980 AD, Erik the Red headed farther west when he was banished from Iceland – for murder. He set sail for land that was visible west of Iceland. Three years later, he returned to Iceland and convinced hundreds of others to join him in settling this new country. Some 25 boats set out for what Erik the Red had dubbed Greenland. Only 14 ships survived the seas, but about 450 new colonists set foot ashore.

28.

The land they saw before them was bare, uninhabited, and inhospitable, but Erik the Red's advertisements were not entirely false. A thin green carpet of arctic heath promised support for grazing farm animals. Farms sprang up quickly and, later, churches. One colony, simply called the Eastern Settlement, sat in the toe of Greenland; the Western Settlement lay close to what is now Nuuk, Greenland's capital.

Settlement a Challenge

Settling Greenland posed a formidable challenge. There were no trees large enough to produce timber for shelter or fuel. The only wood was small brush and driftwood. The Vikings settled inland, on fjords resembling those of their homeland. There they built homes of driftwood, stone, and sod. For adequate insulation, the walls of some buildings were made six to 10 feet thick.

29.

Shelter, food, and clothing were, of course, essential to survival. The summer was too short to farm grain crops, so settlers probably went without beer or bread. Although they farmed domesticated animals imported from Europe – goats, sheep, cattle – the settlers ate them sparingly, relying instead on secondary products, such as milk and cheese. In the early days, the Greenlanders' lives differed little from those of their compatriots in Scandinavia. They netted fish and hunted seal and caribou. They wove clothing from wool and linen, sometimes adding the fur of the arctic hare.

Trade with Scandinavia

For about two centuries, Greenland's Vikings had the country to themselves. Yet life was by no means easy, and they relied on a fragile trade with Scandinavia to survive. In exchange for iron, timber, and grain from Europe, they traded pelts of bear and arctic fox as well as narwhale tusks and rope made of walrus hide. Whalebone, too, was traded to Europeans for use in stiffening clothes. According to one account, the Greenlanders even traded live polar bears.

Example R3 (Continued)

30.

At some point during the fourteenth century, Greenland's climate grew colder. With the climate change, glaciers began creeping over the land, bringing with them a run-off of sand, silt, and gravel. That runoff slowly robbed the settlers of valuable pasture-land. To make matters worse, the Black Death hit Iceland, killing some 30 per cent. Although there is still no evidence the sickness reached Greenland, archaeologists believe it left its mark by curtailing the flourishing trade.

31.

The Greenlanders adapted. Recent evidence shows that their diet shifted from land-based foods to marine products. Like their kin in Norway, the Vikings in Greenland had always exploited marine life but, by the close of the fourteenth century, the proportion of their food taken from the sea had risen to 80 per cent.

32.

Between 1100 and 1200 AD, as the colder weather arrived, so did the Thules. These Native Americans, migrants from the area surrounding the Bering Strait began trickling eastward from Ellesmere Island, just northwest of Greenland. It's likely that an uneasy trade between the Vikings and Thules sprang up and that, as living conditions grew harsher for the Vikings, the better-adapted Thules thrived.

Greenland Settlements Abandoned

The Western Settlement was abandoned by 1350 AD and the Eastern Settlement by 1500 AD. When asked what became of the Vikings, Danish archaeologist Jette Arneborg says she thinks they struggled mightily to adapt to the increasingly difficult conditions. But as the weather worsened and life became even harsher, some may have returned to Iceland. And it's easy to imagine that, as trade dwindled, the settle-ments may have become so depopulated the colonists simply were unable to replace themselves.

Example R4 Gept Advanced

SAQ scanning

In this part, there are three passages with eight questions. Please read the questions first and then read the passages **quickly** and **selectively** to find the answers. For each question, mark A, B or C on your answer sheet.

You have **4 minutes** for these questions.

Questions 33–40

First read the following questions. Then read the passages **quickly** and **selectively** to find the answers. For each question, mark A, B or C on your answer sheet.

(**A** = Middlebury; **B** = Bowdoin; **C** = Colgate)

1. _____Which school is located close to a large city?
2. _____Which school has the largest percentage of minority students?
3. _____Which school has announced plans to hire more teachers?
4. _____Which school recently built a new cultural centre?
5. _____Which school did writer Hawthorne graduate from?
6. _____Which school offers students summer research opportunities?
7. _____Which school requires students to take a writing course?
8. _____Which school claims that its strongest programs are in the sciences?

Now scan the following passages to find the answers to the above questions.

Middlebury College

Middlebury College, located in Middlebury, Vermont, is one of New England's leading small, residential liberal arts colleges. It offers students a broad curriculum embracing the arts, humanities, literature, foreign languages, social sciences and natural sciences. In addition, the College's 350-acre campus has been said to be 'among the prettiest in the world'.

Middlebury believes that the purpose of the liberal arts curriculum is to give every student a detailed knowledge of at least one subject, and to correlate this with a broad understanding of the liberal arts. To achieve this objective, students are required to work intensively in one or more departments, while also completing electives in fields outside of their specialization. All students must complete a major, a first-year seminar, a college writing course and two units of physical education.

Middlebury's undergraduate program is greatly enriched by its other programs. Every summer, the main campus is devoted completely to the study of eight foreign languages and cultures. At the same time, at the nearby Bread Loaf campus, the Bread Loaf School of English is in session.

Currently, there are 2,265 students enrolled at Middlebury, of whom 12 per cent are members of minority groups, and 95 per cent are from out of state. By the year 2005, the College plans to increase the size of its student body to around 2,350. Middlebury's full-time faculty of 218 is also expected to increase to nearly 250 by that time, enabling the College to further deepen and strengthen its academic programs.

And to better serve this enlarged community, Middlebury is in the process of constructing major new facilities. In addition to a new hockey rink and a new science center, planned capital projects include an expansion and renovation of Starr Library, new dining facilities, expanded student activities space, new student residence halls, and a new humanities center.

Example R4 (Continued)

Bowdoin College

Bowdoin College's beautiful 110-acre campus is located in Brunswick, Maine. Brunswick, one of New England's most attractive college towns, is just 42 km from Maine's largest city of Portland, and a two-hour drive from Boston.

The *alma mater* of literary giants Nathaniel Hawthorne and Henry Wadsworth Longfellow, Bowdoin has undergone significant changes in recent years. The College now boasts two new, state-of-the-art science facilities and new residential halls. It has gradually phased out its fraternities and sororities, and instituted a new College House system designed to promote interaction among diverse groups of students.

Bowdoin currently enrolls 1,608 students, of whom 13 per cent are members of minority groups, and 82 per cent come from out of state. The school has a full-time faculty of 113, for a student/faculty ratio of 10:1.

Bowdoin's general distribution requirements ensure that all graduates gain a strong foundation in humanities and the arts, natural sciences and math, social sciences, and non-Eurocentric studies. At the same time, Bowdoin is unusual among liberal arts colleges because its strongest programs are in the sciences. Self-designed and double majors have become increasingly popular among Bowdoin undergraduates, and about 80 per cent of juniors and seniors conduct independent study programs with faculty members. Students can also elect unusual research opportunities, such as participation in Arctic archaeological research in Labrador or ecological research in the Bay of Fundy, Canada.

During the non-academic portion of the year, Bowdoin opens its doors to people from all walks of life. Bowdoin College Summer Programs consist of educational seminars, professional conferences, sports clinics, specialized workshops and occasional social events, and they attract several thousand people to the College each summer.

Colgate University

Colgate University is located in the village of Hamilton, at the northern end of the Chenango Colgate Valley, in upstate New York. Its 515 acres of campus begin at the village edge on the valley floor and rise to a forested hill.

Colgate currently enrolls 2,866 students, of whom 68 per cent come from outside of New York State, and 14 per cent are members of minority groups. Its full-time faculty of 230 gives Colgate a student/faculty ratio of 11:1.

Colgate is currently in the process of expanding and renovating its campus. Case Library was recently renovated, new housing has been built, and a social sciences academic building, cultural center and fitness center have been added. Residence hall renovation continues, and a new academic facility for the arts is under construction.

Colgate offers 50 undergraduate concentrations (majors), in four academic divisions: Humanities, Natural Sciences and Mathematics, Social Sciences and University Studies. Competence must be demonstrated in a foreign or classical language, and in English composition. First-year students enroll in a first-year seminar during the fall term.

In addition, Colgate offers a small graduate program leading to the Master of Arts (MA) in several academic fields, and the Master of Arts in Teaching (MAT) degree.

During the summer, Colgate encourages its students to take part in one of the many research projects being carried out on campus. Each year, more than 100 Colgate undergraduates receive summer research assistantships, enabling them to work full-time on research or scholarly projects in close collaboration with faculty members. Typical research appointments are for eight- to ten-week periods. During this time, partially subsidized on-campus housing is available, and special academic and recreational events enhance this scholarly community.

Comment on SAQ/information transfer (Examples R3–4)

Information transfer tasks are a useful variant of short-answer questions. The guiding principle here is to keep the answers brief and to reduce writing to a minimum to avoid possible contamination from students having to write answers out in full.

The questions set in this technique normally try to cover the important information in a text (overall gist, main ideas and important details). The nature of the technique and the limitations imposed by capacity at lower levels of ability will constrain the types of things students might be expected to read for in the early stages of language learning. In the first year of learning a language, reading will normally be limited to comparison and contrast of the personal features of individuals and extracting specific information from short, non-personal texts often artificially constructed. At higher levels more complex, more authentic texts will be used and most skills and strategies in expeditious reading can be assessed.

All of the performance conditions identified in Chapter 6 can be taken account of in employing this technique and in contrast to indirect techniques (such as R1) the normal purposes for which people read can be more easily accommodated. However, a good deal of care needs to be taken that the non-verbal task the students have to complete does not itself complicate the process or detract from the authenticity of the experience. In some of the more sophisticated tasks using this format, there is sometimes a danger that students may be able to understand the text but not be totally clear what is expected of them in the transfer phase. There is also a danger that in order to fit more neatly into such techniques texts are sometimes expressly written for this purpose and the conditions of an authentic text are accordingly not met (Weir 1990).

The superiority of the short-answer and information transfer techniques over all others is that texts can be selected to match performance conditions and test operations appropriate to any level of student, and the techniques are likely to activate almost all the processing elements we discussed earlier in our model of reading. They are accordingly likely to generate the clearest evidence of context- and theory-based validity.

8.2   Techniques for testing listening comprehension

We will now consider a variety of techniques that should be useful in testing the various components of listening comprehension. You will have to examine these examples of tests designed to measure listening to see how far they match *the frameworks* we have detailed in Chapters 6 and 7 above. These are examples that have been constructed for specific students in specific contexts. They are taken from a variety of levels, from elementary to advanced.

The particular context- and theory-based validities illustrated by some examples may well be inappropriate for your own students. The purpose of the exercise is to become aware of these techniques, their advantages and limitations, and to think critically about them so that you can decide what would be most appropriate (with modification where necessary in terms of your own framework) for the students you are responsible for in your particular context.

The examples represent some of the more valid options for testing listening ability along an indirect/direct continuum. Read the texts/tasks and complete the test items set on each. As a way of assessing the relevance of these tests and test items for your students, while you are completing the items, think hard about the skills/strategies you are using to answer them. For each technique consider:

- What can you say about their context-based validity?
- What can you say about their theory-based validity?

The testing of intensive listening: indirect tests

The first two tests below are *indirect*. They do not directly test a range of desirable operations, nor do they incorporate a reasonable coverage of relevant conditions, and would thus seem to measure only a limited part of what might constitute listening proficiency. To the extent that they do not match the operations and the conditions under which these might normally be performed by the intended target group, then the tasks are indirect. The more indirect they are, the more difficult it is to go directly from performance on the test task to statements about capacity to carry out future real-life activities.

You should refer back to Chapter 7 and in particular look at the model of the listening process, and to Chapter 6 for the context validity part of the socio cognitive framework.

Example L1 Matching Responses

Read the following answers. Then, listen to the tape and number the answers to the questions as you hear them. Not all statements will be numbered. You will listen to each set of questions twice.

A

_____At 8 o'clock.
_____It's nice.
_____No, I don't.
_____No, I don't think so. I think he's much older.
_____I will go to England to study.
_____It's about 30 miles.
_____It's Arthur's.
_____She is 20 years old.
_____To Ireland. They don't want to go to England.
_____After the garage, turn right and then take the second turn on your left.
_____Spring.
_____No, I'm not. I like horror films.
_____In December.
_____Sleeping.
_____She is very beautiful.
_____Why don't we go swimming?

Tapescript Set A

1. Where do they want to go to study?
2. Whose is this book?
3. Which is your favourite season of the year?
4. What will you do after you finish secondary school?
5. What were you doing when the film started?
6. How far is Oxford from Reading?
7. Can you tell me how to go to the nearest bank on foot?
8. What do you think of my new haircut?
9. When is your birthday?
10. What time does the film start tonight?
11. I think John is only 16, what do you think?
12. What shall we do on Sunday?
13. Do you like cricket?
14. You are frightened!!!

Comment on Example L1

Because of the large number of items that can be tested efficiently through this procedure it is possible to cover a wide range of structure, lexis and functions. It suffers from the fact that the candidate is only listening to single utterances and so discourse-level skills are not called upon. Achieving a situationally authentic purpose for such a task is not easy. A number of the interlocutor variables in task demands can be addressed satisfactorily, for example, variety of accents, gender and speech rate.

In Example L1 the candidate has to process meaning fully in order to be able to select the right answer in this multiple-matching format rather than possibly relying on decoding skills alone. Little recourse is made to content knowledge and the monitor is limited in what it has to achieve. The fact that the answer has to be retrieved visually from a list of possible answers obviously raises questions about the interactional authenticity of the processing that is called upon.

As with other indirect tasks it is difficult to report on what test scores mean. Performance at the micro-linguistic level gives no clear idea of how a candidate might perform on more global comprehension tasks. We cannot tell from this technique, or from dictation and listening recall, whether a candidate could understand the main idea(s) of a text, recall important detail, understand the gist of a passage, or determine the speaker's attitude to the listener. Thus, though such indirect tests are related to listening ability they cannot be said to be representative of it.

The big danger of using such indirect techniques in tests is the poor washback this will have on the teaching that precedes the test. Time spent in practising for such indirect tests could be much more profitably spent in preparing candidates for the real-life listening activities they will later have to cope with. The more test tasks reflect such real-life activities in terms of appropriate operations and conditions, then the more positive the washback of testing on teaching might be.

Example L2 Dictation

(Weir 1993)

Instructions to students

Situation: You are in a lecture and the lecturer concludes with a brief summary. He then gives you details of an assignment you have to do, and a reference to some reading which will help in the assignment.

Task: Write down in AS MUCH DETAIL as you can

- The lecturer's summary
- Details of the assignment
- The reference he gives

You will hear the text only once. There will be pauses. During the pauses write down what you have heard. You will have **2 minutes** at the end to check what you have written.

When you hear numbers you can use figures.

N.B. This is a test of your ability to grasp detail while listening in English. You will not be penalized for spelling or grammar mistakes. Do not worry about punctuation.

First we will give you a short piece for practice. Write down what you hear. We will **not** mark this.

_____
_____
_____

The practice session is now finished.

Now write down what you hear on the tape. Remember you will hear it only **once**.

Write here

1. _____
2. _____
3. _____
4. _____
5. _____
6. _____
7. _____
8. _____
etc._____

_____

Comment on Dictation Example L2

Given that candidates should be asked to perform operations as close as possible to those they might encounter in the target situation, this means listening to dictated material which incorporates oral messages typical of those they might have to process in this way in real life. Thus in EAP tests candidates might, for example, listen to definitions, references, details of assignments being dictated to them at reduced speed – all as might occur in the normal context of a lecture. Care must be taken not to make the chunks dictated too short; otherwise it involves mere transcription of simple elements. By progressively increasing the size of the chunks more demand is placed on working memory and linguistic knowledge to replace forgotten words.

The technique is restricted in terms of the number of conditions for listening that the tester is able to take account of. There are restrictions on the speaker variables (speed, pausing, built-in redundancy) as the candidate normally has to write everything down. There are also severe limitations on the organizational, propositional and illocutionary features of the text(s) that can be employed, as even native speakers are restricted in the length of utterances they can handle in this format. Similarly, the conditions of channel and size can only be partially accounted for. In short, the conditions under which this task is conducted only in a very limited sense reflect the normal conditions for reception in the spoken language.

Quote 8.3   Buck on dictation

[A]dvocates of integrative testing argued that it was a good test of expectancy grammar...Angela Oakeshott-Taylor (1977) examined the errors test takers made when taking dictation tests and found that they related to interpretation of the acoustic signal, phonemic identification, lexical recognition, morphology, syntactic analysis and semantic interpretation. On the basis of this she argued that dictation tests assess performance at all stages of the 'speech perception' process.
(2001: 74)

In terms of efficiency these indirect tests score highly. They are relatively easy to construct, easy and quick to administer and, with adequate training, relatively quick and easy to mark. It may be considered necessary in certain situations to improve the overall reliability of a listening battery by including a technique such as dictation, which can enhance this through the large number of items that can be generated, as well as being partially valid for specific situations where dictation might feature as a target group activity.

Marking may be problematic if one wishes to adopt a more communicatively oriented marking scheme where a mark is given if the candidate has understood the substance of the message and redundant features are ignored. However, training and standardization of examiners can normally overcome these problems. Using this method, one mark is given for each segment that is re-encoded in a semantically acceptable form. No marks are deducted for use of recognisable standard or personal abbreviations, omissions of communicatively redundant items, e.g., articles, or mechanical errors of grammar, punctuation or spelling. The decision the marker has to make in awarding a mark is whether the candidate demonstrates that he has understood the dictated utterance or not. If yes, then one mark is to be awarded. There are no half marks. This is a yes/no decision. If in doubt, mark it wrong! The use of a semantic scoring scheme as against an exact word system should further enhance a test's validity. One would not want to penalize for mechanical accuracy errors in a candidate's answers as to do so would interfere with the measurement of listening ability to the extent that performance is contingent on written production.

The central problem remains how performance on an indirect test of this type, which appears to measure only a limited part of listening ability in terms of our processing model described in Chapter 7, can be translated into a direct statement of proficiency. The tester cannot easily decide on what would constitute a satisfactory performance. Quantitative indicators of language ability do not easily translate into qualitative descriptors.

Quote 8.4   Buck on what dictation tests

Clearly, given the lack of context and no obvious communicative situation, dictation does not seem to require the ability to understand inferred meanings. Or to relate the literal meaning to a wider communicative context. Dictation operationalizes listening in the narrower of the two level view of listening. Dictation also clearly tests more besides listening: it requires good short-term memory as well as writing ability, and it seems fair to say that it is far more than a test of listening skills.
(2001: 78)

Next we turn to examples of listening tests which are considered to be more communicative, in so far as the listener is not concerned simply with decoding the linguistic information in the message but is also expected to interpret the meaning of that information in terms of the wider communicative context it is uttered in. It is felt that:

- Texts used should at least have the characteristics of target language use texts, i.e., be as authentic as possible in terms of salient performance conditions (context-based validity: see Chapter 6) in the real world target situation. Bachman and Palmer's *situational authenticity* (1996: 43) and our context validity.
- Task processing should also be as authentic as possible – though obviously in most real-life situations the listener just assimilates the information and stores it for later use. At the very least the cognitive processing involved in interacting with the task should reflect what happens in similar tasks in real-life purpose (theory-based validity: see Chapter 7). Bachman and Palmer's *interactional authenticity* (1996) and our theory-based validity.

In listening tests we will nearly always have to determine whether candidates have understood by getting them to do something with the information they have heard. This will involve other abilities, such as reading printed questions or writing answers, which are obviously construct-irrelevant. As long as the method itself (e.g., writing answers) does not lead to variance between candidates we need not worry overmuch. If all candidates have equal ability in these other skills then scores should not be affected and the risk of construct-irrelevant variance in scores should be minimal. A range of task types in a test would also help guard against construct-irrelevant variance.

Example L3 Short-Answer Questions

(Based on an example in the SATD manual, Khalifa (ed.) 2003)

Listening (15 minutes)

I. First look at the questions below for **1 minute**, then listen carefully to a dialogue between an interviewer and a space scientist in a TV programme. You can take notes while listening. You will hear the tape only ONCE. You will have **3 minutes** after listening to write your answers.

1. Why do many space scientists prefer unmanned spacecraft?

_____

2. Why is cleanliness important in building a spacecraft?

_____

3. What is the biggest problem in launching a spacecraft?

_____

4. What happens to the rocket engines after finishing their work?

_____

5. What do shuttles use in order to land?

_____

Text Example L3

First look at the questions below for **1 minute**, then listen carefully to a dialogue between a woman and a man in a TV program. You can take notes while listening. You will hear the tape only ONCE. You will have **3 minutes** after listening to write your answers. (One mark for each correct answer) *(allow 1 minute pause)*

Now listen to the tape.

Woman: Welcome to the program Professor Porter. Could you first please tell us what kinds of vehicles are used in space exploration?

Man: There are two kinds: first there are manned spacecraft. There are also unmanned spacecraft . . . which are preferred by many space scientists.

Woman: Why are unmanned spacecraft preferred?

Man: I suppose the main reason is that human lives are not in danger. However unmanned spacecraft cannot react to – umm – unexpected happenings.

Woman: How does the preparation for a space mission begin?

Man: First of all, space vehicles are built in special factories under extremely clean conditions.

Woman: Why this concentration on cleanliness?

Man:	Any dust could cause an explosion...that's why cleanliness is absolutely essential. After it has been built, the vehicle is then transported to the launch site – umm – by truck, rail, aircraft or ship.
Woman:	Is it then used immediately by astronauts?
Man:	Not really! Crews must first test the spacecraft to make sure it is in working order.
Woman:	Are they trained in using it?
Man:	Sure...of course they are...
Woman:	I understand that there are great difficulties in launching a spacecraft.
Man:	Yes. Gravity's the biggest problem.
Woman:	And how do you overcome gravity?
Man:	There are different rocket engines that lift the spacecraft at different stages of launching until it reaches its orbit. These engines then separate from the craft.
Woman:	So, they separate from the craft?
Man:	Yes, when they are not needed anymore.
Woman:	When the spacecraft finishes its mission, how does it return?
Man:	A spacecraft uses small rockets to come into the atmosphere again. This action is called de-orbit. Once the spacecraft is back into the atmosphere, air resistance slows it down more and more.
Woman:	How do spacecraft land?
Man:	Shuttles use – umm – shuttles use their wings to land on the runway, they land like an airplane. The wings are very much like those of an airplane.
Woman:	Professor Porter, I would like to thank you very much.

Comment on Example L3

First, the test developer needs to check that the discourse selected as input is valid in terms of the *conditions* appropriate to the particular context it is being developed for. In testing proficiency for known real world contexts, the texts should reflect appropriate features of the future target situation and in achievement testing reflect the salient features from discourse modes previously encountered in a course. As we noted above for reading, this response format allows us to satisfactorily address nearly all the elements of task setting and task demands. Texts can normally be selected to match performance conditions and test operations appropriate to any level of student, and the technique is likely to activate almost all the processing elements we discussed earlier in our model of listening. The format is accordingly likely to generate the clearest evidence of context and theory-based validity.

It is difficult to evaluate listening texts without actually listening to them. However, even on a visual inspection of the above texts it would seem that due care would need to be taken with interlocutor-related variables such as phonological modification, accent, degree of pausing (hesitation and false starts), adequate redundancy and speed of delivery in recording the text.

Buck argues that test developers should attempt to get away from closely scripted, formal, written language (2001: 246) and 'use spontaneous speech situations, but also ensure they have the linguistic characteristics of unplanned oral discourse', although he does admit that we should not underestimate the problems in delivering these. Nearly all the examples he cites from published tests such as Test of English for International Communication (TOEIC), TOEFL, and First Certificate in English (FCE) fail to do this.

Quote 8.5   Buck on appropriate listening comprehension texts

Tests must have characteristics suitable for the construct definition: if you need to assess automatic processing, you need fast texts; if you want to assess phonological modification, then you need texts with suitably modified pronunciation; and if you want to assess discourse, then you need longer texts. The particular text characteristics will obviously vary from one situation to another, but at the very least texts must use realistic spoken language. If the strategy is to focus on what is unique to listening, then it becomes even more important to use texts with a range of realistic oral features. (2001: 253)

To the extent that key features of real world spoken language are absent from the texts we employ, then construct under-representation occurs.

SAQs are a realistic activity for testing EAP listening comprehension, especially in those cases where it is possible to simulate real life activities where a written record is made of the explicit main ideas and important details of a spoken message (e.g., listening to a lecture, recording information for personal use, such as train times, etc.). The responses produced by the candidate can be limited and so the danger of the writing process interfering with the measurement of listening is restricted. Questions requiring a greater deal of propositional inferencing (passage-dependent) will mean we have to decide in advance what is an acceptable interpretation of the text and what constitutes an adequate response in a written answer. Though this is more complex than marking items which have unambiguous responses, the way the question is framed should enable the test developer to control the number of these. Piloting should help determine the range of acceptable answers. In those cases where the number of responses seems infinite, this suggests that there may be something wrong with what the question is asking or the way it has been structured.

It is crucial that test writers map a text whilst listening to it in advance of writing the questions in order to ensure they do not miss out on testing any of the explicit or implicit main ideas or important details, where this is the *purpose* of the particular listening exercise. As long as the initial mapping exercise is carried out with due care and attention, then the questions the candidates receive after they have listened to the text and taken notes should represent a reasonable summation of the information (main points and important details) that could have been taken away from the text.

If the candidate has to answer written questions while listening to continuous discourse, there is a danger that some of the main ideas or important details might be missed while an answer to a previous question is being recorded. Questions will need to be spaced out appropriately in the text to avoid this.

By providing candidates with a framework of statements questions in the example above, the tester has actually given away the main elements of the structure of the text. If we want to test a candidate's ability to extract unaided the main ideas and important detail from spoken input this might be better served by candidates first making notes while listening to the lecture or interview and then answering questions after they have finished listening. This then would involve note taking abilities as well as listening comprehension.

Example L4 Information Transfer Techniques

You are in Britain on holiday and you would like to see a Shakespeare play performed by the Royal Shakespeare Company at Stratford-upon-Avon. You phone the Royal Shakespeare Company Theatre at Stratford to find out what plays are being performed. You need to discuss which play you are going to see with your friends, so you have to take down the details you are given on the phone. Write down the information about the performances that you need, to help your friends decide. The first one is done to help you.

Text

Thank you for calling. We're sorry there is no one in the office at the moment. This recording gives you information about the plays that are being performed in Stratford this week. On Monday at 2 o'clock the *Three Sisters* will be performed and seats are available at £5. This play can also be seen in the evening on Thursday at 8 o'clock when seats are available at £10. On Wednesday there is an afternoon performance of *Julius Caesar* at half past two and the price of tickets is £6. *Julius Caesar* will be performed again on Saturday evening at 8 o'clock and tickets will be £15. We are pleased to announce that on Tuesday and Friday this week there will be performances of *Hamlet*, one of Shakespeare's most famous plays. On Tuesday it will be performed at 2 o'clock in the afternoon and on Friday there will be an evening performance at the usual time. Tickets will cost £12 for the evening performance and £6 for the afternoon. Should you require any more information please ring this number between 10 o'clock in the morning and 2 o'clock in the afternoon.

Example L4 (Continued)

Information about plays on at the Royal Shakespeare Company

	Time starts	Play	Price
Monday	2.00	*Three Sisters*	£5
Tuesday	2.00		£
Wednesday		*Julius Caesar*	£
Thursday	8.00		£
Friday		*Hamlet*	£
Saturday	8.00		£

Information transfer techniques

In classroom testing the information transfer technique will usually involve drawing or labelling diagrams or pictures, completing tables, recording routes or locating buildings etc. on a map. At lower levels of ability we need to keep the actual transfer operation simple, as in Example L4. The nature of the technique and the limitations imposed by communicative capacity in the early stages of language learning constrain the types of things students might be expected to listen for. These are normally going to be limited to identification, comparison and contrast of the personal features of individuals, or distinguishing features of various physical items or of events. The students could also be asked to follow a set of instructions, where the teacher reads instructions and the students complete a drawing and label it.

In using this technique you should try to keep answers brief and to reduce writing to a minimum, so as to minimize any demands on productive skills. In the questions, cover the range of information in the text and if possible, even with short texts, try to establish what colleagues, or students in the same ability range as the intended test population, would consider important in terms of main ideas/important details to extract from the listening experience.

With more advanced students a wider range of skills can be tested through this format. It is particularly efficient for testing an understanding of sequence, process description, relationships in a text and classification. The technique does not, however, lend itself easily to testing the skills of inferred meaning comprehension or determining the speakers' attitudes. If the purpose for listening to spoken discourse involves these skills then this particular technique may not be suitable. To ask a question on overall gist or the speaker's attitude or the connotation of words this might best be done through a multiple-choice question which asks for the best inference from three options. However, our earlier reservations about this technique should be borne in mind (see Chapter 6 on response formats). If it is possible to test this skill through SAQ (see L4 above) then this is generally preferable.

A particular advantage of using the information transfer technique in testing listening is that the student does not have to process written questions while trying to make sense of the spoken input, and the amount of writing the student has to produce can be even more constrained than in SAQs.

There is, however, a problem of securing authentic texts which match the conditions one might wish to include. There is a danger that the text will relate more to the written than the spoken medium and listenability will be impaired. Shohamy and Inbar (1991) suggest that texts that more closely resemble spoken language are easier to process than those that exhibit more 'written' features. Care must be taken to select text types that reflect the purpose of the test.

Beyond the elementary level it is quite difficult to find spoken texts that fit neatly into the information transfer format. For example, pure classificatory texts are very rare. Whereas, in reading, a certain amount of editing of texts is feasible (though not necessarily desirable) and in general a greater variety of texts are more readily available, this is not the case for listening texts taken from authentic sources. It is extremely difficult to locate and record suitable authentic spoken discourse for this technique at an advanced level. This must put a serious question mark against its potential validity.

In terms of the types of texts suitable for use in this format, many such as narratives and argumentative texts may be inappropriate. If these are identified as important in particular testing contexts then other techniques may need to be adopted to sample understanding of these.

Teachers are most likely to use the information transfer technique at lower proficiency levels than the level of academic listening, not least because of the problems of replicability referred to above in the discussion of its use in reading tests. Understanding of complex classification or description of state and process are normally dealt with at the higher levels of ability. Constructing information transfer tasks to match these texts could entail a level of draughtsmanship or drawing ability normally beyond that of the average teacher. The most serious factor limiting its use in the classroom is the issue of achieving reasonably clear drawings, as most teachers simply do not have the abilities required to produce the illustrations used. The illustrations are at the same time one of the strengths of this approach and a potential Achilles' heel.

8.3 Techniques for testing speaking

The range of techniques below embraces the more direct types such as interaction between students (Example S3), and the face-to-face interview (Example S5), and the more indirect types such as mini-situations (Example S1). Directness here is a function of how closely a task relates to real-life performance (in terms of context and theory-based validity), and how far performance on the task can be assessed in terms that allow of direct comparison with that target performance. The more indirect the task the more difficult it will be to translate test results into statements about what candidates can or can not do in terms of the real-life activity under review.

The examples have been constructed for specific students in specific contexts. They are taken from a variety of levels from elementary to highly advanced. The particular conditions or operations in some examples may well be inappropriate for your students. You should think critically about them so that you can decide what would be most appropriate for the students you are responsible for in your particular context, or what alterations might be necessary before you could use them.

Test techniques to be reviewed

Indirect
(S1) Mini-situations on tape
(S2) Information transfer: narrative on a picture sequence.

Direct
Interaction is student with student
(S3) Information gap exercise
Interaction is student with examiner or interlocutor
(S4) Free interview/conversation
(S5) Controlled 'interview'
(S6) Monologic tasks

Example S1 Mini-Situations

Candidates have to respond to a number of remarks that might be made to them or to situations that they might find themselves in when they are in Britain.

A.

First, you will hear a number of remarks which might be made to you in various situations when you are speaking English. Some are questions and some are comments. After each one, reply in a natural way.

Here is an example:

Sorry to keep you waiting.
That's all right.

Now are you ready? Here is the first.

1. Where've you been? We started ten minutes ago.
2. It's hot in here.
3. Didn't you see the red light?

Etc.

B.

You will hear descriptions of a number of situations in which you might find yourself. Say what seems natural in each situation. Here are some examples:

1. You are late for an appointment at the doctor's surgery. What might you say to the receptionist when you arrive?
2. Your examination result was not as good as you expected. You would like to discuss your work with your tutor, and you would like to see him about it as soon as possible. What might you say to him?
3. Someone asks you what sort of weather you have in your country at this time of year. How might you answer?
4. You don't know where the local Health Centre is. Ask another student the way there.
5. You are not sure of the time of the next class. How might you ask your friend for the information?

Etc.

C. TSE Test of Spoken English ETS

Now you will be asked to respond to a co-worker.

Imagine that you happen to meet a colleague who has recently received a promotion. Greet your colleague and be sure to:

- mention the recent promotion,
- express your positive reaction to the promotion, and
- extend appropriate wishes to the colleague.

You will have **30 seconds** to prepare your response. Do not begin speaking until I tell you to do so. (60 seconds)

Comment on example S1A–C

This test type may have some advantages in terms of the conditions the tester is able to build into it. Perhaps the main benefit if the material is recorded is that it is possible to expose the candidate to a wide variety of linguistic and interlocutor task demands (for example, different interlocutors, accents, gender, settings, roles, topics, functions) in a short space of time. Against this it might be argued that because this test type involves a high degree of flexibility in jumping from situation to situation, we may be placing unfair demands on candidates.

All candidates receive exactly the same input and so the task dimensions are equivalent for all. This is a desirable condition of uniformity of administration that is much more difficult to attain in the more direct tasks we will examine below. The contaminating variable of the effects of co-construction of discourse prevalent in more interactive tasks is controlled in this response format.

If the candidate's responses are recorded, reliability can be enhanced. Double marking is possible and the recording can be replayed. Reliability is further enhanced by the large number of items that this technique can incorporate. In normal face-to-face, examiner–student interaction it may also be difficult to make reliable judgements about the candidate's ability to operate appropriately in a variety of situations. The tape technique lends itself to this more readily. Thus, in terms of sampling, this technique has the advantage over a number of the later examples.

A big advantage of this technique is its practicality. In those situations where language laboratory booths are available, as many as 60 candidates can be examined at any one time. As the performances are recorded they can be marked at a time and a place suitable to the examiner(s).

In terms of a number of the performance conditions we might want to build into a test example, S1A and S1B are, however, limited, e.g., in terms of reciprocity. As a result of these limitations the quality of output can only be assessed by a restricted range of criteria. The TSE examples are potentially more productive and they are likely to allow judgements to be made on linguistic, discoursal and sociolinguistic aspects of language competence.

Example S2a Information Transfer

Description of a chart or a figure

Test of Spoken English Sample Test

The graph below shows the number of workers in five different occupations in the United States in 1990 and the projected number for the year 2005. Take **15 seconds** to look at the graph.

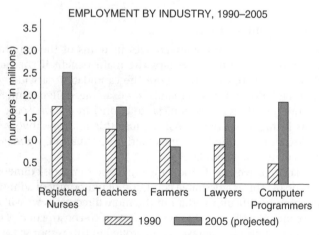

EMPLOYMENT BY INDUSTRY, 1990–2005

1. Tell me about the information given in the graph. (60 seconds)
2. What do you think might be some of the reasons for the changes represented in the graph above? (60 seconds)

S2a is a common task in many professional and study settings (Weir 1983a provides details of this). Luoma (2004: 148–50) argues that 'to do well on the task, the speakers need to set the scene and identify parts of the information or stages in the process that they are explaining and present them in a coherent order. They also need to explain the significance of the important parts or stages, so that the listeners understand what the explanation is about and why it is being given....

A particular point to check with graphs is complexity, as many graphs are too complex for examinees to understand under stressful test settings. Appropriate graphs contain enough information to give material for a sustained explanation, butnot too much so that they are easy enough to interpret.'

Example S2b Narrative on a series of pictures

The candidate sees a panel of pictures depicting a chronologically ordered sequence of events and has to tell the story in the past tense. Time is allowed at the beginning for the candidate to study the pictures.

Test of Spoken English Sample Test

Please look at the six pictures below. I'd like you to tell me the story that the pictures show, starting with picture number 1 and going through picture number 6. Please take **1 minute** to look at the pictures and think about the story. Do not begin the story until I tell you to do so.

1. Tell me the story that the pictures show.
   (60 seconds)
2. The man in the pictures is reading a newspaper. Both newspapers and television news programmes can be good sources of information about current events. What do you think are the advantages and disadvantages of each of these sources?
   (60 seconds)

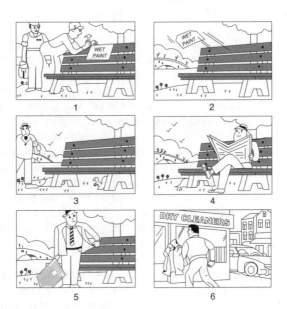

Comment on Example S2a and b

The information transfer technique is straightforward and much favoured by school Exam Boards in Britain. In the study of suitable techniques for a spoken component for TOEFL (Clark and Swinton 1979) this proved to be one of the most effective techniques in the experimental tests. The task required of the candidates is clear. It does not require them to read or listen and thereby avoids the criticism of contamination of measurement. An important proviso is that the value of the technique is dependent on the pictures being clear and unambiguous and free from cultural or educational bias.

The picture sequence can be an efficient procedure and one of the few available to get the candidate to provide an extended sample of connected speech, a long informational routine, which allows the application of a wide range of criteria in assessment including coherence as the organization of discourse in long turns. It is also useful for eliciting the candidate's ability to use particular grammatical forms, such as the past tense for reporting.

Luoma (2004: 144) emphasizes that when using a picture sequence the examiner must ensure that candidates demonstrate control of the essential features of narratives:

- setting the scene;
- identifying the characters;
- referring to them consistently;
- identifying the main events;
- telling them in a coherent sequence.

Because all candidates are constrained by common information provided by pictures, graphs or drawings (the same dimensions of input), it is possible to make a comparison of candidates which is relatively untainted by background or cultural knowledge, given that the drawings themselves are culture-free.

If the quality of the pictures is in any way deficient, then the candidate may not have the opportunity of demonstrating his best performance. Differences in interpretation might also introduce unreliability into the marking.

Our comments on information transfer tasks in the reading and listening sections provide evidence of the value of this technique in screening out the potential impact of other skills on the measurement of the skill under review. The main problem we identify, of the difficulty teachers may have in being readily able to produce the visual non-verbal stimuli, applies here as well. This in the end may be the biggest limitation of the use of this technique in the classroom and teachers may, as a result, resort to student prepared talks with all their associated problems.

The extended picture description lacks situational authenticity and one might seriously question when students ever need to do this kind of thing in real life, i.e., what is its purpose? However, claim might be made for interactional authenticity in that the technique may well be tapping into the informational routine of reporting, particularly in the case of the description of the contents of the graph, which might well happen in an oral presentation, talk or lecture.

Describing something that has happened may well be an important operation in some contexts, but, generally speaking, this task tells us very little about the candidate's ability to interact orally or to use skills such as negotiation of meaning or agenda management. The technique does not allow the tester to incorporate the important condition of reciprocity, which can only be tested in a more interactive technique.

Example S3 Student–Student Interaction

In this type of test where the examiner takes no part, candidates should be more at ease and may mean they have more opportunity and inclination to speak. They can also select in advance whom they wish to do the test with so that they are interacting with somebody they know and feel happy communicating with. This may well lead to a positive affective response as we discussed in Chapter 5 and possibly enhance performance.

In these tasks students normally work in pairs and each is given only part of the information necessary for completion of the task. They have to complete the task by getting missing information from each other. Candidates have to communicate to fill an information gap in a meaningful situation.

As a development from this interaction an interlocutor appears after the discussion and the candidates might, for example, have to report on decisions taken and explain and justify their decisions. The interlocutor is normally known to the students and might be their teacher.

Tasks should be explained clearly to students before they start. The teacher should interfere as little as possible and only prompt where absolutely necessary. Prompts should be in L1 in monolingual situations and no direct clues should be given to pupils about what to say.

In the example below, candidates in groups of two or more have to organize and maintain some kind of discussion in which each student is to have more or less an equal amount of speaking time. The task involves taking information from written texts and arriving at a consensus on certain matters through interaction. If it is an achievement test, then the content may well have already been practised in class in a comprehension exercise and the vocabulary and structures pre-taught. The students would not have seen the actual spoken language task before the test but may well have practised on similar activities. The task is normally set up so that there is no single correct solution.

Interaction with peers

The situation is that one of the candidates (student B) has won a competition and the prize is £90. He or she would like to buy a camera. The two candidates are asked to decide between four cameras and decide which is the best camera to buy. Student A has information on two cameras and student B has information on another two. They have to exchange this information verbally (only) and decide which camera to buy. Tell them they have **10 minutes** to complete the task.

Example S3 (Continued)

Student's prompt sheet A
You will find below information on two cameras, A and B. Your friend has information on two more cameras C and D. Your friend has won some money in a competition and wants to buy a camera. Using the information you both have, you must help him/her decide which camera to buy. Make sure you check all the information before deciding. When you have finished discussing, you should tell your teacher which camera you would buy, and why. Wait for the other person to start the conversation.

	Price (£)	Weight (gm)	Size	Flash
Camera A	90	250	small	+
Camera B	80	300	medium	+

Student's prompt sheet B
You have won some money in a competition and want to buy a camera. You have £90 to spend. You will find below information on two cameras, C and D. Your friend has information on two more cameras A and B. Using the information you both have, you must decide which camera you would buy. Make sure you check all the information before deciding. When you have finished discussing you should tell your teacher which camera you would buy. **You must take the responsibility for starting the discussion and reaching a decision. You only have 10 minutes for this.**

	Price (£)	Weight (gm)	Size	Flash
Camera C	60	250	small	–
Camera D	80	550	small	+

(Weir 1993)

Alternative

It would be possible to adapt this task for use with four students at a time. Each student would be given a prompt sheet with only one of the four sets of details filled in. Each student would be asked in turn by a different member of the group about the various elements: cost, weight, etc. and the other students would complete the details on their own sheets. In this way each student would get the opportunity to both ask and answer questions. Next, any student would be allowed to ask for any missing information on any of the cameras. The final stage would be a discussion on which camera should be bought. This could be structured by first having A/B talk and then having C/D talk and finally the group as a whole coming to an agreement.

Further alternatives could easily be constructed using cars, motorcycles, watches, pens, etc. Cambridge ESOL has employed pictures in their main suite examinations to the same effect; see Milanovic and Weir (2003: Chapter 7) for a discussion of the development of these tasks.

Comment on Example S3

Tasks of this type can be interesting and incorporate real materials from everyday life. In example S3, the students have to solve a problem, report conclusions to a third party and support these in argument, thus covering both interactional and informational routines.

The task is interactive and as such comes much closer than most other tasks under discussion to representing real communication. It recognizes the unpredictability of communicative situations and demands an ability to generate original sentences and not simply the ability to repeat rehearsed phrases.

As a normal feature of the interaction elicited by S3, candidates use question forms, elicit information, describe, make requests, make comparisons, give opinions, state preferences, give explanations, persuade, come to decisions, etc. They perform a range of the operations we identified earlier as occurring in normal spoken interaction. The range of operations is likely to be more extensive than occurs in the interviews in S4 and S5 below (see Fulcher 2003 for discussion of this).

The interaction is purposeful but unpredictable. Negotiation of meaning is required to arrive at a suitable outcome and the tasks are designed to encourage cooperation and a desire to arrive at a consensus. Because the candidates' contributions are unpredictable, they are less likely to have been rehearsed beforehand, as happens in many traditional interview situations. The candidates have to monitor and respond to the discussion spontaneously. An appropriate level of explicitness is required in order to decide on the best choice of camera.

Some improvisational skills may well be called upon, e.g., candidates may need to indicate purpose, check on understanding, ask the other person for forgotten information, ask for and give opinions, check common ground, clarify by summarizing, indicate understanding by gestures and other para-linguistic means, indicate uncertainty and/or lack of comprehension, express agreement or reservation, negotiate meaning by making and/or responding to clarification requests in order to succeed in the task, correct misinterpretations, and make themselves understood.

The task allows candidates to develop the activity in their own way and each participant has to respond and adjust to interlocutor feedback. There may well be agenda management even when done in pairs and this can easily be built into the task explicitly through the test instructions. In classroom testing it is perhaps best if one candidate is given a primary responsibility for this, as in the example above (this role can then be swapped around during the course). Candidates need to ensure adequate cooperation and participation from their partner in the task in order to complete it.

The task will certainly involve turn taking and candidates will have to signal when they want to speak, recognize the right moment for taking a turn, know how not to lose their turn, recognize others' signals of a desire to speak and know how to let other people have a turn. The candidates could be warned in advance which aspects of negotiation of meaning and agenda management would be monitored in any assessment of improvisational skills.

Additionally, by providing students with all the information they need one is attempting not to disadvantage those with lack of knowledge about the topic.

In terms of the conditions under which the task is performed there can be few test tasks which represent the act of communication better than this particular type as it fulfils most of the criteria for what makes a test communicative: that it should be purposeful, contextualized and interactive. Normal time constraints obtain, allowing performance to be assessed for fluency in terms of smoothness of execution. Both participants have a responsibility for keeping the interaction going until the objective is realized, so reciprocity is a marked feature of this task with both contributing, taking what the other person says into account and reacting to it. The role, setting and purpose are reasonably realistic for most teenagers and the task has the advantage of allowing them to interact with peers who are familiar to them. The task dimensions for S3 were appropriate for the original target group for the test and were closely checked against the course book and previous learning experiences in the classroom in terms of the length of the discourse, its propositional and linguistic complexity and the range of structures and lexis that were needed.

Perhaps the biggest advantage of this task type is a practical one, namely its replicability. *Such tasks can easily be reproduced by teachers in a multiplicity of forms by varying the details of the items to be discussed.* With a word processor this would take very little time and would make a valuable contribution to test security.

The topic may affect performance and fluency of contributions in particular and care must be taken in piloting to ensure that this task demand is addressed. The familiarity of the candidates with each other could also have an effect and in general it is felt that it is better if candidates can interact with people known to them, whom they feel comfortable with (see Chapter 5 for discussion of this). The contributions of individuals may vary as a result of these factors and though this is true of real-life discussions, it may affect the assessment of certain individuals if they say relatively little.

There is a potential problem with the reciprocity condition if one of the participants dominates the interaction, as the other candidate may have a more limited opportunity to demonstrate communicative potential (see discussion of introversion and extroversion in Chapter 5). Similarly, if there is a large difference in proficiency between the two, this may influence performance and the judgements made on it. There is also a problem if one of the candidates is more interested in the topic or the task, as the interaction may become one-sided as a result. If candidates are being assessed on their performance in a single situation on a task such as this, and extrapolations are made about their ability to perform in other situations, the resulting generalization may be equally one-sided.

The whole emerging area of the co-construction of discourse is crying out for investigation in relation to spoken language examinations (see Fulcher 2003: 44–6 for a discussion of the area). Examiners have little control over what candidates say to each other so there is an issue of variability in input across candidates and in co-construction. The real problem is that an individual's performance is clearly affected by the way the discourse is co-constructed with the person they are interacting with. How to factor this into or out of assessment criteria is yet to be established in a satisfactory manner.

Practical constraints on this type of task include the time available, the difficulties of administration and the maintenance of test security where parallel forms are not readily available. There also needs to be some suspension of disbelief, as the natural tendency would be for candidates to show each other the information each is given as a prompt.

In terms of our framework, this technique comes much closer than any of the others to allowing the test writer to deliver on a wide range of the theory and context-based elements that currently appear to characterize spoken interaction.

Interaction of student and examiner

Example S4 The Free Interview/Conversation

In this type of interview the conversation unfolds in an unstructured fashion and no fixed set of procedures is laid down in advance.

Comment on Example S4

The unstructured interview is a popular means of testing the oral skills of candidates. These interviews are like extended conversations and the direction is allowed to unfold as the interview takes place. The discourse might seem to approximate more closely to the normal pattern of informal social interaction in real life, where no carefully formulated agenda is apparent.

The candidate is able to take the initiative, change the direction of the interaction and introduce new topics. It at least offers the possibility of the candidate managing the interaction and becoming equally involved in negotiating meaning. The free interview indisputably involves interaction. In general the development of the interaction will be unpredictable and processing will normally take place in real time.

The free conversation to a certain extent provides a predictable context (in terms of formality, status, age of the interviewer, etc.), but the interviewer will affect the context created by the attitude adopted and the role selected. The candidate will have to react to this. In addition he or she will have to interpret and produce language that is cohesive and coherent in terms of the linguistic environment of the interaction. The candidate and the interviewer will have to react to the communicative value of various utterances.

One of the drawbacks of the interview is that it cannot cover the range of situations candidates might find themselves in and interlocutor variables are restricted to the one interlocutor.

The flexibility of the free interview is a major strength. The interview can be modified in terms of the pace, scope and level of the interaction. The good candidate can be pushed to the level of her/his ability in the hands of a skilled interviewer. Such flexibility of stimuli is not possible with other more structured forms of oral assessment. The assessment of speaking and listening in this integrated fashion covers what Carroll (1980) described as 'the constructive interplay with unpredictable stimuli'. The technique should enable the examiner to apply all the criteria outlined below in Chapter 9 for handling routines, improvisation and micro-linguistic skills if appropriate.

A particularly effective oral interview can occur when the candidate is interviewed and assessed by both a language examiner and a subject specialist who have been standardized to agreed criteria. The procedures followed in the UK General Medical Council's PLAB oral interview which assesses both medical knowledge and spoken English merit consideration in this respect.

In interviews it is sometimes difficult to replicate features of real-life communication such as motivation, purpose and role appropriateness. The language might be purposeful but this is not always the case and there may be exchanges in which the questioner has no interest in the answer. This is particularly so when the questioner already knows the answer (a problem with asking questions on a single picture). Normally, we are communicating because we are interested in what somebody is saying, rather than how he is saying it. The intrusion of the latter into a conversation might have a dampening effect. The purpose of assessment is not in itself communicative, except of course for language testers.

It is often difficult to elicit fairly common language patterns typical of real life conversation, such as questions from the candidate. Interviewers often manipulate conversations to get candidates to say things employing a variety of structures. This might reduce the authenticity of the discourse. It is unlikely, however, that a trained examiner would produce simplified language (slow rate of delivery or lexical or structural simplification) except where this is necessary with very weak candidates. This would need to be taken into account in the assessments made.

As there are no set procedures for eliciting language, candidate performances are likely to vary from one interview to the next, not least because different topics may be broached and differences may occur in the way the interview is conducted, with obvious implications for reliability. The procedure is time-consuming and difficult to administer if there are large numbers of candidates. The success of this technique is heavily dependent on the skill of the examiner. The shy, more inhibited candidate might not do as well as the more extrovert, more garrulous one. The problems of the co-construction of the discourse impacting on the performance assessment of the candidate are particularly prominent in this open-ended response format.

Example S5 The controlled interview (Advanced Level)

In this technique there are normally a set of procedures determined in advance for eliciting performance. The interviewer normally has been standardized in the use of an *interlocutor framework* of questions, instructions and prompts (see Weir and Milanovic 2003: Chapter 7). He or she normally manages the interaction and retains the initiative in selecting and developing the topics. The candidate normally only speaks in response to stimuli from the examiner. The interview is usually face-to-face. It normally starts with personal or social questions designed to put the candidate at ease. It may then enable the candidate to speak at length about familiar topics and perhaps finish at the higher levels with more evaluative routines such as speculation about future plans or the value of an intended course of study.

Increasingly, exam boards around the world are moving towards a common technique for the 'Interview' which as in the case of UCLES main suite examinations consists of a combination of activities usually involving:

- an interview phase between examiner and candidates as Part 1;
- an interactive phase between candidates as Part 2;
- a presentation phase as Part 3.

The first two phases account for a wide range of interactional routines and the final phase focuses mainly on extended informational routines. The hybrid 'interview' thus seeks to address most of the components discussed above under context and theory-based validity.

Comment on Example S5

During the interview, processing can take place under normal time constraints and the purpose of the interaction is acceptable to many candidates who may well face such a role in the future. It can put the candidate in the position of having to interact with somebody they do not know, of higher status and of either gender. These may be conditions which need to be built into the test to reflect the future use of the language. It is possible to test the candidate's ability to perform a variety of informational and interactional routines, and the examiner is in a position to assess improvisational skills as well, for example by asking for repetition or clarification of responses.

It remains difficult, however, even in a semi-structured interview, to satisfy such conditions as reciprocity which mark normal conversation, as the student is mainly cast in the role of respondent and there is little opportunity for him to take the initiative, manage the agenda, or take on responsibility for keeping the discussion going. In any interview the candidate is unlikely to walk in and say to the examiner 'there are a number of questions I'd like to put to you'. Few demands are put on turn taking ability either, when the candidate is cast solely in the role of respondent.

Example S5 differs from S4 in that in Parts 1 and 3 an *interlocutor framework* means there is a better chance of candidates being asked the same questions. Thus it is easier to make comparisons across performances, and reliability is enhanced. Unlike some of the more direct tasks examined above, one can be more confident that the input dimensions will be reasonably similar across candidates. The open interview in S4 does not share this advantage and different candidates may be expected to demonstrate their proficiency under a range of different task *conditions*. However, even when the procedures for eliciting performance are specified in advance there is still no guarantee that candidates will be asked the same questions, in the same manner, even by the same examiner and the linguistic demands made on the candidate will vary to the extent that this is the case – and concerns about the effects of the co-construction of discourse on performance come into play.

Parts 2 and 3 of this 'interview' further expand the range of operations and conditions the candidates have to deal with. Part 2 is similar to S3 above. Part 3 is similar to the examples in S6 below. As a group of activities, most elements of context and theory validity can be satisfactorily addressed by this hybrid format.

With carefully prepared and agreed criteria, together with a reasonable measure of standardization to these, a reliable and valid idea of a candidate's level can be formed. This hybrid interview is easy to set up and administer and has potentially high context and theory-based validity. It has been shown that with sufficient training and standardization of examiners to the procedures and criteria employed, reasonable reliability figures can be reached with both techniques, so scoring validity can be achieved too. It can be efficient in diagnosing specific weaknesses.

It is, however, time-consuming and expensive to administer when conducted on a large scale (the advantage of the semi direct test such as the mini-situations in Example S1 is obvious here). In situations such as the CET in China where there are over ten million candidates a year less direct response formats may be unavoidable and informational routines (as in Part 3) rather than interactional may be preferred.

It may be difficult for a single examiner to concentrate on what the candidate is saying and to reply accordingly as well as listen for how he or she is communicating. Thus in the FSI and Cambridge ESOL oral examination there is a separate examiner and interlocutor. The virtue of having the two trained people in the room means that the advantages of double marking for scoring validity can be utilized (see Chapter 9 below for discussion of this).

Example S6 Monologic Tasks

In a number of the examples above (S2 information transfer and S5 Part 3 Controlled Interview) the candidate has to deliver an extended monologue. The following further examples are taken from the specimen materials for the new TAST, the TOEFL Academic Speaking Test. They offer a number of useful and varied ways of examining the candidate's ability to deal with an extended informational routine.

a. Text version of Sample Question 1: Personal Experience

Narrator: You will now be asked a question about a familiar topic. After you hear the question, you will have **15 seconds** to prepare your response and **45 seconds** to speak.

Narrator: Choose a teacher you admire and explain why you admire him or her. Please include specific examples and details in your explanation.

Preparation time: 15 seconds

Response time: 45 seconds

b. Text version of Sample Question 2: Personal Preference

Narrator: You will now be asked to give your opinion about a familiar topic. After you hear the question, you will have **15 seconds** to prepare your response and **45 seconds** to speak.

Narrator: Some students study for classes individually. Others study in groups. Which method of studying do you think is better for students and why?

Preparation time: 15 seconds

Response time: 45 seconds

c. Text version of Sample Question 3: Reading/Listening/Speaking Situation

Narrator: You will now read a short passage and then listen to a talk on the same topic. You will then be asked a question about them. After you hear the question, you will have **30 seconds** to prepare your response and **60 seconds** to speak.

Example S6 (Continued)

Narrator: The administration at National University feels it needs to find a way for more people to be able to attend sporting events. Read the article from the university newspaper. You will have **45 seconds** to read the article. Begin reading now.

New Stadium Plans

The university has decided to accommodate more people at sporting events and is considering two alternative plans to accomplish this goal. One plan is to expand the current stadium, doubling it in size. The other plan is to build a new, larger stadium on the empty southern edge of the campus. The expansion of the current stadium would be by far the less expensive of the two alternatives.

Narrator: Now listen to a student who is speaking at a student government meeting about the stadium plans.

Student: I'm all for saving money, but money isn't everything. If you look at the area around the stadium, you'll see that expansion would cause the main street to be rerouted right around a main classroom building. Can you imagine the extra noise? Also, they'll have to build where there are now student parking lots – and we barely have enough parking spaces as it is. And you know that it'll take up part of the large open area next to the Student Center and that's become a really popular place for students to hang out in good weather. *This* is what they should be worried about, *not* money.

Narrator: The student expresses her opinion about one of the university's plans for a stadium. State her opinion and explain the reasons she gives for holding that opinion.

Preparation time: 30 seconds

Response time: 60 seconds

d.   Text version of Sample Question 5: Listening/Speaking Situation

Narrator: You will now listen to a conversation. You will then be asked a question about it. After you hear the question, you will have **20 seconds** to prepare your response and **60 seconds** to speak.

Narrator: Now listen to a conversation between two students who are in the same chemistry class.

First student: So, Pete, have you worked on any of those review questions Professor Gibbons gave us?

Second student: You know, I waited too long to start on them – I just started last night, and wow are they hard! If the questions on the exam are like this, I'm sunk.

First student: I did the same thing. I figured I wouldn't have trouble doing them, since I didn't have that much trouble doing the homework assignments…but these review questions…

Second student: Yeah, me too. I worked out the first question OK – the one on hydrocarbons – but I absolutely could *not* figure out how to do number two.

First student: Oh, *I* got number two. But I'm still trying to figure out the hydrocarbon question.

Second student: Well, I can help you with it if you want. In fact, maybe we should work on the rest of the questions together?

First student: Yeah. If we each understand different parts of the material, maybe between the two of us we can figure out everything we need to know for the exam. I don't think I could do it alone by Tuesday – I just didn't leave myself enough time.

Second student: Yeah, OK. I'd thought about maybe trying to get some help from Professor Gibbons on Monday when she has office hours, but since the exam is on Tuesday, that wouldn't leave a lot of time. So let's try to do it together.

Narrator: Describe the problem the students are discussing and how they decide to solve it. Then explain what you think they should do and why.

Preparation time: 20 seconds

Response time: 60 seconds

e.   Listening/Speaking Academic

Narrator: You will now listen to part of a lecture. You will then be asked a question about it. After you hear the question, you will have **20 seconds** to prepare your response and **60 seconds** to speak.

Narrator: Now listen to a part of a talk in a market research class.

Professor: So let's talk about a couple methods of doing a survey or poll. Remember we use surveys to gather information about a subject we're interested in from a large population.

One way to get information is to *mail out your survey* in the form of a set of written questions. To make your survey a success, you want to try to get back as many responses as possible. How do you do this? Well, one way is to make your survey official-looking, so people will feel it's important for them to respond and send it back to you. Another way to increase response rate is to offer a chance to win a small prize to those who answer and return your survey.

Now you could also conduct a *telephone* survey, where you call people and ask them a series of questions to get the needed information. Using this method, it's easy to reach a large number of people – you keep calling until you get the number of people you need. But it's clear that the sample of people here who respond could be different from the group that responds by way of the mail. First some people might not be reachable

Example S6 (Continued)

at all, because they don't have telephones. Or they might work during the hours a phone interviewer is calling. This might create variations in information based on social or economic status. Second, some people simply won't cooperate on the phone, feeling it is an invasion of privacy.

Narrator: Using points and examples from the talk, describe the two survey methods presented by the professor.

Preparation time: 20 seconds

Response time: 60 seconds

Comment on Examples S6a–e

This set of specimen materials from ETS offers an interesting variety of methods for getting students to speak at length. Because they are monologic they lend themselves easily to being delivered over the phone or in the language laboratory thus ensuring that input is the same for all candidates. For mass oral test administration as in the CET in China they are certainly more efficient than face-to-face interview or peer/peer interaction.

They are likely to produce a wide sample of student speech and thus facilitate the application of multiple criteria. In particular, organization of discourse over an extended turn can be measured. In most interactional routines, and especially closed tasks, this is not. In the TEEP test (see Weir 1983) the one-minute extended monologue proved to be the best single predictor of overall speaking performance in the whole 30-minute-long battery of speaking testlets.

As we noted for Example S3 monologic tasks are situationally authentic in many contexts and in particular the academic. Task demands and setting can be geared to the requirements of Target Situation Use in all respects, and internal processing can mirror closely that of such activities. The integrated nature of some of the activities is also attractive in that it approximates more closely to the setting students will find themselves in when they get to university where they may have to combine information from a variety of sources to present in seminars. By providing such information in common for all candidates variability in content knowledge is controlled for.

The focus on monologic informational routines avoids the complications of the co-construction of discourse that may bedevil judgements on performances on all but the most tightly controlled interactional tasks. It also means that the test developer is able to investigate the effects of intra-task variation in terms of task demands and setting more easily. Key considerations such as the effects of varying planning time, planning conditions (planned/unplanned), amount of talking time and audience can each be systematically researched (see Case study 1, section III for ways this might be done). It is rather surprising that almost no research has been carried out on monologic speaking tasks even though they are an important element in many national and international high stakes ESOL tests. Research into intra-task variation is critical for all high stakes tests because if we are able to manipulate the difficulty level of tasks we can create parallel forms of tasks at the same level (see Chapter 9 and Case study 4, section III). It would also contribute to establishing a principled methodology for establishing appropriate versions of tasks across the ability range.

8.4   Techniques for testing written production

We next consider examples of tests designed to measure writing that have been constructed for specific students in specific contexts. They are taken from a variety of levels from elementary to advanced. The particular *conditions*, or *operations*, in some examples may well be inappropriate for your students. The purpose of the exercise is to think critically about them in terms of the frameworks so that you can decide what would be most appropriate for the students you are responsible for in your particular context, and how you would need to adapt them in terms of the conditions and operations involved.

The examples represent some of the more valid options for testing writing ability along an indirect–direct continuum. While you are completing the tasks, think hard about the skills/strategies you are using to answer them. For each technique consider:

a)   What you can say about their context-based validity
b)   What you can say about their theory-based validity

You should refer back to Chapters 6 and 7 and in particular in Chapter 7 look at the model of the writing process and in Chapter 6 the context validity part of the sociocognitive framework.

Ideally, you should try to do each of the items yourself to see what is involved in their completion.

Example W1 Gap Filling

A. Fill in the gaps in the passage below.

I'd like to phone my American friend. _____ a newsreader on American television. He has got a really _____ job. It's seven o'clock here _____ it will be 12 o'clock in America. I _____ phone him at home. He _____ going to work this evening. He's on holiday today. There _____ a big storm in America yesterday. It damaged _____ of the houses and it killed 40 people. It _____ at eight in the morning. News of the storm was _____ television last night. We _____ the homes the fire destroyed.

Example W1 (Continued)

Answer key

I'd like to phone my American friend. **He's** a newsreader on American television. He has a really **interesting** job. It's seven o'clock here **so** it will be 12 o'clock in America. **I can** phone him at home. He **isn't** going to work today. He's on holiday. There **was** a big storm in America yesterday. It damaged **some** of the houses and it killed 40 people. It **started** at eight in the morning. News of the storm was **on** television last night. We **saw** the homes the fire destroyed.

Scoring

One mark to be awarded for each gap appropriately completed.
Total = 10 marks

Comment on Example W1

In our earlier discussion of the testing of reading we looked at selective deletion gap filling, and noted the potential value of these techniques for testing the more specifically linguistic skills such as understanding of vocabulary, structure or cohesion devices. By making the task a selection from a group of possible answers one effectively reduced the importance of writing ability in providing the answer.

It is more accurate, where answers are not provided, to talk of these techniques as testing a mixture of both reading and writing skills. There is obviously a problem in reporting on what is being tested in these more specifically linguistic items. It is by no means clear whether the results of such tests should form part of a profile of reading or of writing ability; nor is it clear how they would contribute to such assessments. Many writers (e.g., see Hughes 2003) avoid this problem by referring to them as tests of general proficiency. The problem of saying what the results mean still remains, however.

The wider the range of conditions to be taken account of in the test, for example, subject areas or topics, the more difficult it is to select discrete linguistic items for testing purposes. In specialized courses, where there is an identifiable, agreed domain, it is easier, but still a choice has to be made as to which items are the most criterial to an understanding of the passage. In those cases where the interest is in achievement related to a course book or a course of instruction, the problems are slightly reduced as lists of structures and lexis covered, and the contexts for these items, are available from course descriptions/syllabi and from scrutiny of materials used by students. The problem of sampling does not go away even then, and an argued case for selection and inclusion needs to be made.

Having selected our passages, how do we decide which items to delete? If such techniques are adopted in tests, the developers must come to a reasoned decision about which lexical items are contributing the most to a reasonable understanding of the passage.

Similar problems occur in the selection of grammatical items. A quantitative survey of the occurrence of the various structural items in the receptive and productive written materials that students will deal with is obviously beyond the scope of most test constructors. What is needed is a more pragmatic, but still reliable, method of selecting items to be included.

You should examine the content of existing tests and course books at an equivalent level to determine what experts in the field have regarded as suitable items for inclusion for similar populations (though the circularity of this approach needs some caution and these data should always be subject to critical scrutiny on the part of teachers and their colleagues). Where the test is an achievement test on a course book or prescribed set of materials, the problem of selection of grammatical items and appropriate contexts is not as great. The decision still has to be made, though, on which items to delete. This is best done through discussing with colleagues the most important items to delete in terms of their contribution to the overall meaning of the passage.

The response format would seem to involve only a limited coverage of the processing elements we noted in Chapter 7. Goal-setting, topic and genre modifying, generating ideas, organizing ideas and reviewing would seem to play only a limited part in this activity but are essential to effective performance in real-life writing. At the lower levels of language ability gap filling is sometimes considered a suitable technique for testing 'productive writing ability' in a very restricted sense. With the prior acquisition of grammatical and lexical skills beyond a certain baseline level, more extended productive tasks are, of course, feasible and, as we argue below, more desirable.

It is extremely difficult to say what scores on indirect tests actually mean. They relate to writing ability, but in no sense are they representative of it. In addition, the backwash effect of such procedures on the teaching that goes on in the classroom may be negative and draw attention away from equipping learners with the capacity for producing extended writing on their own.

It may be sensible to opt instead for carefully graded real writing tasks at a very early stage. These might involve the student initially in simple copying, then, with increased levels of ability, move in a scale of directness to eventual integrated reading into writing or information transfer tasks. Examples of these are discussed below.

Direct tests of writing

Example W2 Open-ended essay tests

a) Holidays

b) Describe what you did on your holidays during the summer.

Example W3

Write a paragraph of not less than 10 sentences (100 words) on the following topic: *Using computers*. You have **25 minutes** for this. You MUST use the following ideas:

- present uses of the computer
- advantages
- disadvantages
- possible future uses of computers

Comment on Examples W2–3 open-ended essay tests

The stimulus is usually written and can vary in length from a limited number of words to several sentences. Setting the tasks is a relatively easy affair. The topics tend to be very general and rely heavily on the candidate providing the context, either through background or cultural knowledge, or imagination. The tasks in W2 and W3 have no clear purpose. Little guidance is given to candidates on who the audience is, how they are expected to answer the question or how their essay will be assessed. Little account is taken of many of the contextual conditions we identified as important in Chapter 6.

The technique can be used for testing ability to carry out a range of the operations we identified in Chapter 7, including developing an extended argument in a logical manner, which cannot be tested through any of the indirect techniques. The big advantage this task type shares with other tests of extended writing (see more controlled tasks below) is that a sample of writing is produced, which as well as enabling the tester to apply a range of appropriate criteria in determining the quality of the output, can also provide a tangible point of reference for comparison in the future. A candidate's work at the start of a course can be compared with work produced at the end. This can be most useful in those cases where sponsors or students themselves require a clear picture of progress as a result of taking a course of instruction (videoed interactions can provide a similar picture in speaking).

This type of free, open-ended writing is problematic, however. An ability to write on such open-ended topics may depend on the candidate's background or cultural knowledge, imagination or creativity. If we are more interested in their ability to produce neutral, transactional, expository prose in defined situations, these may not be factors we wish to assess. If the candidate is not interested in the topic or does not regard it as appropriate, he or she may challenge the task.

Candidates tend to approach an open-ended question in different ways, and may produce quite different text types, exhibiting a wide variety of operations. Examiners will somehow have to assess the relative merits of these different approaches. This increases the difficulty of marking the essays in a precise and reliable manner. Furthermore, where a selection of topics is provided, it is very difficult to compare performances, especially if the production of different text types is involved. Problems for reliability also arise when candidates are allowed to choose different essays to write as we saw in Chapter 1 of the book when describing the history of the CPE, as well as when the task is open or uncontrolled. Compare W2a with W3. The latter is likely to be a much more reliable indicator of writing ability than the former. The downside of this is in terms of the validity of the scoring. By providing an organizational structure for task completion, are we preventing ourselves from using this criterion in the marking scheme? Careful preparation of any prompts is necessary to avoid making the task invalid in this way.

Where feasible we must include a direct extended writing task in our tests because it samples important productive skills which indirect forms of assessment are unable to. It allows the inclusion of operations and conditions other less direct tasks cannot cater for. To omit a writing task in situations where writing tasks are an important feature of the student's real-life needs might severely lower the validity of a testing programme and have an undesirable washback effect on the teaching prior to the test. However, this type of task is more likely to involve knowledge telling than knowledge transformation. As we saw in Chapter 7, this is the mark of a poor writer rather than a good one.

On the face of things, completely free, uncontrolled writing would seem to be an invalid test of the writing ability required for acceptance into most discourse communities, e.g., academic life, the medical profession, the business sector, and is to be resisted because of this until proof is produced that there is a strong link between performance on such tasks and performance on more direct tasks. It is also easier to generalize about writing ability from samples of a candidate's performance, when care is taken in specifying for each task the operations required and appropriate conditions and assessment criteria. When the task is determined more precisely in this manner, it is easier to compare the performances of different students and to improve reliability in scoring.

We should aim to test a candidate's ability to perform certain of the functional tasks required in the future target situation. For students in general English courses, we can include functional tasks they have been exposed to in their language courses or envisaged in the Common European Framework for Languages (Council of Europe 2001). For hospital doctors we might set a task which involves writing a letter to a local GP about a patient on the basis of a set of printed case notes. For a student in an EAP context it might involve search reading of an academic text or preferably texts to extract specified information for use in a written summary (see Example W5 below) or describing information contained in a diagrammatic or non-verbal form (see Example W6). For those studying English as a foreign language in a secondary school, it might involve tasks similar to those included as Examples W4a and b.

Example W4 Responding to given information

a. Responding to a letter

You receive this letter from a friend. Write a short reply to it. Give your friend all the information he asks for. You should write in complete sentences.

Alexandria, Egypt

5 May

Dear friend,

We are going to visit London in September. Can we see you then? What's the weather like then? Do we need to bring our warm coats? Liz would like you to tell us what we could visit in a week. What sort of food will we be able to eat? Finally, can you suggest a good hotel for us to stay in?

Love,

Tim

Write your reply here:

London

6th July

Dear Tim,

_____

_____

_____

_____

_____

_____

Love

b.

You are asked to write a paragraph for a wall chart in your class. Look at the information below, where Egypt and the United Kingdom are described. Write a paragraph of eight sentences comparing Egypt to the United Kingdom. You may write your ideas on the back of this paper. *Only the answer written in the lines below will be marked.* Marking will be based on: relevance and adequacy, organization, spelling, punctuation, grammar and use of vocabulary (equal marks to each one).

	Egypt	United Kingdom
Location:	North Africa	Europe
Population:	62 million	60 million
Language:	Arabic	English
History:	More than 5,000 years	2,500 years
Exports:	Raw materials	Financial services
Imports:	Computers, medicine	Raw materials
Currency:	Egyptian pound	Pound sterling
Sport:	Football	Rugby/cricket

Comment on Examples W4a–b

Most of the interactional and informational operations identified earlier could be built into this type of format, even at the lower-ability levels. W4a is particularly suited to the production of social and service texts.

By careful construction of the input the candidate receives, the conditions under which the task is to be performed can be largely controlled and thus made more appropriate for the candidature than might be the case in more open-ended pieces of writing. The candidate does not have to invent a response out of thin air. There is a person to write to, for a particular purpose. The topics can be carefully selected to ensure contextual appropriateness, and the technique provides the means of exerting some control over the organizational, propositional and illocutionary facets required in writing the response to the stimuli.

There is a question mark over the difficulties that having to process a written stimulus might cause, but to the extent that the task represents real-life interaction, this should not trouble the tester unduly. In order to respond to letters in real life we have to be able to read them. It does not seem to be the case that competent writers are unable to read, though the reverse may be quite common.

Most of the criteria we might wish to apply to a writing task can be catered for, with the possible exception of organizational ability in the more structured examples. Controlling the tasks in this fashion makes it easier to make reliable judgements on the relevancy and adequacy of content. There are a number of points in the stimulus material the candidate receives that have to be answered in the response.

Example W5 Information Transfer Tasks

GEPT Advanced Writing Test Task 1 LTTC Taiwan

General instructions

In this test, you will have an opportunity to demonstrate how well you can extract main ideas from both verbal and non-verbal input, organize these ideas effectively in writing tasks and make clear your own viewpoint on these main ideas. There are two

Example W5 (Continued)

task in this test. Each task has a different time limit. You must complete both tasks or your test will not be marked. Detailed instructions will be given to you at the beginning of each task.

Read these instructions carefully and plan ahead so that you can complete all the requirements within the time limit. Insufficient development of any part of either task will result in a lower score for that task. Your performance will be scored according to the following criteria: relevance and adequacy, coherence and organization, lexical use, and grammatical use.

The entire writing test takes 105 minutes.

Task 1

You are going to take part in the GEPT Composition Contest and the winning prize is an NT$5,000 book voucher. The title of the composition is 'The Advantages and Disadvantages of Advertising'. Information about this topic is provided in the two articles on the following pages.

- First, read each text to establish the main points the writer is making. You can use the space provided on your test paper to make notes.
- Then, *in your own words* as far as possible, write a composition that summarizes the *main ideas of both texts* concerning the pros and cons of advertising. If you use more than three consecutive words from the articles, use quotation marks (' '). **Plagiarism will result in failure.**
- In the final part of the composition, you should make clear your own viewpoint on these main ideas and come to a conclusion.

Your composition must be about **250 words**. You have **60 minutes** to complete Task 1.

The Disadvantages of Advertising

Anyone who lives in America is aware of advertising. Reading newspapers and magazines, we see full-page ads urging us to buy clothes, autos, cigarettes, and kitchen appliances. Television and radio programs include commercials; we all have heard the phrases 'brought to you by' and 'sponsored by' hundreds of times. If we drive, we see road signs or billboards proclaiming the qualities of products or the location of restaurants or motels. If we commute on a transit system, we cannot help but notice the prominent signs displayed on the buses and subways. And in our mail, along with the bills and the letters, come shiny flyers and circulars promoting products and announcing sales.

Advertisements in some form intrude into nearly every waking minute of our lives. We simply cannot get away from their pounding, incessant messages. Because ads permeate radio and television, we find ourselves singing their silly jingles and repeating their 'cute' lines. Sellers admonish us to buy through a profusion of techniques: hard sell, soft sell, music, comedy, and appeals to all our emotions and fears.

Some ads are even potentially harmful. Perplexing or misleading sales pitches may lure unwary buyers into financial trouble. It is always best to remember: 'caveat emptor' – let the buyer beware. Many commercials go far beyond the mere transmitting of information when they attempt to transform our values and attitudes. Cigarettes ads, for example, often imply that smoking is a manly or sexy habit. It is neither.

Because of these problems, many people have become extremely critical of commercials, especially those directed at children. As adults, we are often skeptical of what we read or hear in advertisements. Children, because they are not as mature or experienced as we are, cannot judge how reasonable or accurate ads are. If the man on TV says chocolate-covered, sugar-coated wheat toasts are healthful and nutritious, children may very well believe it. Many parents feel sellers take unfair advantage of children's inability to evaluate what they see or hear.

Unfortunately, despite their problems, commercials and ads are an established part of modern life. Providers of goods and services will always try to persuade us to purchase what they are selling. As consumers, we must learn not to believe everything we hear or read, so that we will not be fooled into buying things we don't need.

NOTES

Advantages of Advertising

Advertising plays an extremely important role in our society. Perhaps most obviously, it keeps us informed about the latest products and services, thus enabling us to buy intelligently. Advertising also has a positive impact on our economy, by providing funding for the media and stimulating competition among goods and service providers. In addition, advertising can be used to promote public welfare, thus exerting a positive social impact on society.

We as consumers benefit greatly from advertising. By reading bank ads, for example, we might decide to transfer our money from our current bank to one offering better rates or more convenient hours. When traveling, we can save hundreds of dollars on transcontinental airfares by comparing the ads in the travel section of the newspaper.

Advertising can also be used to increase awareness in society about particular issues, and in so doing, it becomes a form of education. Anti-drug advertising such as 'Just say NO', and drunk driving campaigns are just two examples of how society uses the advertising industry as a means to promote public welfare.

In addition to the social benefits, advertising also brings huge economic benefits to society. Without advertising, the media – including newspaper, television, radio, etc. – would be much less vigorous. Advertising provides revenue for commercial mediums, which would otherwise need to be funded by the actual consumer of these mediums For example, a newspaper would cost up to three times as much money (since advertising provides two-thirds of the revenue of the print media), or all television, bar government-funded networks, would be pay-TV (since nearly all revenue for television is currently provided by advertising). The price a consumer may have to pay to receive very cheap, or even free, news and entertainment may include sitting through a 30-second commercial break while watching a television program, or flicking a couple of extra pages in a magazine, to get through the advertisements to the articles.

Although advertising might appear to raise the prices of goods and services, a closer look will show that it actually helps to keep prices low. Advertising stimulates economic activity, with vigorous competition between institutions and higher buying rates of products. This, in turn, leads to lower product costs for the consumer.

NOTES

Comment on Example W5

Great care needs to be taken in ensuring that the conditions relating to text type and method factor are discussed rigorously at the moderating stage. The views of subject specialists and of a sample from the test population need to be elicited to try to ensure that any bias is kept to a minimum. The subject specificity of certain input texts might create too many problems for non-specialists in the subject, and the test might prove unsuitable for them. In the end one may have to resort to generally accessible scientific texts of the sort that appear in *New Scientist* for science and engineering students, and topics such as health education or other aspects of society if the test population is to include arts and social science students.

The LTTC GEPT Advanced test is aimed at students in Taiwanese universities. An EAP task needs to match with generalizable writing operations if a subject-specific test is not possible because of heterogeneity of population. A generalized academic writing task should include the following features: provision of topic/assignment prompt; an indication of audience expectation; specified and accessible source(s) of data; lexis constrained (to some extent) by all of the above. The candidate has to search for and extract data relevant to the question. Furthermore, the candidate has to reorganize and encode these data within the conventions of academic discourse so that the reader's expectations of relevance, adequacy, coherence, appropriateness and accuracy are fulfilled (see Hyland 2002, Weigle 2002: 187–190, Weir 1983 for further discussion).

This response format is suitable for testing a student's writing ability in terms of the tasks he or she has to cope with in an academic situation. This example represents one of the few attempts in public examinations to build greater task validity into a prompt for an academic writing test. In terms of theory-based validity this task is likely to involve authentic goal-setting, topic and genre modifying, generation of ideas, organization and reviewing. It is likely to involve knowledge transformation rather than simple knowledge telling in the better candidates. In terms of the elements of task setting and task demands both this response format and W6 below are able to address all these appropriately with regard to the TSU the test is designed for. Together, they offer a context- and theory-based valid approach to assessing academic writing in an exam context. The relationship of performance on these tasks to performance on more extended University assignments in terms of construct validity (see Chapter 10 for discussion of criterion-related validity) is still however, in urgent need of investigation.

A common difficulty with an integrated writing component of this type, however, is making the marking reliable. To assess students' responses reliably one needs to formulate the main points contained in the extract, construct an adequate mark scheme and standardize markers to it using explicit criteria and a script library. Some subjectivity inevitably remains and it is easy to underestimate the difficulty of marking reliably. Whether such written work should be marked by specialists from the target discourse community or by language specialists needs to be thought about. The simple solution might be to involve both.

A further difficulty we noted earlier is how to treat cases where students plagiarize the original text. Taking decisions as to what does and does not constitute plagiarism may differ from marker to marker and needs standardization.

Example W6 Non-Verbal-Verbal

GEPT-Advanced Writing Test

Task 2

A local English newspaper has just printed some worrying statistics on the traffic accidents that occurred in the downtown area in June. The data are shown in Figures 1 and 2 below. As a citizen, you would like to help improve the situation.

Write to the Opinion section of this local English newspaper:

- Firstly, summarize what you think are the **main findings** from the reported data and discuss the possible causes.
- Secondly, make suggestions about what can be done to reduce the number of accidents in the downtown area.

Your report must be about **250 words**. You have **45 minutes** to complete Task 2.

Example W6 (Continued)

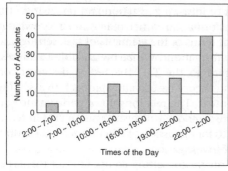

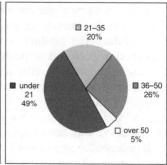

Figure 1. Number of accidents in the downtown area in June

Figure 2. Percentage of accidents involving drivers in different age groups

Comment on Example W6

With concise, clear, accessible stimuli (tabulated data, graphs, pictures and drawings) the candidate does not have to spend a long period of time decoding an extended written text. The more visual and the less verbal these stimuli are, the more efficiently they can be decoded.

As in the previous task in terms of theory-based validity, it is likely to involve authentic goal-setting, topic and genre modifying, generation of ideas, organization and reviewing. It is likely to involve knowledge transformation rather than simple knowledge telling. It can satisfactorily address the demands of context validity as set out in Chapter 6.

As with prompts in all writing tasks, care needs to be taken in the selection of topics. Problems have arisen in this technique when, in an attempt to avoid bias arising from background knowledge, a test has resorted to extremely specialized, arcane areas for visual stimuli, for example, castle crenellations in the fifteenth century or door frames in the eighteenth century. This is a problem familiar from our discussion of testing reading and the spoken skills. In all skills testing, care must be taken in selecting topics to ensure that candidates are in a position to process language productively and receptively as they would in real-life contexts. This entails that the writing tasks we set students should not make undue or unequal demands on the background knowledge of candidates.

Sometimes candidates are unable to cope with the mental challenge of decoding complex non-verbal stimuli and the equally complex rubrics that sometimes accompany these. The need to understand a very complex set of instructions and/or visual stimuli to produce a relatively straightforward piece of writing sometimes causes the candidate to resist or fail the task. This was a problem we referred to in discussing this technique in relation to reading above. The cognitive complexity of the non-verbal input should never be allowed to interfere with the measurement of language skills or we face the problem of construct irrelevant variance. Checks should be made concerning the familiarity of the intended population with graph or graph-related tasks and piloting should ensure that sufficient time is available for interpreting them in the test task. In the piloting some candidates might take the task in their own L1 to check on its transmissibility.

Another major difficulty we referred to in the discussion on reading was that the drawing ability required is likely to be beyond the reach of most teachers, and the *replicability* of such items by teachers must be checked, though with the onset of packages like SPSS (see Chapter 11), drawing pie charts and histograms is relatively straightforward.

Example   W7 TOEFL new generation integrated writing task

Example of writing item based on reading and listening

RLW2 Task

RLW – Reading then Listening then Writing.

You will first have **5 minutes** to read a passage about an academic topic and take notes on the topic if you wish. Then you will put away the passage and listen to a lecture about that same topic and take notes while you listen. Then you will have **20 minutes** to write a response that summarizes the main points of the lecture *and* explains the ways in which points made in the lecture cast doubt on points made in the reading passage. The question does **not** ask you to express your opinion. Try to answer as completely as possible from the information in the lecture and the reading passage. You *will* be able to see the reading passage while you write and you can use the notes you have taken as well. Typically, an effective response will have between 150 and 225 words. Your response will be judged on the quality of your writing and on the completeness and accuracy of the content.

Narrator: You will have **5 minutes** to read the following passage and take notes on it on the Notes page if you wish. After that you will put the passage away and listen to a lecture about the same topic. You may take notes on the Notes page while you listen. After the lecture is over, you will have **20 minutes** to write about the lecture and how the lecture is related to the reading. At that time you will be able to look again at the passage and use your notes. Your response will be judged on the quality of your writing and on how well your response presents the points in the lecture and their relationship to the reading passage.

Narrator: Begin reading now. You may take notes on the notes page as you read.

Example W7 (Continued)

RLW2 Reading passage (reading time 5 minutes)

Altruism is a type of behavior in which an animal sacrifices its own interest for that of another animal or group of animals. Altruism is the opposite of selfishness; individuals performing altruistic acts gain nothing for themselves.

Examples of altruism abound, among both humans and other animals. Unselfish acts among humans range from the sharing of food with strangers to the donation of body organs to family members, and even to strangers. Such acts are altruistic in that they benefit another, yet provide little reward to the one performing the act.

In fact, many species of animal appear willing to sacrifice food, or even their life, to assist other members of their group. The meerkat is often cited as an example. In groups of meerkats, an individual acts as a sentinel, standing guard and looking out for predators while the others hunt for food or eat food they have obtained. If the sentinel meerkat sees a predator such as a hawk approaching the group, it gives an alarm cry alerting the other meerkats to run and seek shelter. By standing guard, the sentinel meerkat gains nothing – it goes without food while the others eat, and it places itself in grave danger. After it issues an alarm it has to flee alone, which might make it more at risk to a predator, since animals in groups are often able to work together to fend off a predator. So the altruistic sentinel behavior helps ensure the survival of other members of the meerkat's group.

Narrator: Stop reading now. Please put the reading passage away until the lecture is over. (2 seconds)

[*Beginning here is the RLW2 lecture proper*]

Narrator: Now listen to a professor's response to the reading passage. (2 seconds)

Let's consider the question about whether there are any truly altruistic acts. Are there really unselfish acts or do all such acts, in the final analysis, bear rewards? To take an extreme case, suppose a person donates a kidney to a complete stranger. Doesn't the donor receive appreciation and approval from the stranger and from society? Doesn't the donor gain an increased sense of self worth? Such non-material rewards might be very valuable. Such acts *are* very generous, but can it be said there's *no* gain?

And what about meerkats? Well often in science, new findings force us to re-examine earlier beliefs and assumptions. And a recent study of meerkats is having exactly this effect. The study examined the meerkat's behavior quite closely, much more closely than had ever been done before. And some interesting things were found ... like about eating habits ... it showed that typically meerkats eat *before* they stand guard – so the ones standing guard usually have a full stomach! And the study also found that since the sentinel is the first to see a predator coming, it's the *most* likely to escape ... because the sentinel meerkat often stands guard near a burrow, so it can run immediately into the burrow after giving the alarm. The other meerkats, the ones scattered about looking for food, are actually in greater danger. So, is the sentinel meerkat really acting altruistically?

In fact, it *has* been suggested that alarm calling might actually be *selfish* behavior. When an animal creates an alarm, the alarm call may cause the other group members either to gather together or else to move about very quickly. Both of these behaviors might actually draw the predator's attention away from the caller, increasing that animal's own chances of survival.

[RLW2 Lecture ends here]

Narrator: Summarize the points made in the lecture and explain the ways in which they cast doubt on the points made in the reading passage. You may use your notes and you may look at the reading passage while you write. (2 seconds)

Narrator: Begin writing now. (recommended length: 150–225 words)

20 minutes writing time

Narrator: Stop writing now.

Comment on Example W7

For academic purposes this EAP test comes closer than most other tasks to replicating the context in which writing takes place for tertiary-level English-medium study, so in terms of this aspect of validity it is a refreshing development on what was available before. In addition, it approximates more closely to the processing that takes place in writing an academic essay so in terms of theory-based validity at first sight it is also an improvement on some of the tasks discussed in Chapter 7 and above. Further research would be useful to determine the processing that takes place in task completion particularly in relation to knowledge transformation.

Additionally, it requires a balanced argument text in response and thereby avoids the dangers of a highly personal response which as we saw in Chapter 7 is not required by the particular discourse community such writing is intended for. It is similar in many ways to the TEEP writing task developed by Weir (1983a) for use in admissions to UK-based tertiary institutions in response to the findings of his extensive needs analysis into the language demands placed on students in English medium instruction. The potential positive washback on the teaching and learning that precedes the examination (see Chapter 10) is likely to be considerably better than that occasioned by the structure and written expression element of old TOEFL.

It seems capable of addressing satisfactorily nearly all of the elements we have identified as being important for establishing context- and theory-based validity in a writing task. The only reservations are in terms of the limited length of response and the lack of an audience to construct the writing for. The criteria for marking might also be usefully repeated in the test rubric to aid in goal-setting.

Difficulties may also present themselves in achieving scoring validity (see Chapter 9) to the extent that potential plagiarism of both spoken and written text will require clear ground-rules for markers. Such rules need to be made explicit for candidates as well. In addition, where text is supplied to students for information retrieval purposes this may well enhance student scores on any micro-linguistic assessment criteria.

In the next chapter we further examine scoring validity where the concern is with the extent to which we can depend on the scores we assign to our test tasks.

Further reading

General

Hughes (2003) is the classic volume for testing in the classroom recently updated. A rich source of considered advice for the teacher practitioner.

Reading

Alderson (2000) offers a wide-ranging coverage of reading research, and theory and practice in the assessment of reading.

Urquhart and Weir (1998) discuss testing in the context of reading theory.

Listening

Buck (2001) is thoughtful and accessible treatment of testing listening

Writing

Weigle (2002) is a comprehensive and well-organized treatment of the area.

Speaking

Fulcher (2003) considers the assessment of speaking from historical, theoretical and practical perspectives.

Luoma (2004) is devoted to the testing of speaking and provides many useful examples of speaking tests and scales.

9
Scoring Validity in Action

In Chapter 6 we looked at elements of context validity that need to be considered at the test design stage and made a number of points in relation to test development which could potentially impact on the reliability of our tests. Hughes (2003: Chapter 5) examines a number of these specifically in relation to reliability. He provides a set of guidelines for making the test task itself more likely to produce reliable scores:

- take enough samples of behaviour;
- do not allow candidates too much freedom of choice;
- write unambiguous items;
- provide clear and explicit instructions;
- ensure that tests are well laid out and perfectly legible;
- make candidates familiar with format and testing techniques;
- provide uniform and non-distracting conditions of administration;
- use items that permit scoring which is as objective as possible;
- make comparisons between candidates as direct as possible.

And in relation to the scoring of test performance itself:

- provide a detailed scoring key;
- train scorers;
- agree acceptable responses and appropriate scores at the outset of scoring;
- exclude items which do not discriminate well between weaker and stronger student;
- identify candidates by number, not name;
- employ multiple, independent scoring.

In this chapter we will concentrate on the scoring process itself, but the points made by Hughes in relation to the features of task in terms of the way they have the potential to affect test reliability add further weight to the view expressed in Chapter 2 on the interconnectedness of the components of the validity concept. Context validity impacts on scoring validity as well as theory-based validity.

Scoring involves assigning a mark to a candidate's responses to a test. It is essential that as you construct each test, you draw up a mark scheme. You have to decide how you are going to mark an item and assign the relative weighting of each part as you create tasks. When tasks are moderated prior to test administration, the people involved should consider the appropriateness of the marking scheme as well as the tasks themselves. Murphy (1979) is still a valuable source for drawing up a list of questions which might be asked of the marking scheme. The following are examples of the types of questions moderators might address:

- A full answer key must be provided. Does the mark scheme anticipate responses of a kind that candidates are likely to make? Is there one clear answer to each item? Does the mark scheme allow for possible alternative answers? Alderson argues (2000: 29) that in reading tests: 'Test designers should be open as possible in the range of different interpretations and understandings they accept'.
- Is the key correct and complete?
- Does the marking scheme specify performance criteria to reduce as far as possible the element of subjective judgement that the examiner has to exercise in evaluating candidates' answers, especially in production tasks?
- Are the marks allocated to each task commensurate with the demands that task makes on the candidate? In listening tasks should all parts be weighted equally? In writing tasks for beginners how many marks should be given to a copying task? How many to gap filling, etc.? Does the mark scheme indicate clearly the marks to be awarded for different parts of a question or the relative weighting of criteria that might be applicable?
- Has the mark scheme minimized the examiner's need to compute the final mark for a candidate?
- Are the abilities rewarded those the tasks are designed to assess? For example: if candidates have to write down their answers in a listening test and we take marks off for errors in writing, then writing has become an element of the task. If the criteria do not cover the language ability on show as a result of the test tasks there is a danger of construct under-representation.
- Can the marking schemes be easily interpreted by a number of different examiners in a way that will ensure that all mark to the same standard? Are the criteria for the marking of an essay sufficiently explicit to avoid differences in interpretation? Are marking and markers reliable? Have you limited the number of acceptable answers to short-answer questions? Are all the markers aware and agreed on the acceptable answers? They should be. Is the marker consistent in his/her own standard of marking? He/she should be. Is it agreed that no marks should be taken off for errors in mechanical accuracy such as spelling, punctuation or grammar?

- Perhaps the most important question to ask of any test is: what perform-ance constitutes a pass? In reading, we do not have qualitative descriptors to apply to a concrete product such as speech or writing. We are depending on a quantitative score and trying to translate this into a performance description. This leads us into problems such as: do students have to get all the items in the test right or half of them? Are different combinations of right answers acceptable for a pass? How are we to score the test? Are some items more important than others and therefore to be weighted more heavily? If we set the items at a level of difficulty at which we would expect candidates to get them all right to pass, we have a benchmark to aim at. The combination of items and text should be within the capabilities of anyone we would be prepared to pass. Given the possibility of error interfering with the measurement, it is common practice to set the pass rate at around the 80 per cent mark.
- Such a criterion-referenced approach to making decisions on who should pass is preferable to a norm-referenced approach where for political rea-sons the pass mark is sometimes used to control the numbers passing or failing. If a candidate meets the criterion s/he should pass, if they do not meet it they fail.

9.1   Scoring written production

This section deals with the main approaches to assessing writing and dis-cusses the relative merits of global and analytic approaches to marking for improving the validity of a writing sub-test. Much of what is discussed here in relation to the assessment of writing will also apply to the assessment of spoken language ability, which we will deal with later.

Marking exercise

For the purposes of this exercise we are assuming that you the test writer have con-sidered carefully the operations you want your students to perform in writing and have constructed a writing task in accordance with these which also reflects, as far as possible, conditions appropriate for the test population.

Look below at the marks that 22 MA TESOL students gave to eight exam scripts written by overseas students attending a pre-sessional course at a British university. They were asked to intuitively mark each script out of 20 and were not provided with any specified criteria for doing this. They were only given 15 minutes for this task. In the right-hand column we have indicated the mean mark of each rater and the range used. Below the marks awarded by the raters, at the bottom of the page we have provided the range of marks awarded by different raters to each candidate and the overall mean score for each. **Look carefully at the marks awarded. What conclusions can you draw from these data?**

Scores Awarded out of 20 By MA Students

	1	2	3	4	5	6	7	8	mean	range
A	8	12	12	13	15	8	14	16	12	8–16
B	7	11	12	13	14	7	14	15	12	7–15
C	5	12	11	9	9	4	11	9	9	4–12
D	9	10	14	14	14	6	16	19	13	6–19
E	9	15	15	11	14	8	16	16	13	8–16
F	7	10	11	12	13	14	15	12	12	7–15
G	4	10	15	5	12	3	18	19	11	3–19
H	7	11	10	8	12	6	17	11	11	6–17
I	12	14	17	10	19	10	17	17	15	10–19
J	5	2	3	2	5	1	18	5	5	1–18
K	8	12	14	5	10	13	6	10	11	5–14
L	8	9	11	11	13	9	15	15	11	8–15
M	5	12	15	8	15	9	16	14	12	5–16
N	4	10	12	12	15	3	18	20	12	4–20
O	7	10	10	10	12	15	16	18	12	7–18
P	4	7	12	9	10	3	14	17	10	3–17
Q	5	7	10	8	9	3	11	13	8	3–13
R	3	8	9	9	7	4	17	15	9	3–17
S	8	10	15	10	12	8	15	15	12	8–15
T	3	3	5	5	6	2	8	14	5	2–14
U	12	14	16	13	12	3	19	18	13	3–19
V	10	14	17	14	13	8	18	18	14	8–18
r	3–12	2–15	3–17	2–14	5–19	1–15	6–19	5–20		
m	7	11	12	10	12	7	15	15		

Comment on marking exercise 1

There is a great deal of variability in the marks awarded by the different raters. The most likely reasons for this are the lack of explicit agreed criteria for carrying out the marking task and perhaps also the speed with which it was done. Whatever the reason, candidates would have been seriously affected by the choice of rater assigned to marking their script. Compare the marks of rater **T** with those of marker **I**. Who would you prefer to be marked by? Some of the raters have high average marks (see under **mean** right-hand column) and some have quite low average marks. Some use a narrow band of marks (rater **S**) and some use the full mark range (rater **N**).

The picture is even more disturbing if we look at the range of marks given to each script (see the first set of figures at the foot of the column). Take script 8. The mark range is 5–20, and that for script 6 is 1–15. In nearly all cases the worst scripts, 1 and 6, if they had been marked by certain markers, might have been given higher marks than the best scripts, 7 and 8. This degree of unreliability cannot be tolerated. We must seek ways to bring raters closer together, in terms of the marks they award and in the consistency of their own judgements. This involves the development of appropriate rating scales and the standardization of raters to these scales.

The choice rests between analytic scales where assessments are made in relation to each of a number of separate criteria and holistic scales where an overall composite judgement is made of a piece of writing. Weigle notes the paucity of research on the effects of different scales on outcomes (see Weir 1990 for discussion of some early studies) despite much advocacy in the literature by different authorities for one approach against the other.

Holistic scoring

It is essential that, in developing band scales, they are based on real performances. Mark Scheme 1 below is an attempt to define levels of proficiency, in this case for writing. To the extent that the levels are based on real life performances, then we can have confidence in their applicability (see Hawkey and Barker 2004 on developing the Common Writing Scale at Cambridge ESOL). Teachers of similar year groups can set common tasks and develop criteria-based descriptions to fit different ability levels. Over a period of time it should be possible to develop profiles of ability levels in writing for the students you teach in your context. A similar approach should be adopted for the development of band scales for assessing the other skills as well.

The abiding difficulty is, of course, that candidates may present at different levels in different criteria: for example, a 3 in fluency but a 4 in organization and coherence. A simple solution in high stakes test is that they get the level of their lowest performance but this hardly smacks of 'testing for best', a common refrain among testers in the 1990s. It does, however, accord with the heretical view that we should in fact test for worst especially where the results of proficiency tests might have serious costs for learners and the end users of their test results, as in the case of the PLAB test for doctors from overseas wishing to practise in the UK. Banerjee (2003) carried out an innovative study linking levels of performance on IELTS to costs incurred as a result of acceptance at each level below the normal cut off score for admissions purposes.

General Mark Scheme 1   (Certificate of Proficiency Handbook Cambridge ESOL 2003: 30)

This mark scheme is interpreted at CPE level and is used in conjunction with a task-specific mark scheme for each question.

5 Outstanding realization of the task set:

- Sophisticated use of an extensive range of vocabulary, collocation and expression, entirely appropriate to the task set
- Effective use of stylistic devices; register and format wholly appropriate
- Impressive use of a wide range of structures

General Mark Scheme 1   (Continued)

- Skilfully organized and coherent
- Excellent development of topic
- Minimal error

Impresses the reader and has a very positive effect.

4 Good realization of the task set:

- Fluent and natural use of a wide range of vocabulary, collocation and expression, successfully meeting the requirements of the task set
- Good use of stylistic devices; register and format appropriate
- Competent use of a wide range of structures
- Well organized and coherent
- Good development of topic
- Minor and unobtrusive errors

Has a positive effect on the reader.

3 Satisfactory realization of the task set:

- Reasonably fluent and natural use of a range of vocabulary and expression, adequate to the task set
- Evidence of stylistic devices; register and format generally appropriate
- Adequate range of structures
- Clearly organized and generally coherent
- Adequate coverage of topic
- Occasional non-impeding errors

Achieves the desired effect on the reader.

2 Inadequate attempt at the task set:

- Limited and/or inaccurate range of vocabulary and expression
- Little evidence of stylistic devices; some attempt at appropriate register and format
- Inadequate range of structures
- Some attempt at organization, but lacks coherence
- Inadequate development of topic
- A number of errors, which sometimes impede communication

Has a negative effect on the reader.

1 Poor attempt at the task set:

- Severely limited and inaccurate range of vocabulary and expression
- No evidence of stylistic devices; little or no attempt at appropriate register and format
- Lack of structural range

- Poorly organized, leading to incoherence
- Little relevance to topic, and/or too short
- Numerous errors, which distract and often impede communication

Has a very negative effect on the reader.

0 Negligible or no attempt at the task set:

- Totally incomprehensible due to serious error
- Totally irrelevant
- Insufficient language to assess (fewer than 20 per cent of the required number of words)
- Totally illegible

The ACTFL (American Council for the Teaching of Foreign Languages) scale for assessing foreign language learning in schools and colleges in the USA has been criticized because it appears not to be based on evidence of the acquisition order of the various elements within it (see Bachman and Savignon 1986, Bachman 1988).

In developing scales that represent patterns of acquisition, investigation of linguistic profiles based on actual written work will tell us about possible configurations in terms of specified criteria. It may well be, after sufficient research and development, that at each level in the band scales above we will have a number of different, but clear configurations, in terms of the criteria we might wish to apply. This would provide further evidence of the variability of language acquisition. If this variability is unmanageable, i.e., the pattern of acquisition is too complex or too varied, then we might have to resort to breaking writing down into its constituent parts, as we do for reading. We would then be able to provide a multi-trait profile of a script in terms of analytic features, such as organization and grammatical accuracy.

Analytic scales

By asking markers to be explicit about individual aspects of a piece of written work, it is possible to provide a more detailed profile of a candidate's strengths and weaknesses.

General Mark Scheme 2   TEEP Attribute Writing Scales
(Weir 1983)

1. Relevance and Adequacy of Content

0. The answer bears almost no relation to the task set. Totally inadequate.
1. Answer of limited relevance to the task set. Possibly major gaps in treatment of topic and/or pointless repetition.

General Mark Scheme 2   (Continued)

2. For the most part answers the tasks set, though there may be some gaps or redundant information.
3. Relevant and adequate answer to the task set.

2. Compositional Organization

0. No apparent organization of content.
1. Very little organization of content. Underlying structure not sufficiently apparent.
2. Some organizational skills in evidence, but not adequately controlled.
3. Overall shape and internal pattern clear. Organizational skills adequately controlled.

3. Cohesion

0. Cohesion almost totally absent. Writing so fragmentary that comprehension of the intended communication is virtually impossible.
1. Unsatisfactory cohesion may cause difficulty in comprehension of most of the intended communication.
2. For the most part satisfactory cohesion though occasional deficiencies may mean that certain parts of the communication are not always effective.
3. Satisfactory use of cohesion resulting in effective communication.

4. Adequacy of Vocabulary for Purpose

0. Vocabulary inadequate even for the most basic parts of the intended communication.
1. Frequent inadequacies in vocabulary for the task. Perhaps frequent lexical inappropriateness and/or repetition.
2. Some inadequacies in vocabulary for the task. Perhaps some lexical inappropriateness and/or circumlocution.
3. Almost no inadequacies in vocabulary for the task. Only rare inappropriateness and/or circumlocution.

5. Grammar

0. Almost all grammatical patterns inaccurate.
1. Frequent grammatical inaccuracies.
2. Some grammatical inaccuracies.
3. Almost no grammatical inaccuracies.

6. Mechanical Accuracy I (Punctuation)

0. Ignorance of conventions of punctuation.
1. Low standard of accuracy in punctuation.
2. Some inaccuracies in punctuation.
3. Almost no inaccuracies in punctuation.

7. Mechanical Accuracy II (Spelling)

0. Almost all spelling inaccurate.
1. Low standard of accuracy in spelling.
2. Some inaccuracies in spelling.
3. Almost no inaccuracies in spelling.

Analytic mark schemes have sometimes been found deficient in the choice and delineation of appropriate criteria for a given discourse community. In the design work for the TEEP test it was felt that the assessment of samples of written performance should be based on behaviourally described, analytic criteria, appropriate to the academic discourse community.

The criteria needed to be comprehensive and based on data, collected from the academic discourse community. The criteria in the TEEP SCALE above resulted from a survey of a large number of academic staff at tertiary level institutions in the United Kingdom (see Weir 1983a and b). Academic staff were in favour of procedures that would assess students, particularly in relation to their communicative effectiveness, and in such a way that a profile containing details of candidates' strengths and weaknesses could be made available.

The empirical investigation suggested the criteria of relevance and adequacy, compositional organization, cohesion, referential adequacy, grammatical accuracy, spelling and punctuation as the most suitable for assessing writing tasks. Of these, the first two were rated as highly important and the last two mechanical accuracy features of very little importance. The remaining criteria were rated as being of medium importance. Serious thought might be given in future to omitting any concern with the last two mechanical accuracy features.

Quote 9.1   Weir on TEEP analytic scales

To apply these 'valid' criteria reliably an attempt was made to construct an analytic marking scheme in which each of the criteria is sub-divided into four behavioural levels on a scale of 0–3 (see above). A level 3 corresponds to a base line of minimal competence. At this level it was felt that a student was likely to have very few problems in coping with the writing tasks demanded of him or her by his or her course in respect of this criterion. At a level 2 a limited number of problems arise in relation to the criterion and remedial help would be advisable. A level 1 would indicate that a lot of help is necessary with respect to this particular criterion. A level 0 indicates almost total incompetence in respect of the criterion in question.
(1990: 69–71)

The nature of the problems encountered in the evolution of the criteria provides useful background for the development of similar schemes for assessing both spoken and written production. The first problem in earlier versions of these assessment criteria was that in some an attempt was made to assess two things, namely communicative effectiveness and degrees of accuracy. As a result, great difficulty was encountered in attempting to apply the criteria reliably. It was necessary to refine them so that the first four related to communicative effectiveness and the latter three to accuracy. It may well be that the latter three criteria contribute to communicative effectiveness or lack of it, but attempts to incorporate some indication of this proved unworkable.

Second, distinctions between each of the four levels were only gradually achieved, and it was also necessary to try to establish roughly equivalent level distinctions across the criteria. Great problems were experienced in the trial assessments in gaining agreement as to what was meant by certain of the descriptions of levels within the criteria. Most sources of confusion were gradually eliminated, and this seemed inevitably to result in a much simplified scale for these descriptions of level, particularly in the accuracy criteria 5–7.

In those cases where the candidates are provided with information, as in the TEEP test where the candidates have to extract specified information from an article provided, it may be problematic to employ certain of these criteria. This in some ways equates with the issue of co-construction in spoken language testing we have referred to earlier.

Where all the lexis is provided for the candidates, either through labelled diagrams or in available text (see Chapter 8, Examples W4, W5 and W7), the likelihood is that most candidates will score reasonably well on the *adequacy of vocabulary* criterion. They might in fact score disproportionately better on this criterion than on other criteria, where the same degree of help is not available. One could argue, however, that this help is available in real life, as it is for spelling through spellcheckers on computers. Perhaps this is a strong argument for reducing our criteria accordingly.

A similar argument is put forward in terms of *content* in those tasks where candidates are given this assistance. One might wish to argue more strongly in this case that information is available in real life and what is at issue here is candidates' ability to demonstrate that they can convey relevant and adequate information in their own words. Knowledge transformation is at the heart of advanced expository writing and ability to perform this is a mark of the good writer.

Quote 9.2   Luoma on the number of levels and criteria

The more levels there are, the more specific the feedback will be, and the easier it will be to show progress, for example from the beginning to the end of a semester of language classes. However, since scales are also about measurement, it is important to ask how many levels the raters can distinguish consistently. An easy way of checking this is to see how well raters agree with themselves if they rate the same performances twice with a week's interval between ratings, for example. Another check might be to see how well two raters agree with each other . . .

If the decision is made to use analytic rating criteria, the developers need to decide how many criteria there will be. The *Common European Framework* (Council of Europe 2001: 193) suggests that four or five categories begin to cause a cognitive load for raters and seven is a psychological upper limit. Since it is also important that the analytic criteria are conceptually independent, at least to some extent, 5–6 criteria may be close to the maximum.

(2004: 80)

An important issue is how many distinctions can you make in respect of each criterion? If it is felt that further distinctions can be made, for example between levels 1 and 2, then it will be necessary to provide copies of actual scripts to exemplify these. These concrete exemplifications should assist us in talking about stages, which are really only invented conveniences to help us talk about performance on a continuum. More obviously the scale might be altered by providing a level 4, which would be a perfect performance in respect of a particular feature.

A decision must be taken on how the individually assessed traits relate to each other. In the absence of any indication to the contrary it is probably sensible to weight each facet equally. A possible alternative would be to weight in accordance with proficient users' intuitions. We must also establish what composite mark is equivalent to what level of performance.

The most crucial decision relates to determining the base line for passing a candidate, the most important of mark boundaries. If task conditions and operations are appropriate to the TSU context, and the criteria are approved and seen as criterial by the discourse community the candidate is entering, then we can be reasonably confident in the decisions we take. This approach ensures a close match between the writing to be done and the skills and test facets to be evaluated. Once these have been established, raters, in collaboration with end users of the information in the discourse community, can determine where to draw the line in terms of pass and fail. This is a matter of defining a minimally adequate candidate in terms of the tasks being carried out, under specified conditions, to a certain level of output on specified criteria. Selecting sample scripts from these tasks to form a script library illustrating the various distinctions we wish to make can enable us to be even more confident in our subsequent judgements.

Single global impression versus multi-trait analytic marking procedures

The relative merits of single, global impression and multi-trait analytic approaches to marking, for improving the validity of a writing sub-test, are examined briefly below (see also Hamp-Lyons 1991: 241–76). Many of the points raised are also applicable to the testing of spoken language.

In discussing the examples of extended writing in Chapter 8 above, it was argued that by controlling the writing tasks we might improve their validity. We concluded that there was a need for 'controlled' writing tests, in which the context and scope of a feasible, acceptable, appropriate writing task were determined for, and made clear to, the candidate. It was felt that this would facilitate marking and allow a more reliable comparison across candidates. We will now examine how the application of single, global impressionistic and multi-trait analytic approaches to marking might also aid us in our attempt to improve the validity of our writing tasks.

In the global impression method of marking, candidates are placed at a single level on a scale, based on an impression of their written work as a whole. In global marking no attempt is made to evaluate a text in terms of separate criteria. Each grade on the scale is usually equated with a distinct level of achievement which is closely described in terms of a number of criteria.

The method is quick to use and this often encourages the use of two markers who have to agree on a final single grade. It has found favour with admissions tutors because the descriptions are easy to handle administratively: for example, all candidates at band 7 or above can be accepted. No interpretation or computation is required.

Quote 9.3   Weigle on disadvantages of holistic scoring

One drawback to holistic scoring is that a single score does not provide useful diagnostic information about a person's writing ability...This is especially problematic for second language writers, since different aspects of writing ability develop at different rates for different writers .... Another disadvantage of holistic scoring is that holistic scores are not always easy to interpret, as raters do not necessarily use the same criteria to arrive at the same scores...Holistic scores have also been shown to correlate with relatively superficial characteristics such as length and handwriting...Holistic scoring has also come under criticism in recent years for its focus on achieving high inter rater reliability at the expense of validity.
(2002: 114)

A danger is that a marker's impression of the overall quality might have been affected by just one or two aspects of the work. In some ways this is similar to the halo effect reported in relation to analytic scales where the possibility exists that the rating of one criterion might have a knock-on effect in the rating of the next. If a major preoccupation of a marker is with grammar, and the candidate exhibits a poor performance on this criterion, are the marks awarded in respect of other criteria contaminated by the grammar mark? With careful standardization of markers and checking of marking it should be possible to counteract this possibility.

A more deep-rooted problem is that the global approach fails in practice because it does not cater for learners whose performance levels vary in terms of different criteria. ESL writers quite often acquire differential control over the components of writing ability, for example, some have much greater fluency than accuracy and vice versa, some have greater syntactic control than lexical, etc.

The real problem with most global impression band scales is that they are not empirically derived. They appear to represent levels of proficiency, but as yet we do not have a clear idea of the order of acquisition of various skill attributes in writing or even whether there is such an order. Until adequate research is carried out, and scales are empirically founded on the scripts produced by real candidates, then they are at best tentative in their implications. (For examples of empirically-driven scales, see Hawkey and Barker 2004 for writing, and Hasselgreen 1998 for speaking).

In multi-trait, analytic marking, a level is recorded in respect of each criterion, and the final grade is a composite of these individual assessments. This method avoids the potential flaw in global impression band scales of uneven development in the different criteria. Hamp-Lyons (1991: 242) has argued:

> In order to reach a reasonable balance among all the essential elements of good writing, readers need to pay conscious attention to all those elements. A detailed scoring procedure requiring the readers to attend to the multi-dimensionality of ESL writing is needed.

It would, then, be interesting to see if the judgements produced matched the global impressions of proficient users. One would hope that judgements of a good piece of writing resulting from the analytic approach accorded with what reliable native writers thought was a good piece of writing.

This method has the added advantage that it lends itself more readily to full-profile reporting and could perform a certain diagnostic role in delineating students' strengths and weaknesses in written production. It can tell the end user of the information whether a candidate has a flat profile or whether it is in any sense marked by particular strengths or weaknesses (see Hamp-Lyons 1991: 253–5). This information cannot be supplied through a global impression scheme.

This diagnostic function, when based on more than one sample script, might be particularly beneficial for placement purposes, opening up the possibilities of targeted remedial tuition. It might also be of value in a formative role during a course of instruction.

Such a diagnostic function might also help to provide clearer information on the areas of language gain during a course of instruction. Thus it could be useful in providing both educational, illuminative information, as well as establishing evaluation data for accountability purposes.

Hamp-Lyons (1990: 81) emphasizes the importance of a further dimension of assessment. She stresses that we need to investigate ways of rater training to improve on the present situation (see Fulcher 2003: Chapter 4 for sound advice on this in relation to testing second language speaking). *Rater training* is a systematic process to train raters to apply the rating scale and the mark scheme in a consistent way. This will involve careful consideration of the context in which training occurs, the type of training given, the extent to which training is monitored, the extent to which rating is monitored and the feedback given to raters.

Quote 9.4   Weigle on rater training

Shohamy *et al.* (1992) found that rater training was a more significant variable than experience in terms of rater reliability, although they did not report any difference in terms of relative severity. Weigle (1994) found that rater training improved the reliability of raters but did not completely erase individual tendencies to be severe or lenient in rating.
(2002: 71)

Although analytic schemes may facilitate agreement amongst examiners as to the precise range of qualities that are to be evaluated in an essay, the actual amount of individual marker variation involved in the assessment, i.e., degree of unreliability, in many schemes may be reduced very little if there is a lack of explicitness with regard to the applicable criteria, or a use of vague criteria. Hamp-Lyons' work on the development of multiple-trait scoring procedures for specified topics, in particular contexts, shows how these dangers can be avoided (see Hamp-Lyons 1991: 248–61).

She argues that the raters should focus only on the most salient criteria as established through careful test development, well grounded in actual data, in the context where measurements are to be made (see discussion of the establishment of the TEEP assessment criteria above).

Weir (1990: 68) reported that a multi-trait analytic mark scheme is seen as a useful tool for the training and standardization of new examiners. By employing an analytic scheme, examining bodies feel they can better train and standardize new markers to the criteria of assessment (for an extended discussion on the standardization and training of examiners, see Murphy 1979). A measure of agreement about what each criterion means can be established, and subsequently markers can be standardized to what constitutes a different level within each of these criteria. Weir (1990) cites research where analytic schemes have been found to be particularly useful with markers who are relatively inexperienced. There is, however, a downside to using an analytic approach, not least in the additional time it takes to mark analytically as against holistically because more than one judgement is required per script.

Hughes (2003: 103–4) also points out some difficulties with using such scales. He mentions:

- the time it takes to apply;
- concentration on individual aspects may divert from overall effect;
- when an additional impression score is required to counteract this, discrepancies may well arise.

Choice of rating scale, as always, depends on the prevailing situation in the context of administration. In those cases where large numbers of scripts have to be marked fairly quickly and there are serious human resource implications (e.g., the College English Test in China with ten million candidates a year) practicality might lead us to using a holistic scale because of its speed and ease of application. Alternatively, computers are sometimes used in the rating process – though how one marks for coherence and relevance and adequacy of content, the two key criteria according to many test users, may be the stumbling block for this particular technological advance.

Where practicality considerations are less important, validity considerations are paramount and feedback to learners is desired, analytic scales are preferable.

9.2 Scoring speaking tests

There are enormous practical constraints on the large-scale testing of spoken language proficiency. These include the administrative costs and difficulties and the sheer logistics of testing large numbers of candidates either individually or in very small groups. The extent to which the demands of validity can be met through direct tests of spoken language ability will depend on the particular situation test developers find themselves in.

Despite these problems with reliability and practicality, the essential task for the test designer is to establish clearly what operations the candidate is expected to perform and the conditions under which these tasks are to be carried out. Appropriate criteria for assessing the product arising from the elicitation procedures have to be agreed upon at this test design stage. These criteria need to reflect the features of spoken language interaction the test task is designed to generate.

It would be useful if the criteria employed in the assessment of language production on tasks could be related in a principled way to the criteria for the teaching of a skill: after all, conditions, operations and assessment should be relevant factors in helping the development as well as the summative assessment of skilled performance. If this relationship between teaching and testing could be strengthened, the important washback effect of test tasks on the teaching that precedes it would be enhanced.

The relationship between a task and the criteria that can be applied to its product is an essential factor in taking decisions on what to include in a test of spoken or written production. *Tasks cannot be considered separately from the criteria that might be applied to the performances they result in.* Having established suitable tasks and appropriate assessment criteria to accompany them, consideration needs to be given as to how best to apply the criteria to the samples of task performance.

Just as in the rating of written tasks, so too in the measurement of spoken language there is a need to establish clear criteria for assessment and to standardize examiners in their use of these criteria.

Quote 9.5   Luoma on the rating process

The rating process determines exactly how the criteria will be applied to the performances. Do the raters rate the performances task by task? Do they pay attention to all the criteria on all tasks, or should they use some criteria on some tasks and other criteria on others? If both holistic and analytic criteria are used, which rating should they give first? These practical decisions clarify the meaning of the criteria, and the process design may lead the developers to make some further modifications to them.
(2004: 171)

The assessment of spoken language is potentially more problematic than the rating of written scripts, given that no recording of the performance is usually made. Whereas in writing the script can be reconsidered as often as is necessary, assessments have to be made in oral tests, either during or shortly after the test. If the examiner is also an interlocutor, then the problems are further compounded. You need to work out how the examiner will record the marks. The importance of double marking for reducing unreliability here is undeniable.

In oral testing, as in the assessment of written production, there is a need for explicit, comprehensive marking schemes, close moderation of test tasks and marking schemes, and training and standardization of markers. They will all make a contribution to the reliability of the marking. In assessment of written samples scripts are made available for rating practice. In speaking, if videos can be made of candidates performing test activities, these can subsequently be used for training and standardization of marking in a similar fashion. The procedures outlined below for rating written scripts are (*mutatis mutandis*) for the most part applicable to the assessment of spoken production.

In order to measure the quality of spoken performance, we first need to establish criteria of assessment. Normal spoken interaction is performance-based, i.e., it involves memory limitations, distractions, shifts of attention and interest, and errors. We must not lose sight of this in assessing non-native speakers. Native speaker speech is characterized by compensation features such as self-correction, false starts, repetition, rephrasing and circumlocutions. The processing conditions of oral language result in these common features so they should not feature in assessment scales to the detriment of candidates. The presence of accuracy as a criterion in some of the published scales included below (TEEP and TSE) needs some attention in this respect.

As we discussed for writing above, testers also need to decide whether they will treat these criteria separately in an analytic scheme (lots of separate impressions) or try to collapse them into some form of global impression banding. The decision on whether to use an analytical or a global impression band scale will largely rest on the degree to which one can describe in behavioural terms the different levels of proficiency that student performances will result in.

If we apply analytical criteria to the spoken product of test tasks, the issue still remains of what the profile of achievement of a successful candidate is. In other words, we have to be explicit about the level of performance expected in each of the specified criteria (see below). In addition, there is a question mark hanging over analytic schemes, as to whether they result in repeatedly assessing the same thing, the halo effect. Does awarding a top grade on your favourite criterion influence the grades you give on the other criteria?

One potential advantage of the analytical approach is that it can help provide a profile of a candidate's weaknesses and strengths which may be helpful diagnostically, and also make a formative contribution in course design.

The Educational Testing Service (2002) *Test of Spoken English* provides a complex scale in a number of different versions for administrators, the public and examinees, and examiners. The concise version for administrators consists of the **lines in bold** in the Table A below, and that for examinees and the public contains the additional statements underneath each of these bold statements. Table B is for markers new to the scales and provides a further level of detail with descriptions of the type of language that might manifest itself. This meets with Alderson's (1991) concern that different scales might need to be prepared for different audiences.

A The Test of Spoken English Rating Scale

60	**Communication almost always effective: task performed very competently**
	Functions performed clearly and effectively
	Appropriate response to audience/situation
	Coherent, with effective use of cohesive devices
	Use of linguistic features almost always effective; communication not affected by minor errors

A   The Test of Spoken English Rating Scale   (Continued)

50   **Communication generally effective: task performed competently**
Functions generally performed clearly and effectively
Generally appropriate response to audience/situation
Coherent, with some effective use of cohesive devices
Use of linguistic features generally effective; communication generally not affected by errors

40   **Communication somewhat effective: task performed somewhat competently**
Functions performed somewhat clearly and effectively
Somewhat appropriate response to audience/situation
Somewhat coherent, with some use of cohesive devices
Use of linguistic features somewhat effective; communication sometimes affected by errors

30   **Communication generally not effective: task generally performed poorly**
Functions generally performed unclearly and ineffectively
Generally inappropriate response to audience/situation
Generally incoherent, with little use of cohesive devices
Use of linguistic features generally poor; communication often impeded by major errors

20   **No effective communication: no evidence of ability to perform task**
No evidence that functions were performed
No evidence of ability to respond to audience/situation
Incoherent, with no use of cohesive devices
Use of linguistic features poor; communication ineffective due to major errors

B   The Test of Spoken English Band Descriptors for Overall Features (ETS)

60 Communication almost always effective: task performed very competently.	Speaker volunteers information freely, with little or no effort, and may go beyond the task by using additional appropriate functions. • Native-like repair strategies • Sophisticated expressions • Very strong content • Almost no listener effort required
50 Communication generally effective: task performed competently.	Speaker volunteers information, sometimes with effort; usually does not run out of time. • Linguistic weaknesses may necessitate some repair strategies that may be slightly distracting • Expressions sometimes awkward • Generally strong content • Little listener effort required

40	Communication somewhat effective: task performed somewhat competent.	Speaker responds with effort; sometimes provides limited speech sample and sometimes runs out of time. • Sometimes excessive, distracting, and ineffective repair strategies used to compensate for linguistic weaknesses (e.g., vocabulary and/or grammar) • Adequate content • Some listener effort required
30	Communication generally not effective: task generally performed poorly.	Speaker responds with much effort; provides limited speech sample and often runs out of time. • Repair strategies excessive, very distracting, and ineffective • Much listener effort required • Difficult to tell if task is fully performed because of linguistic weaknesses, but function can be identified
20	No effective communication: no evidence of ability to perform task.	• Extreme speaker effort is evident; speaker may repeat prompt, give up on task, or be silent. • Attempts to perform task end in failure • Only isolated words or phrases intelligible, even with much listener effort • Function cannot be identified

The 'tasks' and 'functions' in the scale descriptors refer to the test tasks.

Weir (1993) provides the analytic scale below for the assessment of speaking in preference to a banded impression scale for the reasons expressed in relation to the assessment of writing above.

Analytic speaking criteria (Weir 1993)

Fluency

4. Generally natural delivery, only occasional halting when searching for appropriate words/expressions.
3. The student hesitates and repeats himself at times but can generally maintain a flow of speech, although s/he may need an occasional prompt.
2. Speech is slow and hesitant. Maintains speech in a passive manner and needs regular prompts.
1. The student speaks so little that no 'fluent' speech can be said to occur.

Analytic speaking criteria (Weir 1993) (Continued)

Pronunciation

4. Occasional errors of pronunciation a few inconsistencies of rhythm, intonation and pronunciation but comprehension is not impeded.
3. Rhythm, intonation and pronunciation require more careful listening; some errors of pronunciation which may occasionally lead to incomprehension.
2. Comprehension suffers due to frequent errors in rhythm, intonation and pronunciation.
1. Words are unintelligible.

Vocabulary

4. Effective use of vocabulary for the task with few inappropriacies.
3. For the most part, effective use of vocabulary for the task with some examples of inappropriacy.
2. Limited use of vocabulary with frequent inappropriacies.
1. Inappropriate and inadequate vocabulary.

Grammatical accuracy

4. Very few grammatical errors evident.
3. Some errors in use of sentence structures and grammatical forms but these do not interfere with comprehension.
2. Speech is broken and distorted by frequent errors.
1. Unable to construct comprehensible sentences.

Interactional strategies

In this criterion, the term 'interactional strategies' means using strategies such as initiating the discussion, asking for clarification, expanding the topic, turn taking and concluding the discussion.

4. Interacts effectively and readily participates and follows the discussion.
3. Use of interactive strategies is generally adequate but at times experiences some difficulty in maintaining interaction consistently.
2. Interaction ineffective. Can seldom develop an interaction.
1. Understanding and interaction minimal.

The criteria in each of the tables need empirical validation in the particular situation testers find themselves in. First the tester would need to specify appropriate tasks in terms of conditions and operations and decisions are then taken on the criteria that are applicable to the output generated and the levels of performance within each of these. Intuition among professionals may provide a good starting point for developing scales, but this will need to be supported empirically either by qualitative analysis of performances and or quantitative analysis of features occurring at different levels of performance to help further refine and concretize these (see Fulcher 1993, 1996a, Hasselgreen 1998 for rigorous approaches to this). The dimension of practicality cannot be ignored here and the criteria developed would need to be readily deployable by teachers. It would have to be established how many criteria teachers could reliably handle in any one particular assessment. The criteria developed would need to be accessible to other teachers and the number of levels within each criterion would have to represent real distinctions in the performance of actual candidates.

It may well be that in any one situation not all the criteria suggested for assessing the routine skills, improvisation skills and micro-linguistic skills above would be applied by the assessors. The criteria used would depend on the nature of the skills being tested and the level of detail desired by the end users. The crucial question would be what the tester wants to find out about a student's performance on appropriate spoken interaction tasks. This is the crucial issue of test validity. Once the tester is clear about what to find out, then decisions on the appropriate level of analysis to be applied to the output from test tasks are easier to make.

It is increasingly recognized that discourse in spoken interaction tasks is co-constructed (e.g., Lumley and Brown 1997; Brown and Hill 1998, Brown 2003), but ratings at present are invariably given to individuals. Luoma (2004: 190–1) draws attention to the pressing need for research in this area.

Quote 9.6   Luoma on the need to address co-construction of meaning in oral interaction

In pair or group tasks, or even when an examinee interacts with an interlocutor, the performance of one speaker is likely to affect the performance of the other(s). In discourse analysis, this is discussed under the heading of co-construction of meaning. What we need to understand better is exactly how one person's performance affects the others. We also need to know what it is about an examinee's talk and his or her accommodation to the conversation partner that should be appreciated in order to make evaluations in a fair way. Tests sometimes use a criterion such as 'discourse skills' to evaluate this, but the scale descriptors are usually rather vague, and they concentrate on a rater's perception of the flow of the conversation. This needs to be supplemented or replaced by descriptions of what the examinees actually say and do. The patterns that make a difference are likely to include recycling of phrases and structures from previous turns and the explicit and implicit development of themes and topics between speakers. However, only concrete analyses of test performances combined with ratings of discourse competence can provide accurate detailed descriptions of this.
(2004: 190–1)

We have examined briefly the contribution rater training could make to scoring validity (see Fulcher 2003: Chapter 6 for a full treatment). We now look at two further procedures that should also help.

Standardization

This is the process of ensuring that markers adhere to an agreed procedure and apply rating scales in an appropriate way. Even if examiners are provided with an ideal marking scheme, there might be some who do not mark in exactly the way required. The purpose of standardization procedures is to bring examiners into line, so that candidates' marks are affected as little as possible by the particular examiner who assesses them.

Examiners should be requested to attend a standardization meeting before beginning marking proper. Here the marking criteria would be discussed to ensure the examiners fully understand the criteria that are to be applied. The marking scheme is examined closely and any difficulties in interpretation are clarified. Tape or script libraries may be set up to provide examples of performances at the prescribed levels. It is important that any scales that are employed have been systematically calibrated across the range of possible scores on real performances. Benchmark scripts can then be selected for training writing examiners. At the pre-marking meeting the examiners have to conduct a number of assessments. In respect of an oral test this might involve listening to and/or watching audio tape or video tape recordings of candidates' performances on the test, at a number of different benchmark levels.

The examiners are asked to assess these performances and afterwards their assessments are reported in plenary and compared to see if they are applying the same marking standards. Reasons for the scores awarded are discussed in order to make explicit the basis on which decisions have been made. The aim is to identify any factors which might lead to unreliability in marking and to try and resolve these at the meeting. In this way any potential ambiguities in interpreting the marking scheme can be exposed and appropriate application of criterion levels to performances determined.

In the case of new examiners there might also be extensive discussion with the supervisors about how to conduct an examination, how to make the candidate feel at ease, how to phrase questions, what questions to ask in an interview situation, the type of prompts they might give to weaker students and how to react to candidates.

Once the standardization has been completed there must still be checks. In tests of writing, sample scripts should be sent in to be marked again by the supervisors so that the process of ensuring reliability can be continued. In oral tests supervisors may sometimes sit in unannounced on a number of oral tests, observe how they are conducted and discuss the allocation of marks with the examiner subsequently. They might discuss how improvements could be made either in technique or marking.

Moderation of scores

It is often argued that work marked independently by two different markers, with their marks being averaged, is a more reliable estimate than if it were marked by a single marker. This is of course true only if the markers are equally consistent in their own marking (see Chapter 4 for a discussion of this). If this is not the case the reliability of the more consistent marker on his own might be better than the combined reliability estimate for two markers who exhibit unequal consistencies. With an adequate marking scheme and sufficient standardization of examiners, however, a high standard of inter-marker and intra-marker reliability should be possible. The advantages of a double as against a single marker system would then be clear. The use of multi-faceted Rasch (MFR) analysis can now provide a very clear picture of whether markers are behaving consistently with themselves and with other markers and can detect any bias against individual candidates.

Recent research in the language testing literature on speaking and writing tests recognizes that interactions between other *facets* within the assessment procedure can also impinge on the outcomes (e.g., task variability). In order to account for these features in estimating reliability of speaking and writing tests, it is now becoming common to use statistical models, such as MFR. The procedure of MFR analysis allows investigation of the influence of tasks compared with other facets of the testing procedure, such as the rater and the rating scale. You can download *minifac* free from www.winsteps.com/minifac.htm. This is a demo version of the Facets software with built-in limitations to the number of facets and data points – though more than enough for the novice user to work with. (see McNamara 1996: Chapters 5–8, Myford and Wolfe 2000, 2003, 2004 for an accessible treatment of Rasch analysis).

Below is an example of an accreditation report from an MFR analysis of a standardization procedure. This shows that these raters are all doing well (though other analyses would also have been called into play before a final decision could be made).

In MFR analysis we look out for the Infit and Outfit mean square scores. It is often recommended that they should be in the range 0.5–1.5 for tests of production. If the scores are low, it might suggest that the rater is not using the range of scores (and is sticking pretty much to one section of the scale). So, for example, with a rater who is both harsh and has a low 'infit mean square' estimate we find that even when a candidate is of a high level of proficiency (and other judges have recognized this) the rater still gives a low score. If they are high (i.e., over 1.5), it indicates that the rater is not applying the scale in a manner consistent with the other raters.

MFR has clear importance for detecting inconsistent individual rater behaviour both over time and in comparison with other raters. MFR can take into account all of the factors that might affect the final score of a student: for example, the ability of the student, the severity of the rater and the

Rater Measurement Report from Test Accreditation Procedure (FACETS output)

Table 7.2.1 Raters Measurement Report (arranged by N).									
Obsvd Score	Obsvd Count	Obsvd Average	Fair-M Average	Model		Infit		Outfit	
				Measure	S.E.	MnSq	ZStd	MnSq	ZStd	N Raters
242	44	5.5	5.46	.51	.25	0.9	0	0.9	0	1 Rik
205	36	5.7	5.65	−.10	.28	1.1	0	1.1	0	2 Jane
285	44	6.5	6.38	−2.32	.26	0.8	0	0.9	0	3 Annie
247	44	5.6	5.56	.19	.26	0.7	−1	0.7	−1	4 JonP
251	44	5.7	5.64	−.07	.26	0.9	0	1.0	0	5 Noel
253	44	5.8	5.68	−.20	.26	1.2	0	1.1	0	6 Angela
218	44	5.0	5.06	2.01	.25	0.8	0	0.8	−1	7 Charles
243.0	42.9	5.7	5.63	.00	.26	0.9	−0.4	0.9	−0.4	Mean (Count : 7)
23.9	2.8	0.4	0.36	1.18	.01	0.1	0.7	0.1	0.7	S.D.

RMSE (Model) .26   Adj S.D. 1.15   Separation 4.44   Reliability .95
Fixed (all same)   chi-square: 147.9   d.f.: 6   significance: .00
Random (normal)   chi-square: 6.0   d.f.: 5   significance: .31

difficulty of the task. As long as the raters are consistent in themselves it becomes possible to adjust scores for the differences occasioned by the harshness/leniency of a large cohort of raters. It thus enhances the possibility of a fair measure of the candidate's ability.

The procedure is recommended to determine raters' severity, to guard against bias, and to inform any decisions to be made concerning score adjustment before grade setting. (See McNamara 1996: 283–7, Myford and Wolfe 2000: 7, 2003, 2004 for a useful introduction to MFR.)

The *rating conditions* under which marking takes place, e.g., temporal, physical, psychological, are increasingly seen as having a potential impact on scoring and need to be standardized too. Papers marked in the shady groves of academe may receive more considered treatment than those scored on the 5.30 pm rush hour tube out of London on a Friday afternoon.

Estimating marker reliability: classical analysis

If MFR analysis is not possible, then a classical analysis correlation coefficient will provide a rough estimate of the degree to which a marker (or different markers) are consistent in their assessment of candidates' performance. Inter-marker reliability is the consistency with which two or more judges rate the work or performance of test takers. Intra-marker reliability is the consistency of a single marker with him or herself. This is not the same as test reliability as this must account for other sources of unreliability additional to that occasioned by less than perfect scoring.

Calculating marker reliability

This is usually calculated through the correlation statistic which can be done by hand (see below) or with less hassle by using a spreadsheet program such as Excel, using the formula = CORREL(array 1, array 2), where array is the column of scores. The Statistical Package for the Social Sciences (SPSS) is even easier to use for all the statistics discussed in this chapter (see Bryman and Cramer 2001, and SPSS Inc. 2002).

$$r = \frac{N\Sigma xy - (\Sigma x)(\Sigma y)}{\sqrt{[N\Sigma x^2 - (\Sigma x)^2][N\Sigma y^2 - (\Sigma y)^2]}}$$

Where:

N = number of pairs of scores
Σxy = sum of the products of paired scores
Σx = sum of x scores
Σy = sum of y scores
Σx^2 = sum of squared x scores
Σy^2 = sum of squared y scores

The symbol **r** stands for the correlation, which will always be between −1.0 and +1.0. If the correlation is negative, we have a negative relationship; if it's positive, the relationship is positive. A correlation of 0.9 or above is normally considered a desirable level of marker reliability as when this level is reached we get an overlap of 81 per cent (square of the correlation) between the markers.

However, as we saw earlier, correlation is notoriously sample-dependent and if the mark range is restricted, i.e., where candidates are scoring within a band or so of each other, such correlations may well be depressed. Similarly, if there any very high or low scorers in the sample this can distort correlations in the opposite direction. Furthermore such correlations say nothing about relative levels of marking, nor do they tell us whether A is a hard marker or B a lenient one (see Fulcher 2003: 201–3).

Such correlations are now fast going out of favour. As we described above, MFR now offers a more sophisticated way of looking at degree of overlap between raters but also it provides evidence on level of marking and provides a systematic method for calibrating scores to iron out differences occasioned by inter marker differences.

9.3   Internal reliability of receptive tests

As we saw in Chapter 4, in *receptive* tests we are often concerned with the extent to which test scores are internally consistent rather than with marker reliability *per se*.

Item analysis

In the classroom we need to investigate procedures for investigating properties of test items (especially facility and discrimination) prior to development of their final format and content. We are interested in the difficulty of individual items because if they are too easy or too difficult they may be contributing little to the information a test can give us about any differences between individuals. Item facility can be estimated by finding the proportion of correct responses, using the formula:

$$IF = \frac{\Sigma C_r}{N}$$

Where, IF = item facility

ΣC_r = sum of correct responses

N = number of test-takers

We are also very interested in whether items discriminate between strong and weak candidates. We would expect good students to get an item right and weak students to get it wrong but not vice versa. Calculating an item discrimination index will tell us the extent to which this is the case. The formula below enables us to do this:

$$IDis = \frac{H_c}{H_c + L_c}$$

Where, IDis = item discrimination

H_c = number of correct responses in the high group

L_c = number of correct responses in the weak group

We calculate the item discrimination by first sorting the students by their total score on the test. Two groups are then identified, a top scoring group and a bottom scoring group. Normally we take the top and bottom thirds when we have a small test population but Henning (1987: 51) suggests about 28 per cent or even a bit lower for a very large population.

Negative results would tell us that the item is being answered correctly by weaker students and incorrectly by better students – clearly something is wrong. Maybe the item is too difficult and the top group does not answer it while the weaker group are simply guessing. Whatever the reason, the item needs sorting out.

Internal consistency

In Chapter 4 we discussed when we might use internal consistency measures and when we thought they were inappropriate. In those tests where the items are considered homogeneous then this statistic obviously has a place in providing us with information on the degree to which the items are pulling in the same direction, i.e., how internally consistent the test is. We also noted that in certificated exams such as the main suite of Cambridge ESOL, given the limited range of candidates taking the exam at a particular level in the main suite, such correlations are likely to be depressed.

Internal consistency/reliability is thus a feature of a test, which represents the degree to which candidates' scores on the individual items in a test are consistent with their total score. Estimates of internal consistency can be used as indices of test reliability; various indices can be computed, for example, KR-20, alpha. The formula for KR-20 is:

$$r_{tt} = \frac{n}{(n-1)} \times \left(\frac{s_t^2 - \Sigma s_i^2}{s_t^2} \right)$$

Where, r_{tt} = KR-20 estimate of reliability

n = number of items in the test

s_t^2 = variance of the test scores (population variance)

Σs_i^2 = sum of the variances of all items (sometimes Σpq)

Most calculators will enable you to work out easily averages and the standard deviation for an item. To get s_t^2 you just square the standard deviation.

Quote 9.7   Weir and Milanovic on internal consistency in Cambridge Examinations

In recent years Cambridge ESOL has set target levels for the internal consistency reliability for the item-based components of the Main Suite examinations – Paper 1 (Reading), Paper 4 (Listening) and, where applicable, Paper 3 (Use of English). These target levels are routinely used in the test construction procedures and the predicted operational reliability for each paper is based on the type and quality of the tasks that are chosen according to the test specifications. The information used includes the Rasch-based difficulty estimates and other data obtained during the item writing and pre-testing processes. In practice this means that the estimates which are obtained operationally in 'live' test administrations typically fall between an acceptable minimum value and the intended target value (which is also sometimes exceeded).

The range of alpha values is as follows:

Paper 1	Reading	0.80 to 0.85	(test papers with 40 items)
Paper 3	Use of English	0.85 to 0.90	(test papers with 55–60 items)
Paper 4	Listening	0.75 to 0.80	(test papers with 25–30 items)

Quote 9.7 (Continued)

This pattern is to be expected for examinations that measure across a restricted range of ability and where the length of the paper, in terms of number of items, and the kind of item type varies. Note that Paper 3 is the longest paper, with 55 items and this has the highest estimate. The estimates are lower for Paper 1 with 40 items and for Paper 4 which has only 25–30 items.
(2003: 107–8)

Error of measurement

This statistic is concerned with the difference between an observed score and the corresponding true score, or proficiency. (American Educational Research Association *et al.* 1999). In Chapter 4 we described its usefulness when looking at an individual's performance on a test.

Concept 9.1   Reliability of scores for the individual: Standard Error of Measurement (SEM)

The SEM, also known as the standard error of a score, is another way of reporting the reliability of a test. It is computed from the reliability coefficient:
$$SEM = SD\sqrt{1 - r}$$
Where SD = is the standard deviation of the obtained scores on the test
    r = the reliability coefficient
Nitko (1996: 71) illustrates how:
'For a fixed value for the reliability coefficient, SEM becomes larger as SD increases.
For a fixed value for the SD, SEM becomes smaller as the reliability coefficient becomes larger.'
We can state with certain degrees of confidence the reasonable limits within which an individual's score on a test will fall, independent of the variability of the group on which the SEM has been based. We could add and subtract the SEM from an individual's obtained score to provide the boundaries of a 'score band'. It does not matter whether it is a homogeneous or heterogeneous group. It is thus more suitable for interpreting individual scores.

Hughes points out that using IRT provides an even better estimate of probable error in a student's score. In classical analysis described above we only have a single estimate of SEM for all candidates, whereas 'IRT gives an estimate for each individual, basing this estimate on the individual's performance on each test item' (Hughes 2003: 42).

Weir and Milanovic (2003: Chapter 8) advise that in taking decisions on pass or fail in the CPE writing test consideration should be given to double marking at least those candidates who fall within one standard error of the pass/fail boundary. Hughes (2003: 42) in a similar vein argues: 'this should make us very cautious about making important decisions on the basis of the test scores of candidates whose actual scores place them close to the cut off point....We should at least consider the possibility of gathering further relevant information on the language ability of such candidates.'

Criterion-related decision consistency

In criterion-referenced tests we are often more interested in the consistency in judgements of whether a set criterion has been met, decision consistency, rather than consistency of scores *per se*.

Concept 9.2   Criterion-related decision consistency

We want to know whether a test is consistent in deciding whether or not the candidates have or have not reached the criterion. Imagine a case where 50 candidates take a test (perhaps two alternate forms of it) twice. Those who reach a criterion may be called 'masters'...and those who do not reach it may be called 'non-masters'. Of the 50 candidates:

    18 are masters on both occasions

    15 are non-masters on both occasions

    9 are masters on the first occasion but non-masters on the second

    8 are non-masters on the first occasion but masters on the second

So out of 50 candidates, 33 are assigned to the same category (master or non-master) on both occasions. Thirty three out of 50 can be expressed as a percentage (66 per cent) or as a proportion (0.66)...an accepted estimate of decision consistency..

(Hughes 2003: 42)

9.4   Scores, grading and post-exam validation procedures

The final part of the scoring process is where grades are decided and checks carried out to ensure that the test was not biased against any group of candidates.

Quote 9.8   Wood on the reliability of grades

The reliability of grades is, in an important sense, the bottom line of the examining system: all other reliabilities of markers...and items, feed in to produce outcomes which are more or less reliable, and therefore just. There exist direct relationships between the reliability of the examination, which usually means the reliability of the overall marks, the number of grades on the scale, the reliability of the grades and the severity of the consequences of misclassification.

(1991: 134)

Weir and Milanovic (2003: 102–3) describe how, once all examination papers have been marked and a series of checks to ensure that all candidates have been assessed accurately and to the same standards have been carried out, grading takes place. Grading is where the cut-off score for the various

grades, with A, B, C passing and D and E failing, according to the performance criteria defined for that grade are set. At this meeting reports and analyses
that have been carried out on the score data (the way the examination materials have worked in practice as predicted by the pre-testing, and standards
fixing activities which were carried out during the question paper production
cycle), and similarly, reports and analyses in relation to various groups of
candidates, are reviewed according to an established procedure.

Grading should always be done in relation to explicit benchmark criteria.
Some authorities introduce norm referencing for political reasons where a
fixed percentage of passing candidates determines the cut off score. The latter
procedure has obviously nothing to contribute to the validity of testing; in
fact, quite the reverse.

After the grading meeting, results in terms of grades are generated. At this
stage procedures and results are reviewed to ensure the fairness of the final
results before they are issued to candidates. As part of this procedure an Awards
Committee looks particularly closely at the performance of candidates who
are close to the grade boundaries – particularly the pass/fail boundary.

The last part of our framework deals with the external validity of the test.
When we have generated sufficient evidence on the context, theory-based
and scoring validities we should also be interested in going outside the test
and evaluating its impact and its relation to other measures of the same ability.

Further reading

Brown (1991) provides an accessible introduction to statistics for testers.
Bryman and Cramer (2001) provide a good introduction to SPSS.
Council of Europe (2001) provides a number of scales that might be useful as a basis
for customizing to your own needs.
Crocker and Algina (1986) provide a comprehensive explanation of the statistics
and concepts discussed in the chapter.
Hughes (2003: Chapter 5) provides a refreshingly accessible overview of all aspects of
reliability, including worked examples of using IRT in Appendix 1.
Weigle (2002) provides numerous examples of scales for writing and Luoma (2004)
does the same for speaking.

10
External Validities in Action

Once a test has been successfully developed, administered and the results shown to be reliable, there still remains the question of what other evidence needs to be generated to demonstrate that it is valid. Two further steps need to be taken. The first involves looking for an external criterion beyond the test in question against which it might be measured.

10.1   Criterion-related validity

A test is said to have criterion-related validity if a relationship can be demonstrated between test scores and an *external* criterion which is believed to be a measure of the same ability (see Chapter 4 for further discussion). Information on criterion relatedness is also used in determining how well a test predicts future behaviour (ALTE 1994). The statistical procedures for doing this were discussed in the last chapter under 'correlation' and 'Rasch analysis', so treatment of these external validity relationships will be brief.

The procedures detailed below will generate evidence on the similarity in construct between two measures (concurrent validity) and also the extent to which we can depend on the results of a test (criterion-related reliability). As such they indicate clearly the case for integrating such reliability estimates into a validity framework.

Comparison with other tests/measurements

Traditionally conceived in the literature as *concurrent validation*, this involves the comparison of the test scores with some other measure for the same candidates taken at roughly the same time as the test under consideration. This other measure may consist of scores from some other tests, or candidates' self-assessments of their language abilities, or ratings of the candidate by teachers, subject specialists, or other informants (see Davies 1983, Alderson *et al.* 1995 for a detailed discussion of this). Significant correlations above 0.9 would indicate a strong relationship between the two measures with over 80 per cent of the variance being shared.

A test is also said to have criterion-related validity if a relationship can be demonstrated between test scores obtained from different versions of a test administered to the same candidates in the same conditions on two different occasions. Two or more versions of a test are considered interchangeable, when they measure the same constructs in the same ways, are intended for the same purposes, and are administered using the same directions. *Alternate forms* is a generic term used to refer to any of the following three categories. *Parallel forms* have equal raw score means, equal standard deviations, equal error structures and equal correlations with other measures for a given population. *Equivalent forms* do not have the statistical similarity of parallel forms, but the dissimilarities in raw score statistics are compensated for in the conversions to derived scores or in form-specific norm tables. *Comparable forms* are highly similar in content, but the degree of statistical similarity has not been demonstrated. (American Educational Research Association *et al.* 1999). The approach is discussed in detail in Chapter 11, Case study 4.

High indices of alternate-form reliability in a test do not necessarily yield a significant meaning, unless a consistent content coverage over test forms is also established and full validity is confirmed (i.e., context- and theory-based too). Inconsistent test content across test forms can potentially impact on test scores, consequently causing bias against candidates and harming fairness in the test (see Chapter 11, Case study 4 for further discussion of this).

The difficulties of putting this into practice operationally mean that this form of evidence is seldom made available. Exam Boards tend to rely on more sophisticated methods such as item response theory (IRT) to try and ensure two versions of the tests are measuring the same ability at the same level of difficulty. However, in the classroom it is always prudent to compare results obtained through continuous assessment over a period of time with those obtaining in a one-shot test, particularly if the latter is for high stakes.

Quote 10.1   Saville on parallel forms reliability

Each edited item is pretested on a representative sample of candidates (usually involving around 200 learners who are about to take one of the live examinations) so that data can be statistically analysed. In this way pretesting plays an important role in achieving reliability in terms of parallel forms of the tests.

All the materials which are pretested can be related to the underlying scale of difficulty in the item bank by the use of 'anchor' items; these are items with known measurement characteristics which provide the basis for calculating the difficulty of the new items to go into the bank. UCLES EFL uses IRT models (mainly the Rasch model) to construct the common scale which underpins the item bank and which provides the basis for the construction of parallel forms of the tests at the different levels of the system. (2003: 91–2)

Comparison with future performance

Predictive validity involves the comparison of test scores with some other measure for the same candidates taken some time after the test has been given. This other measure may consist of scores from some other test (not necessarily language, e.g., degree results), or candidates' self-assessments of their language abilities, or ratings of the candidate by teachers, subject specialists, or other informants (see Alderson *et al.* 1995, Criper and Davies 1988, Cotton and Conrow 1998, Hill *et al.* 1999 for exemplification of this). Banerjee (2003) provides a full and innovative discussion of the whole area of predictive validity and argues for considering the external criterion in terms of cost to students and other stakeholders if admitted at various levels of test performance, as against degree of overlap with the criterion course result.

Predictive validity is, however, in general beset with problems because of the variables that may interfere with the comparison over time.

Comparison with external benchmarks

Saville (2003) details how Cambridge ESOL has linked its examinations closely to the levels laid out in external internationally accepted frameworks. However, when this is done for example with reference to the Council of Europe's Common Frame of Reference, the question must remain as to the validity of such a model when it is premised on an incomplete and unevenly applied range of contextual variables; little account is taken of the nature of cognitive processing at different levels of ability; and performance of the 'Can-Dos' is rarely criterion-related to actual quality of performance.

Quote 10.2   Saville on calibrating examinations to external criteria

Assessment is carried out at *a variety of different criterion levels*, from the level of beginner up to the level of a highly proficient user, with a series of intermediate levels in between. The Main Suite of examinations from UCLES EFL has five separate examinations each targeted at a different level, and linked to a framework used for a wide range of other languages.

A key feature of the approach is that each examination is benchmarked to a specific criterion level and can be interpreted within the context of the overall framework of levels. In the context of ALTE, these levels are interpretable internationally and have been empirically linked to the Common European Framework of Reference (see discussion of this in the Council of Europe's *Common European Framework of Reference*, 2001, Chapter 9, Assessment and Appendix D).

The ALTE scale of levels which is used by UCLES EFL provides a set of common standards and is the basis of the *criterion-referenced approach* to the interpretation of examination results.

In particular it requires:

- the *vertical* mapping of the continuum of language ability from low to high;
- the detailed specification of examination content at each criterion level together with examples of criterion performance in terms of candidates' performance in speech and writing (i.e., the *horizontal* dimension).

This approach allows individual results on any one examination to be situated in relation to the total 'criterion space', i.e., the much wider continuum of ability.

Referencing to the criterion is undertaken by means of scalar analyses using the Rasch model to relate the results from the whole range of Cambridge examinations to the Common Scale. In addition, the ALTE *Can Do* scales provide criterion-related statements at each level in relation to the specified domains which are covered in the examinations (situated language use for social, tourist, work and study purposes).

The criterion scale and the *Can Do* descriptors provide the external reality which helps to ensure that the test results mean something to the key stakeholders (the candidates, their sponsors and other users of examination results).

... The approach to *Grading* the examinations, which is based on principles of criterion referencing, allows candidates' results to be compared from session to session and from year to year to ensure that grades in a particular examination remain constant. This aspect of fairness is of particular importance, not only to the candidates themselves, but also to universities and employers looking to recruit people with a specific level of language ability, which they can rely on.

(2003: 62–4 and 101)

10.2 Consequential validity

As we saw in Chapter 4, increasingly high stakes tests are paying more attention to establishing evidence relating to consequential validity. It is now seen as de rigueur that the adequacy and appropriateness of interpretations and actions based on test scores should be supported by both empirical evidence and theoretical rationales (Messick 1989).

As we saw in Chapter 4, consequential validity can be considered in three main areas.

Differential validity

In discussing test fairness, bias may refer to construct under-representation or construct-irrelevant components of test scores that differentially affect the performance of different groups of test takers (American Educational Research Association *et al.* 1999).

Bachman (1990) is concerned with four potential sources of test bias:

- cultural background
- background knowledge

- cognitive characteristics
- native language/ethnicity/age and gender.

Clearly, attempts should have been made before the test was implemented at the context and theory-based validation stages to ensure that none of these potential sources of bias are allowed to interfere with the measurement. After the test it is useful to check up on this statistically and this is where candidate information (on L1, familiarity with topics, etc.) is useful as it can be collected as appropriate before or after the examination and electronically recorded and compared to test scores.

Weir and Milanovic (2003: 103) describe how at Cambridge ESOL Grade Review and Awards meetings: 'The performance of large groups of candidates (or cohorts) is compared with cohorts from previous years, and performance is also compared by country, by first language, by age and a number of other factors, to ensure that the standards being applied are consistently fair to all candidates, and that a particular grade "means" the same thing from year to year and throughout the world.'

Additionally, Bachman (1990: 278) rightly cautions that group differences must be treated with some caution as they may be an indication of differences in actual language ability rather than an indication of bias.

In Chapter 11 Case study 5 we will look further at some background variables that might be investigated to determine whether they have impacted on test scores, e.g., gender, learning style, previous experiences, and others.

Washback

Recent validation projects in Australia (Burrows 1998), Hong Kong (Cheng 1997) and Sri Lanka (Wall 2004) have addressed the influence of tests on teaching and learning in a variety of settings. A similar project is underway to monitor the impact of Next Generation TOEFL. While some studies examined the impact of testing innovations (Wall and Alderson 1993, Cheng 1997, Burrows 1998), others have compared test preparation courses with other settings, such as general English courses (Alderson and Hamp-Lyons 1996). Green's study (2003) is of the latter type and examined practices and outcomes on IELTS examination preparation courses with other EAP courses such as university pre-sessional courses.

Quote 10.3   Green on backwash studies

Early research into backwash from language tests (Hughes, 1988; Khaniya, 1990) was criticized for a lack of empirical data (Alderson and Wall, 1993); relying instead on insights from interested participants. More recent research has therefore triangulated quantitative data with qualitative descriptions of educational practices derived through ethnographic methods (Burrows, 1998; Cheng, 1997; Watanabe, 1996b). This has allowed the development of theoretical models of backwash that recognize a wide variety of moderating variables interacting with test influence (Burrows, 1998, Hughes, 2003). (2003: 1–3)

Few studies have tried to analyse how we might go about trying to achieve beneficial backwash. In a refreshing change, Hughes (2003: 53–7) offers some suggestions for achieving beneficial backwash:

- Test the abilities whose development you want to encourage.
- Sample widely and unpredictably.
- Use direct testing.
- Make testing criterion-referenced.
- Ensure the test is known and understood by students and teachers.
- Where necessary, provide assistance to teachers.

The major research studies carried out by Wall (2004) and Cheng (2004) emphasize the centrality of Hughes' last criterion if beneficial washback is to occur:

- Training teachers in the new content and methodology required for the test is essential. If teachers are untrained in the new knowledge skills and attitudes required for effective teaching towards the examination, why should we expect backwash?
- Support in the forms of appropriate teaching materials must be freely available.

Green (2003) suggests a number of other conditions that need to be in place (see Chapter 4 above for extended discussion):

- There needs to be a considerable overlap between test and target situation demands on language abilities.
- Success on the test is perceived to be important.
- Success on the test is perceived to be difficult (but both attainable and amenable to preparation).
- Candidates operate in a context where these perceptions are shared by other participants.

In designing and developing high stakes tests, the more these factors can be taken account of at the development stage the more positive the backwash of the test is likely to be.

> ## Quote 10.4   Saville describes the Cambridge ESOL perspective on impact
>
> Procedures also need to be put into place after an examination becomes operational to collect information which allows impact to be estimated. This should involve collecting data on the following:
>
> - who is taking the examination (i.e., a profile of the candidates);
> - who is using the examination results and for what purpose;
> - who is teaching towards the examination and under what circumstances;
> - what kinds of courses and materials are being designed and used to prepare candidates;
> - what effect the examination has on public perceptions generally (e.g. regarding educational standards);
> - how the examination is viewed by those directly involved in educational processes (e.g. by students, examination takers, teachers, parents, etc.);
> - how the examination is viewed by members of society outside education (e.g. by politicians, businessmen, etc.).
>
> (2003: 75)

Saville argues that, from the evidence collected, it should be possible to demonstrate that the examination is sufficiently valid and reliable for the context in which it is used. This information should be made available in suitable versions of reports to the public and this in itself is a way of ensuring that positive impact is achieved.

Exam boards need to monitor the test's effects on language materials and on classroom activity and to seek information on, and the views of, a full range of stakeholders. Saville (2003: 76) points out how this approach to investigating impact has been developed in relation to IELTS by Cambridge ESOL. A range of integrated processes and instruments were developed to focus on the following aspects of the test's impact:

- the content and nature of classroom activity in IELTS-related classes;
- the content and nature of IELTS text books and related teaching materials;
- the views and attitudes of user groups towards IELTS;
- the IELTS test-taking population.

The first two points concern washback in the more traditional sense, (i.e., the effect of the test on teaching and learning). The second two are concerned with the wider impact of the test, its effects on other systems in the administrative and academic contexts of the tests, and on the attitudes and behaviour of the stakeholders in these.

Effect on society

The effect of a test on the wider community is the third aspect of consequential validity that needs to be investigated in high stakes tests. This is perhaps the most difficult area of all to investigate and the one most likely to be overlooked as it demands going beyond the immediate stakeholders in the testing process. Tests have important effects on people's lives and are thus potentially an instrument of power and control.

Quote 10.5   Shohamy on the power of tests

Pretending that tests are neutral allows those in power to misuse them. Testers must realize that much of the strength of tests lies not only in their technical quality but in their use in social and political dimensions. Studies of the use of tests, as part of test validation on an ongoing basis, are essential for the integrity of the profession.
(2001: 162)

Power and control is not necessarily as one-sided as Shohamy (2001) appears to suggest, however. The validation study of the College English Test (CET) in China details how one Exam Board attempted to generate some empirical evidence on the value of its tests as perceived by a variety of its stakeholders, e.g. end users of results in universities and the business world (see Yang and Weir 1998). In the CPE revision described by Weir and Milanovic (2003) similar attempts were made to elicit feedback on the existing test from participants (the innovation aspect of the book's title) and also there was a conscious effort to involve a variety of stakeholders in the decisions that were taken concerning changes in the five papers of the examination (see also Hawkey 2004 for a description of the CELS examination change process).

The way forward

We have now examined all the elements of our validation framework in action and provided examples of each element from a variety of available sources. To develop the framework further we need help from teachers and researchers in taking specific elements of the framework and determining their importance. We need to find out if the categories are of use to teachers? Underlying all of this is the important research issue: which categories have the greatest effect on performance?

We need to establish a systematic methodology for generating data relating to the categories in our socio cognitive frameworks for test validation described in Part 2 above. Mere inspection of the modules in the test and other self-report data does not necessarily guarantee the identification of the processes actually used by candidates in taking them (see Fulcher 2003: 216–17 for one of the few considerations of the limitations of expert judgements).

In addition, we might for example ask a small sample of the test population to introspect on the internal processes that are taking place in their completion of test items. This can provide a valuable check on experts' surface-level judgements on what is being tested. This is consonant with more general developments in the field of evaluation where the complementarity of quantitative and qualitative paradigms is now generally recognized and tri-angulation of data is encouraged.

It is to these research issues that we now turn in Part 3, where some possible methodologies are outlined.

Further reading

Alderson and Wall (1996) special issue of *Language Testing* devoted to washback.
Banerjee (2003) provides an extensive survey of the literature on predictive validity and an innovative approach to how we might reconceptualize it in terms of cost to students and other stakeholders if admitted at various levels of test performance, as against degree of overlap with the criterion course result.
Green (2003) provides a comprehensive overview of the literature relating to backwash and how to measure it.
Hughes (2003) provides an informative and accessible account of how to achieve beneficial backwash.

Part 3

Generating Validity Evidence

Introduction

Messick (1992: 89) points out that many test makers acknowledge a responsibility for providing validity evidence of the instrumental value of a test but very few actually do it. Ellerton (1997: 80–4) takes this further and catalogues the failings of many tests in relation to the provision of validity evidence; see also Alderson and Buck (1993) and Alderson *et al.* 1995) for similar evidence of deficit.

There does seem to be little excuse for examining bodies delivering high stakes tests that fail to meet the standards for the provision of validity evidence outlined in the previous sections of this book. Exam Boards such as Cambridge ESOL and ETS routinely collect and publish evidence relating to many aspects of the validity of their examinations (see University of Cambridge ESOL Examinations Research Notes, UCRN, www.CambridgeESOL.org, and TOEFL research reports http://www.toefl.org/research/rtfldir.html, many of which are free and downloadable). It is the right of all users of tests to ask for evidence that demonstrates the test is doing the job that it is supposed to be doing. As we have seen, this requires evidence of its context validity, its theory-based validity, its scoring validity and its criterion-related and consequential validity.

The validation procedures we describe below should be applicable in whole or part to the development of any test from classroom to national level. We hope the discussion of these will encourage research on all aspects of the validity frameworks developed in Chapters 5–10. The scope of research into any element of even one framework will obviously be governed by your individual circumstances. Within the constraints of the classroom all of the procedures will certainly not be practical at one particular point in time, but every teacher should be aware that to produce the most accurate picture of a student's ability all have a contribution to make. They can all shed light on what it is that we are measuring and how well we are doing this. The more of these we can embrace in our research investigations the better founded might be our interpretations of test score data.

Though teachers may not be able to generate evidence in all areas for their classroom tests they have the right to expect such evidence from the purveyors of high stakes tests. The more aware they are of these criteria, the more focused the demands they can make for tests to be brought into line with good practice in each element of the framework, and the better able they will be to evaluate evidence in relation to this.

We start the discussion of research in each area of our validity framework by providing a summary of potential focuses and a brief outline of the methods of enquiry and analysis that might be employed in investigating them. Then we describe surface level, highly do-able, broad spectrum, survey-based studies where these seem appropriate for generating validity evidence. Finally, we consider case studies for investigating key elements in depth in the areas of context validity, theory-based validity, scoring validity, and consequential validity.

Even in the case studies, it is possible that you may replicate only a part of the research procedures described. These are not all-or-nothing studies, and even if only a small section of the validity canvas is filled in at a time, then that is still an improvement on a test with no validity evidence attached to it.

A number of the methods suggested in the initial overview of research in each area have already been covered in Part 2 of the book where we provided practical exemplification of the concepts in our framework (for example, how to calculate classical statistics useful for establishing test reliability in Chapter 9), and we will refer you back to this discussion where appropriate.

11
Research Methodologies for Exploring the Validity of a Test

11.1 An introductory note on research

There are many excellent general textbooks available on doing research and you will find references at the end of this chapter. To find out more about qualitative and quantitative research design you are referred to them, and references are also given on specific methodologies such as questionnaire design, interview, and verbal protocols, statistical analysis procedures, and discourse analyses of testee performance.

Specific research articles related to each of the components in our framework are also listed after each case study to provide different perspectives on research in each area. Where possible we give references to articles in the journal *Language Testing*, which is accessible electronically as well as in print and covers the last 20 years of research endeavour in our field.

In brief, any research you do should meet the following criteria:

(a) **It should be believable**. This will in turn depend on the criteria of: acceptability of research designs, sampling (how much is enough to convince your peers?), rigour in methodological procedures and methods of analysis. In other words, how confident will others be in the findings? This is where synthetic small-scale research in the classroom will pay off if it is carried out within a coherent framework.

(b) **It should be logical**. For example, in quantitative studies there should be a clear progression: review of the literature → identification of issues → research question formulation → appropriate methods selected → data collection → analysis → conclusions and recommendations. (This is, of course, only one of the paradigms available in research and, especially in qualitative ethnographic studies, other progressions may be required. However, it does tend to be the most generic, especially in the area of testing, and provides a clear framework for reporting purposes. See Miles and Huberman 1994 for a discussion of other paradigms in qualitative research.)

(c) **It should be feasible.** How does research fit in with your work situation? Will there be problems of confidentiality or ethics? How practical are the methods? How much time will it take? Do you have this time? Is it too wide a study? Is an adequate test sample available? Will there be restrictions on your access to, and use of, data? How much will it cost in terms of time, effort and finance?

(d) **It should be important to the person doing it.** Personal investment is required. Why do you want to do it? How committed are you?

(e) **It should have value/interest.** Is it worth doing, judging from what you have read in the literature? How does it fit into the framework for generating validity evidence laid out in this book?

(f) **It should have relevance.** Is it addressing issues which are important to you and your work situation?

We offer suggestions as to how test developers might go about researching evidence on the major components of validity. In this way we hope to provide the basis for a coherent research programme for generating validity evidence on tests. It may be that you as an individual can only tackle a small number of focuses but Exam Boards obviously will be expected to provide a more complete coverage, given the high stakes of most of the examinations they are charging candidates for.

11.2 *A priori* validation: investigating the specification of the construct and the operationalization of the test

Focuses	Actions and Instruments
STAGE I: DEVELOPMENT	
1.1 Specification of the construct	(1) Theoretical literature review
	(2) Research literature review
I. 1. 1 Context-based validity	(3) Document analysis: curriculum, textbooks, official syllabuses and existing tests
I. 1. 2 Theory-based validity	(4) Needs analysis where necessary
1.2 Specification of the assessment instrument	Items mapped by experts onto characterstics summarized in the left-hand column. (See frameworks described in Figures 1–4 in Part 2).
Context validity	
Purpose	Stakeholders can be asked to confirm these analyses:
Functional/skill requirements	• Expert's judgements (cross-checked where possible)
Linguistic requirements (lexis, structure)	
Type of information	• Student intro/retrospection on how they complete items
Discourse mode	
Method/response format	
Intended operations	

Topic familiarity
Order of tasks/items
Timing/length
Weightings
Interlocutor variables (L/S):
   speech rate/accent/
   acquaintanceship
Addressee (R/W)

Theory-based validity
Executive processing
Executive resources

Scoring validity
Mark scheme
Assessment criteria
Rating scale

The table above outlines the requirements for clear specifications of both the constructs and the test tasks which will be used to operationalize them (see Chapters 6 and 7 above for full details). The starting point for such specifications is through library-based or electronically-mediated research to establish how other researchers have described the constructs we are interested in, or how test developers have specified what they were intending to test. We can review the literature and synthesize the research carried out by others in a particular domain (see the suggested reading at the end of Chapters 6 and 7).

The literature review should tell us what is known about the area we are interested in investigating. It may well be that we can find what we need to know through this library-based research or at least find where the gaps in knowledge are. This should always be the starting point for research into the validity of a test. A quick scan through the contents of over 20 years of the journal *Language Testing* (available electronically, see Chapter 12) or the key references on language abilities, testing and research listed at the end of each chapter and in Chapter 12, should tell you whether anybody has looked at a particular area before. These will tell you what previous investigators have found, and more importantly, how they investigated it, and will also provide follow up on leads to other research.

As well as looking at articles, books and websites in the area of interest there are other forms of documentation which will give you a lot of the information you require. For example, in the USAID School Achievement Test Development (SATD) project in Egypt (see Khalifa (ed.) 2003) there was already a well regarded series of textbooks and official government syllabi in place for teaching and examinations which gave the test writers a lot of information on the language being taught at the various levels within the school system.

In cases where such information is not available to the test writer a needs analysis might be carried out, as Weir (1983a, 1988c) did to establish salient performance conditions and operations for testing the language abilities of overseas students at tertiary level in the UK and as Weir *et al.* (2000) did to establish the reading skills and strategies required by Chinese undergraduates, in the design of the Advanced English Reading Test for China. See also Jordan (1998) for a full treatment of needs analysis in EAP. Bridgeman and Carlson (1983) and Horowitz (1986) carried out a similar study of writing requirements of students at university in the USA. Ferris and Tagg (1996) and Ferris (1998) did something similar for listening. Comprehensive research reports are available from TOEFL (http://www.toefl.org/research/rtfldir.html) which were used as the construct base for designing the Next Generation TOEFL (to appear in 2005); for example, Butler *et al.* (2000), Enright *et al.* (2000), Ginther and Grant (1996), Hamp-Lyons and Kroll (1996) and Waters (1996). Those contemplating developing specifications might find these a useful starting point, not least for the categories of description they provide.

Once specifications have been completed and tests developed, these can be evaluated by *expert scrutiny* using different raters to establish reliability of judgements. At the very least, colleagues in a school can be asked to look at the tests you have developed and relate them to a specification you have provided. The use of checklists may facilitate checking on the degree of agreement between experts on each area. By explicitly formulating questions in advance of any discussion, a structured coverage of all the elements in our framework is made possible and it makes comparison of two versions of the same test easier to handle.

11.3   Establishing context validity

We provide below a section from the *context validity* part of a checklist developed by Akmar Saidatul Zainal Abidin with the author for use in validating a spoken language test at University level in Malaysia. The speaking test consists of two parts: an oral presentation and a group discussion on the same topic area. The complete questionnaire covers all the areas in our validity framework for speaking outlined in Chapters 5–10 above and it can be used in part or whole as one method for establishing the validity of a spoken language test. Obviously, you will need to customize the questions to fit with the types of spoken language task you employ.

Similar survey instruments could be constructed for the other skills with little extra effort to cover most of the areas of our frameworks (with the obvious exception of the hidden elements of automatic processing in our theory-based validity framework). It may be that only one section of the validity framework is investigated at any one time and others are carried out at a later date. Such cumulative research is perfectly acceptable. These checklists can be used in a structured interview format or for wider sampling by post. (See Weir and Roberts 1994 for full details of the use of such instruments.)

Below, you will find the first part of the section of the quest
context validity.

For each of the items below, circle the number that REFLECTS YOUR VIEWPOINT on a five-point scale where:

1 = Strongly disagree, 2 = Disagree, 3 = Undecided, 4 = Agree, 5 = Strongly agree

SECTION A: TEST CONTENT

1. Task A clearly states what I am required to do in the presentation. 1 2 3 4 5
2. Task B clearly states what I am required to do in the group discussion. 1 2 3 4 5
3. Task A is a good test of my ability to communicate orally in an academic 1 2 3 4 5
   context.
4. Task A is a good test of my ability to speak English in social situations. 1 2 3 4 5
5. Task B is a good test of my ability to communicate orally in an academic 1 2 3 4 5
   context.
6. Task B is a good test of my ability to speak English in social situations. 1 2 3 4 5
7. Both task A and task B have equal marks. 1 2 3 4 5
8. The criteria for scoring my performance (Task fulfilment, Language use, 1 2 3 4 5
   Communicative ability) are clear to me
9. The order of the tasks, i.e., task A followed by task B, is appropriate for 1 2 3 4 5
   the test.
10. Two minutes is sufficient time for a candidate to demonstrate his/her 1 2 3 4 5
    ability to present ideas.
11. Ten minutes is sufficient time for a group of four candidates to 1 2 3 4 5
    demonstrate their ability to conduct a discussion.
12. Having written instructions to prepare for tasks A and B is helpful. 1 2 3 4 5
13. The instructions give sufficient information for candidates to prepare 1 2 3 4 5
    for tasks A and B.
14. Tasks A and B involve arguing for or against an idea. 1 2 3 4 5
15. Task A only contains factual/concrete information, e.g., information 1 2 3 4 5
    about physical objects, processes, people, and situations rather than
    abstract concepts such as love, hate, and friendship.
16. Task B only contains factual/concrete information, e.g., information 1 2 3 4 5
    about physical objects, processes, events, and people.
17. Both tasks A and B have a mixture of factual/concrete and abstract 1 2 3 4 5
    information.
18. The topic in tasks A and B is familiar to me. 1 2 3 4 5
19. The instructions for the tasks only contain words that are suitable for 1 2 3 4 5
    my level of language ability.
20. The instructions for the tasks use simple, easy to understand sentence 1 2 3 4 5
    structures.

[Continued]

In addition to these methodological procedures (literature review, document analysis, interview and questionnaire), you might want to investigate certain areas in a more precise quantitative fashion to determine the effect of certain conditions on task performance. We now turn to an example of the type of small-scale studies that might be carried out with this in mind.

Context validity Case study 1: small-scale research into elements of the framework

The case of speaking

We argued in Chapter 6 that test performance is affected by the conditions under which a task is carried out, i.e., context validity considerations. A number of empirical findings in the research on the direct testing of spoken performance support this view (for example, Foster and Skehan 1996, O'Sullivan 2000, Wigglesworth 1997). Skehan and Foster (1997) have suggested that foreign language performance is affected by task processing conditions. In their research they have attempted to manipulate these conditions in order to modify or predict difficulty. For Skehan (1996) *task* difficulty is a function of the following moderator variables:

- Code complexity, which for him is 'concerned with traditional areas of syntactic and lexical difficulty and range' (p. 52). Placing a task on this difficulty continuum involves identifying the relative complexity or simplicity of the language code that is required receptively and productively for task success.
- Cognitive complexity, which is affected by both cognitive processing and cognitive familiarity. 'Processing is concerned with the amount of on-line computation that is required while doing a task, and highlights the extent to which the learner has to actively think through task content. Familiarity, in contrast, involves the extent to which the task draws on ready-made or pre-packaged solutions. It is implicated when all that is required is the accessing of relevant aspects of schematic knowledge if such knowledge contains relevant, already organized material, and even solutions to comparable tasks, e.g., sensitivity to macro-structures in narratives' (p. 52). Cognitive complexity is concerned with the content of what is said, and relates to the conceptualization stage of Levelt's (1993) model.
- Communicative stress, which includes time pressure, modality (reading, writing, speaking, or listening), scale (number of participants or relationships involved), stakes (either low or high, depending on how important it is to do the task and to do it correctly), and control (how much learners can 'control' or influence the task) (pp. 52–3).

A number of empirical findings have revealed that task difficulty has an effect on performance, as measured in the three areas of accuracy, fluency, and complexity (Mehnert 1998, Skehan 1996, Skehan and Foster 1997, 1999, O'Sullivan and Weir 2002, Wigglesworth 1997).

Establishing task difficulty

Norris *et al.* (1998: 59) argue that task difficulty can be based on subjective assessment of the variable contributions of the components suggested by Skehan (1996): code complexity, cognitive complexity, and communicative demand. By identifying these components within a given task, variable sources of difficulty can be estimated. They argue that:

> with such a system for estimation of task difficulty, learner performances on carefully sampled tasks can be used to predict future performances on tasks that are constituted by related difficulty components. Empirical support for a system like this could lead to much improved generalizability for task-based L2 performance assessments. Furthermore, comparison of the variable contribution of identifiable sources of task difficulty with the rating of examinee performances according to real-world criteria should provide valuable information regarding the contribution of task difficulty to perceived task success.

Norris *et al.* (pp. 76–7) assert that:

> For a given task, a set of corresponding plus and minus decisions will constitute a general estimate of task difficulty. By applying this new matrix to a set of real-world tasks that have already been selected (again, based on a specific syllabus and curriculum), tasks can be assigned an overall task difficulty index (equal to the total number of pluses). Furthermore, the contribution of particular difficulty characteristics to overall task difficulty can be highlighted and studied after examinee performances are collected and examined *ex post facto*.

In addition to such expert judgements as advocated by Norris *et al.*, it is also possible to investigate the effect of these performance conditions in a more experimental empirical fashion, though, as in most research, a combination of the qualitative and quantitative often proves to be the most beneficial, the illuminative aspects of the former complementing the generalizability benefits of the latter.

Empirical research in this area

A number of researchers at CRTEC, Roehampton University, are carrying out empirical work in this area: Jessica Wu from Taiwan is employing a tape-mediated test (reading aloud, picture description and responding to verbal stimuli) and Tomoko Horai from Japan an oral presentation task to investigate the effects of changes in performance conditions on the difficulty level of these tasks. They are concerned with what happens to performance on a task when, in respect of a single task, you manipulate one of the variables in our context validity box whilst controlling (as far as possible) all the other variables. The thinking behind the research design below derives from discussions with them and from the research in this area to date. The methods of investigation could be extended to many of the elements in our context validity framework. The concern would be the same: does altering one performance condition alter the difficulty level of that task?

The empirical studies we detail below may not be feasible for some of you so first we offer a quick but effective procedure of establishing whether a particular condition may appear to be having an effect on the difficulty level of a task. We include below a checklist for use in 'expert' scrutiny of the performance conditions and their effects that O'Sullivan and Weir (2002) identified from their survey of the research literature on spoken language testing. Teachers in the classroom might simply take two versions of the same speaking task, e.g. information gap test A and information gap B, and discuss both with colleagues, having completed the checklist below. Such broad spectrum, judgemental studies are a useful check on whether this year's exam appears to be at a similar difficulty level to last year's. Areas where differences are clear might then be worthy of further investigation in the type of experiment-based research we go on to discuss in the rest of this case study.

Compare the two tasks by signalling how difficult each is in terms of the various conditions.

MODERATOR VARIABLES	CONDITION	GLOSS (the more difficult the higher the number)	TASK A DIFFICULTY (circle one)	TASK B DIFFICULTY (circle one)
CODE COMPLEXITY	Range of linguistic input	Vocabulary and structure as appropriate to ALTE levels 1–5 (beginner to advanced)	1 2 3 4 5	1 2 3 4 5
	Sources of input	Number and types of written and spoken input spoken source to 1 = one single written or 5 = multiple written and spoken sources)	1 2 3 4 5	1 2 3 4 5
COGNITIVE COMPLEXITY	Amount of linguistic input to be processed	Quantity of input 1 = sentence level (single question, prompts) 5 = long text (extended instructions and/or texts)	1 2 3 4 5	1 2 3 4 5
	Availability of input	Extent to which information necessary for task completions is readily available to the candidate		

			1 2 3 4 5	1 2 3 4 5
		1 = all information of provided 5 = student attempts an open ended task [student provides all information]	1 2 3 4 5	1 2 3 4 5
	Familiarity of information	1 = the information given and/or required is likely to be within the candidates' experience 5 = information given and/or required is likely to be outside the candidates' experience	1 2 3 4 5	1 2 3 4 5
	Organization of information required	1 = almost no organization required 5 = extensive organization required simple answer to a question to a complex response	1 2 3 4 5	1 2 3 4 5
	As information becomes more abstract	1 = concrete 5 = abstract	1 2 3 4 5	1 2 3 4 5
COMMUNICATIVE DEMAND	Time pressure	1 = no constraints on time available to **complete** task (if candidate does not complete the task in the time given he/she is **not** penalized) 5 = serious constraints on time available to **complete** task (if candidate does not complete the task in the time given he/she **is** penalized)	1 2 3 4 5	1 2 3 4 5
	Response level	1 = more than sufficient to plan or formulate a response 5 = no planning time available	1 2 3 4 5	1 2 3 4 5
	Scale	Number of participants in a task, number of relationships involved 1 = one person 5 = five or more people	1 2 3 4 5	1 2 3 4 5
	Complexity of task outcome	1 = simple unequivocal outcome 5 = complex unpredictable outcome	1 2 3 4 5	1 2 3 4 5
	Referential complexity	1 = Reference to objects and activities which are visible 5 = reference to external/displaced (not in the here and now) objects and events	1 2 3 4 5	1 2 3 4 5

MODERATOR VARIABLES	CONDITION	GLOSS (the more difficult the higher the number)	TASK A	
			DIFFICULTY (circle one)	DIFFICULTY (circle one)
	Stakes	1 = a measure of attainment which is of value only to the candidate 5 = a measure of attainment which has a high external value	1 2 3 4 5	1 2 3 4 5
	Degree of reciprocity required	1 = no requirement of the candidate to initiate, continue or terminate interaction 5 = task requires each candidate to participate fully in the interaction	1 2 3 4 5	1 2 3 4 5
	Structured	1 = task is highly structured/scaffolded 5 = task is totally unstructured/unscaffolded	1 2 3 4 5	1 2 3 4 5
	Opportunity for control	1 = complete autonomy 5 = no opportunity for control	1 2 3 4 5	1 2 3 4 5

We need to better understand the effect of the performance conditions one would want to build into a test. For example, does the amount of planning time you allow affect performances in the test? So, if in real life we would have a few days or a week to prepare for an oral presentation, what happens if we cut this right down in our test? If we wish to ensure our reading aloud tests are the same from year to year, does the code complexity of the text supplied to candidates make a difference? Does the cognitive complexity of the topic for use in student–student discussion affect performance, and if it does, how do we ensure equivalence in the tasks given to different students?

If manipulating a specified condition makes a difference we have to get it right for the level of proficiency or achievement the test is aimed at. If it does not make a difference we can worry less about it. At the moment the jury is out on the effect of many of these conditions. We simply do not as yet have the evidence, though our experience and our intuition may suggest strongly that there is an effect.

Exam Boards often administer tests at a number of different levels. The Common European Framework (Council of Europe 2001) posits six levels and defines these largely in relation to empirically derived difficulty estimates based on stakeholder perceptions of what language functions (expressed by 'can-do' statements) can be successfully performed at each level. Useful though this work is, it takes insufficient account of how variation in terms of various performance conditions may affect performances by raising or lowering the difficulty level of carrying out the target 'can-do' statement.

Methods and research methodology design

Hypotheses

From the literature we can identify a number of performance conditions which potentially may affect performance on tests of spoken language. From these we could select those which the limited empirical evidence available suggests are most likely to impinge on task difficulty in a particular speaking test. Thus research might investigate possible sources of variability in task performance in a speaking test along a number of dimensions. In this way we could identify which performance conditions have an effect and may help determine distinctions in proficiency levels.

The conditions under which tasks are performed are treated as the independent variables and we can examine how they impact on the test scores, the dependent variable. Jessica Wu is researching a set of hypotheses which focus on the most promising areas for investigation according to the literature. Her hypotheses include the following:

Hypothesis 1 The complexity of language of the written input to test tasks in terms of syntactic range will have no effect on test task performance, inter-language measures of accuracy, fluency, lexical range, and qualitative self-report estimates of difficulty.

Hypothesis 2 Test takers' familiarity with the propositional content in test tasks will have no effect on test task performance, inter-language measures of accuracy, fluency, lexical range, and qualitative self-report estimates of difficulty.

Hypothesis 3 Guided pre-task planning will have no effect on test task performance, inter-language measures of accuracy, fluency, lexical range, and qualitative self-report estimates of difficulty.

Hypothesis 4 Amount of time allowed for performing a task will have no effect test task performance, inter-language measures of accuracy, fluency, lexical range, and qualitative self-report estimates of difficulty.

Hypothesis 5 Gender of speakers will have no effect on test task performance, inter-language measures of accuracy, fluency, lexical range, and qualitative self-report estimates of difficulty.

Hypothesis 6 The effect of these variables will not be altered by test takers' proficiency level.

One can also see how such a design might readily be applied to the testing of reading, listening and writing as well and to other performance conditions in our context validity framework.

Quantitative studies

Individual research studies could examine whether test takers' scores are significantly affected by changes in any of these independent variables.

MATERIALS TO BE USED
Phase 1: Development and validation of alternate test task forms
(see Case study 4 for a detailed description of this below)

- Two alternate test forms can be developed from the past forms of a speaking test. In order to ensure test form equivalency, 30+ subjects will take forms in the order A then B, and 30+ subjects will take forms B then A, to enable us through post test statistics (e.g., correlations, *t*-tests) to establish the parallel forms necessary for the study.
- The experimental tasks will be based on one of the parallel forms tests. For each hypothesis, one version of the equivalent tasks will be modified in terms of the appropriate processing condition.

Phase 2: Development and validation of post-test instruments

- Questionnaires using Likert Scales for collecting qualitative self-report estimates of difficulty from test takers and subject experts (including raters) can be used (see checklist above).
- Analysis of transcripts for each hypothesis (randomly selected). The analysis can use any of the inter-language measures detailed below.

MEASURES
In addition to statistical analyses such as *t*-tests, correlation and regression, multi-faceted Rasch analysis might be applied to examine the effect of each independent variable on performance (see Chapter 9 for a discussion of MFR).

Qualitative studies

In the qualitative studies, in order to examine whether the test takers' spoken output is significantly affected by task difficulty, a sample of test takers' spoken output might be transcribed and analysed by means of inter-language measures: lexical range, accuracy, and fluency. Below are some of the inter-language measures that we discussed above that might be employed in a study of this type (based on Skehan and Foster 1997).

Fluency based on number of reformulations, replacements, false starts, repetitions, hesitations, and pauses over 1 second (all reported per 5 minutes of performance)

Accuracy based on proportion of error-free clauses (syntax; morphology; word order)

Complexity based on measures of subordination, for example, number of clauses per T-unit or c-unit. Clauses/c-units

---

(Clauses are either a simple independent finite clause or a dependent finite or non-finite clause. A c-unit is defined as each independent utterance providing referential or pragmatic meaning)

Following on the work of Norris *et al.* (1998) described briefly above, post-test questionnaires or checklists (see example from O'Sullivan and Weir above) could be employed to find out how test takers and subject experts perceive the task difficulty in both forms (normal and manipulated). The retrospective data would be used to triangulate the data obtained through the quantitative and other qualitative studies.

All such studies can add to our knowledge about the effects of the task variables (demand and setting) that we dealt with in Chapter 6 and this is an area urgently in need of research.

Further reading

The following are useful references on intra task studies where internal aspects of one task are systematically manipulated to determine how changes to task conditions affect performance levels:

Brown, Anderson, Shillcock and Yule (1984)
Foster and Skehan (1996, 1999)
Mehnert (1998)
Norris *et al.* (1998)
Ortega (1999)
Skehan (1996)
Skehan and Foster (1997)
Wigglesworth (1997)

Next, we turn to the type of study that might be useful for determining more closely the nature of the actual processing that goes on in the test tasks we set our students.

11.4 Establishing theory-based validity evidence

The following table outlines a variety of procedures that may be used to help us more closely establish what is happening when candidates *actually* perform our test tasks.

We divide this case study into two parts. Many of you may feel you are happy just to follow up the qualitative investigations in Stage 1 where expert judgement and introspection/retrospection are used to illuminate the cognitive processing that candidates go through in the test task. You may feel that you want to go on to Stage 2 where the relationship between this processing and test scores is explored through both simple and/or complex statistical analysis. Whatever you decide is suitable for you in your situation it will help deepen your understanding of what students are doing when they are taking your tests.

Theory-based validity

Stage 1A	Qualitative expert judgement of items (e.g., by checklist)
Stage 1B	Qualitative introspection/retrospection by test takers (think aloud/ interview/questionnaire) to validate strategies and skills and the conditions under which the test tasks are performed
Stage 2	Quantitative and qualitative analysis of test performances Basic descriptive statistics Correlation Factor analyses of test results *t*-tests Multi-faceted Rasch Qualitative discourse analysis of test performances in productive tasks

Establishing theory-based validity: Case study 2

Does response format make a difference?

The *response formats* we decide on for testing the various skills and strategies may have a critical effect on the performances that result at both a group and an individual level. We noted in Chapter 6 our serious concerns with multiple choice in this respect. (See also Nevo 1989, Wu Yi'an 1998, Farr, Pritchard and Smitten 1990 for interesting research studies on the process of taking MCQ tests.)

As Exam Boards and commercial organizations begin to experiment with computer-based tests it is now imperative to ascertain how such computer-based approaches impact on theory-based validity, especially when pencil and paper versions are still in use. Weir *et al.* (2004) are carrying out research in the area of theory-based validity comparing pencil and paper-based writing performance with computer-based performance. This case study is based on that work. The central area of interest is the effects of changing modality on theory-based validity.

It is obviously important that receiving institutions can depend on the results of language tests as valid indicators of the English language proficiency of overseas students with respect to the academic courses they are going to follow. The growth in influence of computer technology in the key life skills areas of study, work and leisure, is beginning to emerge in language testing with the introduction by some providers of computer-delivered tests and/or testlets. One key validation area that has only recently begun to receive attention in language testing research is the comparison of performance on computer-based and traditional pencil-and-paper tests of writing.

When viewed in terms of the framework for writing test validation (see Chapter 7), the suggestion that the different output modes may be resulting in significantly different performance becomes an issue of central importance. The fact that there has been no systematic effort to understand the interaction between individual test candidates and theory-based validity raises the possibility that the differences in performance on the two output modes may be such that they are essentially non-comparable as measures. Essentially, what we are hypothesizing is that the different modes may be activating different executive processes within the candidate – therefore making performance on the two modes different on the cognitive processing level.

The review of the literature suggests that before decisions can be made on the introduction of tests which allow for alternative output modes (in this case pencil-and-paper versus computer), you will need to gain a greater understanding of the underlying cognitive processes of, and affective responses to, these modes. In other words, we need to investigate the theory-based validity of test formats employing these modes. In order to do this, we should gather data on the pre-writing and during-writing behaviour of candidates, as well as essential baseline data on their computer readiness. In addition, you will need to pay attention to the nature of the discourse produced to determine whether modality make a difference in performance.

The research questions therefore can be stated as:

STAGE 1

- Do test candidates utilize different cognitive processes when writing on a computer to when they write using pencil-and-paper?

STAGE 2

- Do any of the background variables investigated (computer anxiety, computer attitudes, indices of computer familiarity and experience, gender and L1) have a significant effect on test scores?
- Do they produce discursively distinctive performances?
- Are there significant differences in the scores awarded by independent raters for performances on the two modes?

STAGE 1 METHODOLOGY

Participants
Volunteers from a variety of cultural and ethnic backgrounds need to be recruited to perform the two writing tasks described below.

In addition to a sample of about 30 students, a group of trained and experienced raters need to be recruited in the interests of marker reliability.

Instruments

Participants will need to perform each of two writing tasks on which data exist to indicate that they are similar in terms of difficulty (as measured by test scores achieved by candidates). One will be done in pencil and paper mode the other on computer.

The other instruments might include a computer familiarity questionnaire, a feedback questionnaire on test taking in the different modalities and a cognitive processing questionnaire designed to investigate what actually goes on in the various phases of the writing process. A keyboard skills test might also be considered. Space precludes a detailed description of all the potential instruments here and we will confine ourselves largely to the key instrument concerned with theory-based validity: the Cognitive Processing Questionnaire (CPQ), as this may be new to you.

The development of the Cognitive Processing Questionnaire

Our Cognitive Processing Questionnaire (CPQ) was designed to reflect the underlying concepts identified in the framework of theory-based validity outlined in Chapter 7 above. These, concepts can be seen as reflecting both the Executive Processes and the Executive Resources identified in the framework. The questionnaire might usefully be applied in other studies of writing where different response modes are employed or simply to find out what students are doing when they attempt a piece of writing in your classroom.

In the opening phases the candidate is concerned with pre-writing activities such as goal setting and modifying the topic and genre in relation to their individual schemata. When this has been done, the candidate enters the planning phases where ideas for inclusion (or structuring) are formulated and noted – either formally in terms of a written outline, or conceptualized in the form of unwritten 'mental' notes. Finally, candidates are expected to translate these initial ideas into written language and to review this language once committed to paper or screen. Throughout these phases, the Executive Resources available to the candidate include both linguistic and content knowledge.

A draft version of this questionnaire is included below so you might try it out with your own students in writing classes and customize it for your own research needs. It is also currently being employed as a basis for counselling students who feel they need help in improving their academic writing in a university setting as it hopefully provides a broad ranging review of the processes they have gone through (this checklist was originally devised by the author and Barry O'Sullivan in collaboration with Xiu Xudong of the People's Republic of China and Dr Roger Hawkey).

DRAFT Questionnaire

> Name_____ Gender_____ Student No._____
> College/University_____L1_____

Thank you for your participation in this research study.

Your answers to the following questions should represent *what you did or thought* in answering the academic writing task you have just completed. There are no right or wrong answers to any question in this questionnaire. Your response will not affect the scores you will get on your essay..

Please pay special attention to the **CAPITALIZED** words in the questions when you answer the questions. Please circle the response you feel represents your view.

We will ALSO be grateful for YOUR comments or personal information on these issues IN the space at the end of the questions.

All responses will be anonymous and all personal particulars will be kept completely confidential. ONLY a summary of findings will be reported.

Thank you

Example

Please circle the response ◯

In general, academic writing courses in higher education need improving.
1. strongly disagree   2. disagree   ③ no view   4. agree   5. strongly agree

What I thought of or did before writing this essay

1. I FIRST read the title very slowly considering the significance of each word in it.
   1. strongly disagree   2. disagree   3. no view   4. agree   5. strongly agree

2. I thought of WHAT I was required to write after reading the title and instructions.
   1. strongly disagree   2. disagree   3. no view   4. agree   5. strongly agree

3. I thought of HOW to write my answer so that it would respond well to the title.
   1. strongly disagree   2. disagree   3. no view   4. agree   5. strongly agree

4. I thought of HOW to satisfy readers or examiners.
   1. strongly disagree   2. disagree   3. no view   4. agree   5. strongly agree

5. I was able to understand the instructions for this writing test completely.
   1. strongly disagree   2. disagree   3. no view   4. agree   5. strongly agree

6. I know A LOT about this topic, i.e., I have ENOUGH ideas to write about this topic.
   1. strongly disagree   2. disagree   3. no view   4. agree   5. strongly agree

7. I felt it was easy to produce enough ideas for the essay from memory.
   1. strongly disagree   2. disagree   3. no view   4. agree   5. strongly agree

8. I know A LOT about this type of essay, i.e., I know how to write an argumentative essay.
   1. strongly disagree   2. disagree   3. no view   4. agree   5. strongly agree

9. I know A LOT about other types of essays, e.g., descriptive, narrative.
   1. strongly disagree   2. disagree   3. no view   4. agree   5. strongly agree

10. Ideas occurring to me at the beginning tended to be COMPLETE.
    1. strongly disagree   2. disagree   3. no view   4. agree   5. strongly agree

11. Ideas occurring to me at the beginning were well ORGANIZED.
    1. strongly disagree   2. disagree   3. no view   4. agree   5. strongly agree

12. I planned an outline on paper or in my head BEFORE starting to write
    1. Yes   2. No

If you answered No to Question 12 skip this section

If you answered **Yes**, please continue

13. I thought of most of my ideas for the essay BEFORE planning an outline.
    1. strongly disagree   2. disagree   3. no view   4. agree   5. strongly agree

14. I thought of most of my ideas for the essay WHILE I planned an outline.
    1. strongly disagree   2. disagree   3. no view   4. agree   5. strongly agree

15. I thought of the ideas only in ENGLISH.
    1. strongly disagree   2. disagree   3. no view   4. agree   5. strongly agree

16. I was able to prioritise the ideas.
    1. strongly disagree   2. disagree   3. no view   4. agree   5. strongly agree

17. I was able to put my ideas or content in good order.
    1. strongly disagree   2. disagree   3. no view   4. agree   5. strongly agree

18. Some ideas had to be removed while I was putting them in good order.
    1. strongly disagree   2. disagree   3. no view   4. agree   5. strongly agree

---

While I was writing this essay

19. I felt it was easy to put ideas in good order.
    1. strongly disagree   2. disagree   3. no view   4. agree   5. strongly agree

20. I felt it was easy to express ideas using the appropriate words.
    1. strongly disagree   2. disagree   3. no view   4. agree   5. strongly agree

21. I felt it was easy to express ideas using the correct sentences.
    1. strongly disagree   2. disagree   3. no view   4. agree   5. strongly agree

22. I thought of MOST of my ideas for the essay WHILE I was actually writing it.
    1. strongly disagree   2. disagree   3. no view   4. agree   5. strongly agree

23. I was able to develop any paragraph by putting sentences in logical order in the paragraph.
    1. strongly disagree   2. disagree   3. no view   4. agree   5. strongly agree

24. I was able to CONNECT my ideas smoothly in the whole essay.
    1. strongly disagree   2. disagree   3. no view   4. agree   5. strongly agree

25. I tried NOT to write more than the required number of words in the instructions.
    1. strongly disagree   2. disagree   3. no view   4. agree   5. strongly agree

26. I reviewed the correctness of the contents and their order WHILE writing this essay.
    1. strongly disagree   2. disagree   3. no view   4. agree   5. strongly agree

27. I reviewed the correctness of the contents and their order AFTER finishing this essay.
    1. strongly disagree   2. disagree   3. no view   4. agree   5. strongly agree

28. I reviewed the appropriateness of the contents and their order WHILE writing this essay.
    1. strongly disagree   2. disagree   3. no view   4. agree   5. strongly agree

29. I reviewed and appropriateness of the contents and their order AFTER finishing this essay.
    1. strongly disagree   2. disagree   3. no view   4. agree   5. strongly agree

30. I reviewed the correctness of sentences WHILE writing this essay.
    1. strongly disagree   2. disagree   3. no view   4. agree   5. strongly agree

31. I reviewed the correctness of sentences AFTER finishing this essay.
    1. strongly disagree   2. disagree   3. no view   4. agree   5. strongly agree

32. I reviewed the appropriateness of words WHILE writing this essay.
    1. strongly disagree   2. disagree   3. no view   4. agree   5. strongly agree

33. I reviewed the appropriateness of words AFTER finishing this essay.
    1. strongly disagree   2. disagree   3. no view   4. agree   5. strongly agree

34. I was able to write a draft essay in this test, then wrote the essay again neatly within the given time.
    1. strongly disagree   2. disagree   3. no view   4. agree   5. strongly agree

35. After finishing the essay, I also thought for a while of those statements or thoughts I removed.
    1. strongly disagree   2. disagree   3. no view   4. agree   5. strongly agree

36. I felt it was easy to review or revise the whole essay.
    1. strongly disagree   2. disagree   3. no view   4. agree   5. strongly agree

37. Comments on the above items:

_____

_____

_____

_____

Candidates complete a questionnaire for each of the tasks they perform. Therefore, any differences in the cognitive processes employed in the completion of the tasks under the two conditions (operationalized by alternating the output mode from pencil-and-paper to computer) might be highlighted.

Testee attitudes to different modalities

It would also be possible for you to develop a short, feedback questionnaire to determine how the students felt about the experience of taking the writing test in the two modalities. This would focus on social psychological aspects of the test taking experience as against the cognitive aspects covered in the cognitive processing questionnaire and the familiarity aspects of an *a priori* background questionnaire. (See Hill 1997 for use of questionnaire feedback in relation to speaking and Fulcher 2003: 253–5 for a questionnaire used to investigate the reaction of test takers to task types.)

It might help determine where any differences lay between writing in the two modalities with regard, for example, to:

- any difficulties encountered in accessing input, e.g., in scrolling on the computer;
- how well prepared they were for each task;
- how comfortable they felt working in the modality in and out of the test situation (e.g., experience of fear, frustration, nervousness, willingness);
- how clear were they on what to do from the rubrics provided
- their attitude to the suitability of modality for testing their writing ability
- which they thought the easiest/most difficult/heaviest time pressure/least time pressure
- their views on the whole test experience
- how well they thought they did on the different tasks
- the perceived relevance of the format for their future target situation
- the perceived value of each test task for them
- etc. . . .

This might supplement or be combined with a computer familiarity questionnaire reflecting three indices of computer familiarity:

1. Computer usage
2. Perceived ability
3. Interest in computers

Design

The methodological design is summarized in Table 11.1. As we mentioned at the start of this case study, you may prefer just to focus on the processing part of this study without relating it to the test scores gained in the two treatments under consideration. In this case you would simply analyse the returns to the Phase 5 survey component of the study. Others may want or need to get the whole picture in order to make a decision on which response format to opt for. To do this they will need to determine how scores are affected and analyse these data in the manner suggested below.

Others may be more interested in analysing the output under the differing modalities to see where any differences might lie.

Phase	Instrument	Analysis	Participants
1	Computer familiarity and anxiety questionnaire	Qualitative and quantitative	All
2	Test Occasion 1 Paper-and-pencil version Computer version	All rated and scores analysed quantitatively Qualitative analysis of the output along a number of specified dimensions	All – though a balanced design, so half take one version and the others take the second version
3	Theory-based validity questionnaire Social/psychological questionnaire on test taking experience	Qualitative and quantitative	All
4	Test Occasion 2 Pencil-and-paper version Computer version	All rated and scores analysed quantitatively Qualitative analysis of the output along a number of specified dimensions	All – though a balanced design, inverse of previous phase
5	Theory-based validity questionnaire Social/psychological questionnaire on test taking experience	Qualitative and quantitative	All

Analysis

QUANTITATIVE
Descriptive statistics – are calculated for all items in the questionnaire and the results compared for the response formats.
***t*-test** – the paired *t*-test, allows a comparison of the same group of candidates' scores on two different test forms simultaneously. A comparison of mean scores on different tests can be used as another estimate of the extent to which the same candidates would produce similar results if one task was used as an alternative to another. If the two tasks are equivalent there should be no significant difference in the performance of candidates on the two tests. So if the response format is not having an effect on writing we would not expect there to be a difference in the performance on either. The *t*-tests will tell us whether there is a significant difference between the two.

Correlation – The correlation coefficients between the scores on the various tasks will tell us about the degree of overlap between the tasks. You are reminded about the susceptibility of this statistic to the influence of sampling, as we discussed in Chapter 9 (see also Fulcher 2003: 201–3 for a useful discussion of further limitations).

Factor analysis – Fulcher (2003: 203) provides the following useful definition from Hinofotis (1983):

> A data reduction procedure that allows researchers to collapse large numbers of variables into smaller, more meaningful underlying concepts. The procedure provides a means for conceptually related variables to cluster so that the researcher can come to a better understanding of the relationship among those variables.

Factor analyses enable us to know statistically whether the responses to the different formats load on the same factor. It shows whether there are components that are shared in common by the tasks or whether different components exist underlying the variables under consideration. (See Fulcher 2003: 207 for a clear worked example of factor analysis.)

Multi-faceted Rasch analysis (MFR) – In addition to the above classical statistics, we could also use MFR analysis, which takes into account major sources of variability in the test such as rater harshness and consistency, and task variability (see Chapter 9 for discussion of this and an example of data output). The logit scale produced by the analysis can give us a sample free estimate of the relative difficulties of the two tests or the two response formats. MFR provides a clearer view of the psychometric qualities of the tests.

Use of MFR to include candidates' and raters' views of any format effect – included in the design as a facet along with candidate and marker – to determine whether format has an effect.

Use of MFR analysis to include candidates' affective responses to the test taking experience – again, included as a facet along with candidates, raters and format to determine whether these variables have an effect.

QUALITATIVE

For looking at the discourse produced across a large sample of essays, the type of analysis employed by Hawkey and Barker (2004) and Kennedy *et al.* (2001) might be a useful start. For example, amongst other things Hawkey and Barker used the Wordsmith Tools programme to investigate a number of features, namely:

- whole script, sentence and paragraph lengths
- title use
- vocabulary range, type: token ratio, single occurrence words and word lengths

- behaviour of individual words in concordances and collocations
- candidate errors.

They also got raters to look directly at the sophistication of language and found the following features in the corpus were commented on by the corpus analysts for their impact on the reader:

- (adopting a) style
- use of idiom and colloquial language
- use of rhetoric (words used to influence and persuade)
- rich, lively vocabulary and collocation
- the use of humour and irony
- using personal experience to enhance a general argument and/or strengthen the writer: reader relationship
- variation of pace through sentence and paragraph length.

Finally, they looked at the cohesion and coherence of the written products.

Further reading

Lazaraton (2002), O'Loughlin, (2001), Pavlou (1997) and **Shohamy (1994)** analysed discourse features across different speaking tasks and detail useful methods for analysing such data.
Cumming (1997) provides a very useful summary of the literature that has looked at the characteristics of written texts in language tests.
Scott (2002) Wordsmith Tools website: http://www.lexically.net/wordsmith/version3/index.html
The further reading listed for Case study 1 above (p. 233) also gives useful detail on ways of analysing the discourse produced in different test tasks.

Establishing theory-based validity: Case study 3

Test takers' use of strategies and skills in an Advanced Level Reading Test: are reading skills/strategies distinguishable?

It is important that we endeavour to establish as clearly as we can what students are actually doing in test tasks because the intentions of the test developers may not be realized. What a task *actually* tests is what is central to establishing its validity. In Chapters 6 and 7 we discussed the different performance conditions, especially time pressure and length, which characterize careful, as against expeditious, reading tasks, and we detailed the differences in processing that these various types of reading were likely to activate.

This next case study builds on work done with Jin Yan of the College English test (CET) in China and Joyce Shao Chin of the Language Training and Testing Centre (LTTC) in Taiwan. It differs from the previous case study on theory-based validity in that it aims to investigate any differences, both qualitative and quantitative, that obtain in completing the various reading tasks in different parts of a reading skills and strategies test, rather than focusing on response format *per se*. The response format will be held constant in this next study, i.e., short-answer questions for all parts of the test.

We have discussed theory-based and context dimensions of test validation in Chapters 6 and 7, where we outlined our view of reading strategies and skills in the light of a theoretical model proposed by Urquhart and Weir (1998). It is the existence and distinguishability of these types of reading that we wish to investigate. We wish to investigate the internal cognitive processes involved in completing different reading tasks, and thus provide some evidence for the theory-based validity of an Advanced Level Reading Test, which is undergoing development.

Also, in comparison with the study on contextual variables in speaking that we discussed in Case study 1, this will be based largely on qualitative methods rather than quantitative – so potentially within the reach of every teacher.

Qualitative approaches to test validation

In the area of testing reading comprehension qualitative research can provide a rich source of information about the processes involved, especially if the tasks are organized so that different parts of the test focus on the skills and strategies suggested in our framework in Chapter 7 (see Urquhart and Weir 1998 and Weir *et al*. 2000 for how to set this up).

One of the very few studies that has taken *expeditious* reading into account is the qualitative study on the Advanced English Reading Test (AERT) in China (Weir *et al*. 2000). In order to investigate whether AERT test takers performed different reading tasks (i.e., careful reading global, skimming/search-reading, and careful reading local and scanning tasks), as the test developers intended them to, a concurrent verbal report study on 27 test takers at three levels of ability (top, middle and bottom groups) was carried out. What was interesting was that the top group, i.e., 'successful readers'. processed the tasks in the ways the developers intended but weaker students adopted variant strategies and often resorted to test taking strategies such as wild guessing and attempting to match words in the question stem with words in the passage. We would want to argue that how *good readers* perform on a task should be the benchmark for deciding what is being tested, with obvious implications for sampling.

The major strength of verbal report measures, according to Ericsson and Simon (1993) and Green (1998), is that they are more illuminative with regard to strategy use than other methods. They prefer concurrent reports over retrospective reports, arguing that with such a short time lapse between thought and verbalization they are less susceptible to data loss or alteration than the latter. The problem remains, however, that it is a potentially intrusive technique and may have effects which would not otherwise have emerged in the reading process (see Mann 1982, Stratman and Hamp-Lyons 1994 for discussion of this).

In order to counteract this, retrospective verbal reporting was adopted successfully by Anderson *et al.* (1991), who asked the test takers to provide verbal reports on the reading and test-taking processes *immediately after* answering the questions in separate testlets. More comparative research needs to be done to compare the relative efficiency of these two procedures.

To guard against bias occasioned by any single research method Weir and Roberts (1994) advocate the triangulation of methods and sources where possible. For instance, questionnaires and interviews might be used together (e.g., Phakiti 2003) or in conjunction with verbal report measures (e.g., Weir *et al.* 2000). Less formal interviews can allow the researcher to uncover and probe relevant issues and complement data generated through verbal protocol and questionnaire. Urquhart and Weir (1998: 270–95) provide a detailed account of a range of procedures and methods of analysis, with examples which may be used in studies which attempt to unpack the reading process.

After the initial stages of an enquiry, structured questionnaires allow for a wider sampling and have a greater potential for generating and testing hypotheses, if the questions have been properly piloted. Stage 2 of our research design suggests widening the empirical base and thereby the generalizability of findings by employing this technique. Exam Boards could collect such data as a matter of course.

Overall design of the proposed research

Stage	Participants	Sample size (N)	Methods	Purpose
1. Main study	Candidates	30+	• Test data • Immediate retrospection *or* concurrent verbal report	Comparing the qualitative data collected from candidates and experts with the test developers' expectations in terms of the strategies and skills being tested
			• Questionnaire survey • Retrospective interview	

Overall design of the proposed research   (Continued)

Stage	Participants	Sample size (N)	Methods	Purpose
	Experts	5+	• Questionnaire survey	Establishing whether there are quantitative differences between performance on different parts of the test
2. Large-scale questionnaire survey on the use of strategies and skills	Candidates sampled from the operational population of the test	100+	• Questionnaire survey	Obtaining a larger data set to reflect test takers' views on the strategies and skills being tested

DATA ANALYSIS PROCEDURES

a. *Analysis of verbal reports*

Details of how to analyse verbal reports are provided by Green (1998) who details how to develop an encoding scheme, encoding protocols and establishing inter-coder reliability. The protocols generated through the verbal report procedures can be compared by means of quantitative (number of segments) and qualitative data analyses of reported strategy/skill.

b. *Analysis of questionnaire survey data*

SPSS can be used to compute descriptive statistics and perform reliability analyses.

Frequency computed for the strategies and skills rated by the passing candidates and the experts in terms of their significance to the completion of each reading task.

c. *Analysis of interview data*

The retrospective interviews can be used as qualitative descriptions to verify and clarify what has been reported in the verbal protocols.

d. *Analysis of test data*

Descriptive statistics
Correlation
Factor analysis
t-test
Multi-faceted Rasch Analysis (MFR)
(See Case study 2 and Chapter 9 for detail on these)

Further reading

Urquhart and Weir (1998: 270–95) provide a full account of a range of procedures and methods of analysis, with examples which may be used in studies which attempt to unpack the reading process operationalized through a reading test.
On what happens in the *test taking process* or for further ideas on how to investigate this for yourself, it is worth looking at:
Buck (1991), Hale and Courtney (1994) and **Wu Yian (1998)** on listening.
Anderson *et al.* **(1991), Allan (1992), Crain-Thoreson** *et al.* **(1997) Nevo (1989), Perkins (1992), Phakiti (2003), Storey (1995 and 1997)** and **Weir** *et al.* **(2000)** on reading
Ross (1992) on speaking
Smagorinsky (1994) on writing

On protocol analysis
Cohen (1984, 1988, 1994 and 1997) on verbal reports for investigating test-taking
Gass and Mackey (2000) for a useful theoretical and practical account of verbal protocol analysis
Green (1998) on verbal protocol analysis in language testing research.
Ericsson and Simon (1993) on protocol analysis: verbal report
Pressley and Afflerbach (1995) on verbal protocols for reading
Stratman and Hamp-Lyons (1994) on concurrent think-aloud protocols.

11.5 Establishing scoring validity evidence

Focuses	*Actions and Instruments*
Establishing evidence on rating procedures	
1.1 Rater training	1. Documentation
1.2 Standardization	2. Observation
1.3 Rating conditions	3. Checklist
1.4 Rating	4. Marker reliability studies
1.5 Moderation	

We discussed factors affecting scoring validity in Chapter 9; collecting data on these aspects of test validity is relatively straightforward and has been largely covered in that discussion. Similarly, rating procedures were covered extensively in Chapter 9 and you are referred to that section rather than repeating the same ground here.

We have also dealt in Chapters 4 and 9 with most of the methods for calculating the statistical properties of test items/tasks summarized below (see also Hughes 2003 for an accessible account of their use and value). You are referred to Chapter 9 a for discussion on the importance of each in evidencing scoring validity and for details of how to calculate them by hand. SPSS provides an accessible and efficient way of doing this once the data have been entered onto the spread sheet in the programme (http://www.spss.com/). Microsoft Excel is available in most word processing packages and it also

Focuses	Actions and Instruments
Establishing evidence on scoring validity	
1 Trial on reasonable sample	A trial population will have to be found, that is, a group of people who resemble in all relevant respects (age, learning background, general proficiency level, etc.) the target test population.
2 Statistical analysis	1. Mean
	2. Standard deviation
	3. Item analysis (classical)
	• Facility values
	• Discrimination index
	4. Correlation
3 Estimates of reliability	1. Error of measurement (SEM)
	2. Parallel forms reliability
	3. Internal consistency
	4. Inter-rater reliability
	• Classical true-score correlation
	• Multi-faceted Rasch analysis
	5. Intra-rater reliability
	• Classical true-score correlation
	• Multi-faceted Rasch analysis

enables you to calculate these statistics, albeit with a little extra effort. ETA is a Windows-based IRT analysis package which also provides classical analysis. It is available at http://www.stet.co.uk.

We have described statistical analysis using classical methods rather than IRT as this is more readily available to the individual teacher and for most purposes (with the possible exception of marker reliability where MFR remains the statistic of choice) it is just as good. These basic statistics will tell you whether the items are working in an acceptable fashion. All of these are essential in building up a picture of the statistical properties of a test and we would expect to see publication of all of these as a matter of course on each administration of a high stakes test.

We also described in Chapter 9 the value of SEM for determining how confident we can be that an individual's reported score is his/her 'true' score and described how to calculate this. Internal consistency of items (KR21), and inter- and intra-marker reliabilities (correlation) can be handled using the statistical packages we have recommended, or using the correlation method by hand as described in Chapter 9, so we will not discuss them any further here except to restate their importance in the cumulative set of evidence relating to how a test is behaving statistically, i.e., is it performing in an acceptable statistical fashion as described in Chapter 9? All of this is grist to the scoring validity mill.

Some of you may not have the resources at your disposal, nor the same time as is available to those pursuing academic qualifications, to conduct the type of case study we describe below. You should however be able to join with colleagues and ask questions of any high stakes tests that are administered to their students. For those faced with practical constraints we first provide below a draft of a short but effective checklist on test reliability developed by Akmar Saidatul Zainal Abidin with the author for use in validating a spoken language test at university level in Malaysia. The speaking test consists of two parts: oral presentation and group discussion on the same topic area. Obviously, you will need to customize the questions to fit with the types of spoken language task you employ. If you cannot agree strongly with the following statements in relation to a test, then further investigation of that test's validity is necessary.

Survey of marker reliability

Both task A and task B have the same rating scale. This rating scale consists of three components: Task fulfilment, Language use, Communicative ability.
For each of the items below, circle the number that REFLECTS YOUR VIEWPOINT on the five-point scale.

1 = Strongly disagree 2 = Disagree 3 = Undecided 4 = Agree 5 = Strongly agree

a) The criteria Task fulfilment, Language use and Communicative ability cover all aspects of the performance that the examiner looks for in the presentation.   1 2 3 4 5

b) Three components are enough for markers to use in making a fair judgement of the oral tasks.   1 2 3 4 5

c) The criteria for rating are clear to all markers.   1 2 3 4 5

d) The raters have been given enough information on the procedures for rating the tasks appropriately.   1 2 3 4 5

e) The raters are well trained in using all the rating procedures for the test.   1 2 3 4 5

f) The raters are standardized to benchmark candidate performance levels before marking/rating begins.   1 2 3 4 5

g) The raters were able to work without any disturbance and distraction during the rating process.   1 2 3 4 5

h) Raters' marks are moderated after the test to sort out any differences or problems in the marking.   1 2 3 4 5

i) Statistical analyses are conducted on the marks to check consistency and level of Rating   1 2 3 4 5

j) There are two lecturers present at the test but only the interlocutor interacts with the candidate.   1 2 3 4 5

k) Before the results are issued to candidates, the exam committee checks all results to ensure fairness, especially for those who are close to the pass/fail boundary.   1 2 3 4 5

You may be in a position to carry out more in-depth studies on the reliability of the tests you develop or use with your students. To help you do this we have selected a case study on how to go about ensuring that where alternate versions of the test are in use, from year to year or from test site to test site, you make them as equal as possible. The next case study on establishing the equivalence of tests is probably the most important area in the framework you should investigate. At the very least, all teachers should understand what is involved and demand to see evidence of such alternate form reliability in any high stakes tests their students are entered for. As we discussed in Chapters 4 and 9, if the tests are not equivalent then unfairness results and the consequences could be detrimental to candidates exposed to the more difficult or less valid version.

Parallel forms reliability: a suitable case for treatment

In the area of scoring validity the demonstration of parallel forms reliability, especially in productive tasks, is more complex and seldom carried out. This is an unacceptable situation because it is a *sine qua non* for valid language testing. If you administer a different test from year to year you must establish that the forms you use are the same difficulty level and also are as similar as possible in terms of context, theory-based and scoring validity. Exams like TOEFL and Cambridge ESOL have multiple versions of their high stakes tests so it is critical that these are shown to be equivalent if we are to be fair to candidates and if end users are to make proper sense of the results. Stakeholders have every right to see the evidence that the exam they are taking this year is the equivalent of the one that was taken last year. If they are not, serious validity evidence is lacking and the rule of test fairness violated.

Because of its central importance to validity evidence we have chosen to examine parallel forms reliability in this section. You may say it is not possible to do all of the following strands of the procedure, but even if you did only a part of the study on tests in the classroom it would be a start. Exam Boards should provide evidence in full.

Establishing scoring validity: Case study 4 parallel forms reliability

Few reports are available of how Exam Boards have attempted to establish this form of reliability for their tests and the account below draws on the work of Weir and Wu in connection with the GEPT examination in Taiwan (but see also Yang and Weir 1998 for an account of how it is done before every administration of the College English Test in China). As we discussed in Chapters 4 and 9, traditionally the administration of parallel (alternate) forms of a test in independent sessions provides alternate-form coefficients. The tests must be as similar as possible in terms of the operations tested and the performance conditions of code complexity, cognitive complexity and communicative demand. Thus the same language skills/sub-skills would be tested and any input would be of the same difficulty (see Case study 1 above for discussion of this). The tests would have been constructed to be equivalent but not identical. Such equivalent but not identical tests are known as *parallel forms*.

The results achieved by the learners on the first parallel form would be compared statistically with the results achieved by them on the second parallel form. The resulting correlation would be the *parallel form reliability* of the scores on each of the two forms, i.e., it would be an estimate of the extent to which each of the two forms was awarding the same marks as the other (see Chapter 4 for full discussion). It would indicate how much error variance had resulted due to the context sampling of the two forms. By squaring the correlation, it is possible to provide an estimate of the degree of overlap between the two.

In the study proposed below the aim is to investigate the extent to which two forms of a test are parallel. Both forms A and B are administered to students, with half the group taking A first and half B. The performance data from the different test forms can be analysed by MFR (see Chapter 9), or by classical methods such as correlation, which deals with the extent of shared variance between the two forms, and *t*-tests which indicate whether there is a significant difference in performance level between the two tests for the population sampled. (See Yang and Weir 1998 for one of the few published reports on how large scale tests have attempted to do this.)

Parallel forms reliability may be influenced by errors of measurement which reside in contextual factors. Thus quantitative analysis of test score difficulty needs to be complemented by collection of qualitative data on the degree of difficulty as experienced by candidates, and as perceived by raters with regard to each individual test. As we noted in Case study 1 above, Skehan (1996) attempted to identify factors that can affect the difficulty of a given task and which can be manipulated so as to change (increase or decrease) task difficulty. You are referred to that case study for categories of description that might be checked to ensure parallel content. In evaluating whether test forms are equally difficult, expert judgements can be used in such a study to determine equivalence in the areas of code complexity, cognitive complexity, and communicative demand (the checklist described in Case study 1 is designed for this purpose). We should try to provide evidence on as many of these levels as we practically can.

In speaking tests, context validation has largely depended on transcriptions of the task performance. In a series of UCLES studies on speaking tests (Lazaraton 2002, Young and Milanovic 1992, Ross and Berwick 1992), transcribed performance has demonstrated its usefulness in providing qualitative data for analysis. However, despite its usefulness, such analysis of transcribed performances has its shortcomings, the chief of which is the complexity involved in the work of transcription. As O'Sullivan, Weir and Saville (2002) warned: 'In practice, this means that a great deal of time and expertise is required in order to gain the kind of data that will answer the basic question concerning validity. Even where that is done, it is impractical to attempt to deal with more than a small number of test events – and therefore the generalizability of the results may be questioned.'

Therefore, in an attempt to overcome these practical problems, in a project commissioned by Cambridge ESOL O'Sullivan, Weir and Saville (2002) proposed the use of language function checklists derived from the spoken language and SLA literature as 'an effective and efficient procedure towards establishing the context validity of speaking tests'.

Their aim in using the checklists 'was to create an instrument, built on a framework that describes the language of performance in a way that can be readily accessed by evaluators who are familiar with the tests being observed. This work is designed to be complementary to the use of transcriptions and to provide an additional source of validation evidence'.

Based on their findings, they concluded positively: 'though still under development for use with the UCLES Main Suite examinations, an operational version of these checklists is certainly feasible and has potentially wider application, *mutatis mutandis*, to the content validation of other spoken language tests'. Further, they added that with use of the checklists it would be not only possible to compare predicted and actual test task performance, but also provide 'a useful guide for item writers in taking *a priori* decisions about content coverage'. By taking up this qualitative approach to comparing the predicted and actual performance on the two tests the study can address the *a priori* test development aspect of context validation, as well as the issue of *a posteriori* parallel forms reliability.

Raters can look at Test Forms A and B and predict in advance which language functions they might expect to find in candidates' responses. Then after the test, raters would be asked to observe the functions in candidates' actual performance in the tasks, to determine whether test content was invariant across forms. O'Sullivan, building on the work reported in O'Sullivan *et al.* (2002), is attempting to operationalize a checklist for doing this with glosses and exemplification. After initial piloting and trialling, the draft checklist included below has been used successfully with three groups of teachers to date, with high levels of agreement in its interpretation and use. Brooks (2003) describes how she revised it for successful use with the IELTS test.

Part 1

Analysis of operations:

1. Informational functions

Operation	*Gloss: Does a Test Taker...*	*For Example*
Providing personal information	Give information on present circumstances?	'I'm studying English here in London.' 'I live...' 'I work...'
	Give information on past experiences?	'I studied economics at university.' 'I've been/I went to...before/last week'
	Give information on future plans?	'After I go home,...' 'I hope to qualify in June.' 'I'm going/going to go/I'll go home next week.'
Expressing opinions	express opinions?	Can be *signalled*: 'I don't like English food.' Or Can be *unsignalled*: 'It would be better if schools were given more funding.' Also can be **Positive** or **Negative**.
Elaborating	elaborate on, or modify an opinion?	Can be *signalled*: 'I mean ....' Or 'Maybe not that good, but...' Can be *unsignalled*: 'They could reduce class size, or...'
Justifying opinions	express reasons for assertions s/he has made?	Can be *signalled by the test taker*: 'It's because...' Can be *signalled by the other test taker*: 'Why...' Can be *signalled by the examiner*: ' 'Well, if they are really interested in the work, that in itself will motivate them and they won't mind how much they are paid.' Can be *unsignalled*: 'It's prettier, and cheaper...'
Comparing	compare things/people/events?	'I think X is more useful' 'Both are interesting, but I prefer the style and colours in the smaller one' 'This picture shows .. whereas/while/but this one is busier/more crowded/more interesting.'

1. Informational functions   (Continued)

Operation	Gloss: Does a Test Taker...	For Example
Speculating	speculate?	'She must have paid a fortune for that.' 'I can imagine him spending hours on preparing that.' 'This might/could/should/would/can't be/must be...'
Staging	separate out or interpret the parts of an issue?	'So, first I'll talk about...' 'So, you think he did it, but it wasn't deliberate, or do you think he was provoked and it was an instinctive reaction?' 'But first, we have to...and now, we must choose...'
Describing	describe a sequence of events?	Can be *marked*: 'When she first goes to Italy, she is very innocent. Then...' Can be *unmarked*: 'I went to buy a ticket and found that the ticket office had already closed.'
Summarizing	summarize what s/he has said?	'So, I think we would choose,...' 'So you think...' 'So we have decided/chosen...'
Suggesting	suggest a particular idea?	'We could choose this one.' 'What about...' 'We could (do)...' 'Why don't we (do)...' 'How about (doing)?'
Expressing preferences	express preferences?	'I think this one would be best.' 'I'd rather have a small one.' 'I prefer/like this one better.'

2. Interactional functions

Operation	Gloss: Does a Test Taker...	For Example
Agreeing	agree with an assertion made by another speaker? (apart from 'yeah' or non-verbal)	Can be *marked*: 'Yes, I agree.' 'I think you're right.' Can be *unmarked*: 'But you can't/don't mean...do you?'
Disagreeing	disagree with what another speaker says? (apart from 'no' or non-verbal)	Can be *marked*: 'I don't think that's right.' 'I (don't) agree with you.' Can be *unmarked*: 'But you can't/don't mean..., do you?' 'Well, that depends on your point of view, but I rather think...'

Modifying	modify arguments or comments made by other speaker? Or by the test taker in response to another speaker	'Of course, only is he was forced to go, otherwise...' 'Well, (perhaps) not for this but for that...' Other speaker's input may be **verbal** ('Why?'), **nonverbal** (*raised eyebrow*) or even **paraverbal** (mmm? – *rising intonation*)
Asking for opinions	ask for opinions?	'What do you think?' 'And you? 'Well?' 'What/How about you?'
Persuading	attempt to persuade another person?	Can be *cued*: 'Don't you think?' 'But don't you think that...?' Can be *uncued*: Yes, but he can't spend it all, or he won't have enough left to eat!
Asking for information	ask for information?	'What about you? What are your favourite films?' 'What are your hobbies/leisure activities?' 'Do you know...'
Conversational repair	repair breakdowns in interaction?	Can be 'other repair' – breakdown during other speaker's turn: 'I'm sorry I thought you meant...' Can be 'self repair' – breakdown during own turn: 'What I wanted to say was...' These repairs may be initiated by the person who is speaking (self-initiated) or by the other person (other initiated) and can be verbal ('Pardon.') or non-verbal (*quizzical look*).
Negotiating meaning	check understanding?	'OK?' 'Is that clear?' 'So, do I have to (describe all the photographs)?'
	indicate understanding of point made by partner?	Can be *verbal*: 'Yes, I know what you mean.' 'OK, yes.' Can be *non-verbal: head nod* Can be *paraverbal*: mmm (with or without intonational changes)
	establish common ground/ purpose or strategy?	'Shall we talk about all of them first before deciding?' 'But we have to choose three pictures.' 'So, we both like this one...'
	ask for clarification when an utterance is misheard or misinterpreted?	'Can you repeat that please?' 'What exactly do you mean by 'wealthy?'
	Correct an utterance made by other speaker which is perceived to be incorrect or inaccurate.	'No, we've already decided not to take that one.' 'You mean...' (usually a lexical or grammatical correction)

2. Interactional functions   (Continued)

Operation	Gloss: Does a Test Taker...	For Example
	respond to requests for clarification?	Can be *cued*: 'What I mean is...' Can be non-cued: 'The blue one.' The request itself may be **verbal** ('Which...') or **nonverbal** (*quizzical look*)

3. Managing Interaction

Operation	Gloss: Does a Test Taker...	For Example
Initiating	start any interactions?	'What do you think?' 'Right, so we have to chose the best, what do you think of the blue one?' 'But what about...? 'But this one is (much) more, don't you think?'
Changing	take the opportunity to change the topic?	'Yes, that would be the best, So what about the worst?' 'Talking of sizes, did I tell you about those shoes I saw?' 'I don't like going to a gym, but I like to go for a walk. Last weekend...'
Reciprocating	share the responsibility for developing the interaction?	'What do you think we should do?' 'Have you ever tried to do it?' May simply consist of *verbal* ('Yes'), *non-verbal* (head-nod) or *paraverbal* (uh huh, mm hmm) **support** – used to encourage other speaker to continue.
Deciding	come to a decision?	'So, we have decided...' 'You're right, it's easier that way. That will work.' 'So, let's choose/we've chosen...' 'I would choose...' 'I think we should choose...'

You may, of course, wish to develop your own checklists or customize the one above. The tasks you use may not cover the spread of functions outlined above and they may of course additionally merit the inclusion of other functions we have not listed.

Methods and procedures

QUANTITATIVE APPROACH
Participants should be randomly divided into two groups, 30+ to each group. The two groups should be as equivalent as possible in terms of general language proficiency based on their performance on an external measure. Each group is then invited to take two consecutive tests but in reverse order to each other to guard against order effect.

The tests should be marked by two independent examiners and the results compared to establish inter- and intra-marker reliability. Candidate score data can be analysed by SPSS (SPSS Inc. 2000) for correlation, factor analysis and *t*-test. If MFR analysis is run on the computer program FACETS (www.winsteps.com/minifac.htm), the different versions of the test can be plotted on the same scale of difficulty. Further, by treating rater and task as facets, MFR can provide information on the effect of these facets on candidate ability estimated in a performance assessment setting (McNamara 1996); see Chapter 9 for discussion of MFR.

If FACETS cannot be used, correlations and *t*- tests are an acceptable alternative for the classroom, and ANOVA if more than two tests are considered at the same time. All of these procedures are easily employed using SPSS (see Bryman and Cramer 2001 for an accessible guide to using SPSS).

Summary of analysis procedures
Analysis of test data

- Descriptive statistics
- Correlation
- Factor analysis
- *t*-test
- Multi-faceted Rasch Analysis (MFR)

See Case study 2 and Chapter 9 for detail on these.

QUALITATIVE APPROACH
Both predicted and actual performances can be investigated for the task. For predicted and actual performance on speaking tests the checklist described above can be used and raters asked to map the functions listed in the checklists on to the items/test tasks in versions 1 and 2. We would point out that the checklists provided are not necessarily complete – these were created for use with specific tests and there may be other functions that different tasks/ tests might elicit. (See also Brooks 2003: UCRN 11 for details of how this checklist was converted for successful use with the IELTS test.) Frequency counts then provide details of the relative frequency of occurrence of the language functions and also of the degree of consensus among raters.

In addition to raters' observation of discourse functions in the task, the same group of raters can be invited to familiarize themselves with the tasks and then to provide their views on whether the two were equally difficult, within each task type, in terms of factors which may affect task difficulty (see Norris *et al.* 1998). Accordingly, for each task type, a checklist of task difficulty can be created to elicit raters' judgements on the degree of parallelness of the tests in terms of code complexity (e.g., lexical and syntactical features), cognitive complexity (e.g., content familiarity and information processing required), and communicative demand (e.g., time pressure). An example of such a checklist was provided above in Case study 1.

Exam Boards need to develop a monitoring system, which can serve as an instrument for preventing potential threats to parallel forms reliability and ensuring test fairness. High indices of parallel forms reliability in a test do not necessarily yield a significant meaning, unless a consistent content coverage over test forms is established (theory-based, consequential and criterion-related validity also demand attention however). Inconsistent test content across test forms can potentially have an impact on test scores, consequently causing bias against candidates and harming fairness in the test.

We have focused on productive tasks only in this case study. You are also referred back to the discussion in Chapters 4 and 9, and to Weir and Milanovic (2003: 50–1) for discussion of how MFR can help to develop item banks for discrete test items, thereby allowing the creation of parallel forms at will from items which have been statistically calibrated and stored with known properties.

Further reading

Baker (1997) is one of the few accessible accounts of using IRT analysis.

Bryman and Cramer (2001) is an accessible guide to using SPSS.

Crocker and Algina (1986) provide a solid and accessible account of the statistics you may need.

Fulcher (2003) Chapter 7 provides an accessible account of correlation, factor analysis, multi-trait, multi-method studies and generalizability studies.

Kim and Muller (1978a) There are no easy introductions to factor analysis but this is as close as it gets at the moment.

Kim and Muller (1978b) is the next step up on the previous reference.

McNamara (1996: Chapters 5–8 in particular) is one of the few readable and comprehensive accounts of using Rasch analysis, with examples of how to interpret the output.

Myford and Wolfe (2000, 2003, 2004) for accessible accounts of MFR.

Norris *et al.* (1998) for an extended discussion on how to estimate task difficulty along a number of parameters and a suggested procedure for operationalizing this **SPSS Inc. (2002)** The handbook that goes with the program.

O'Sullivan, Weir and Saville (2002). Describes the rationale and development of the observation checklists described above.

Weir and Milanovic (2003) provide a detailed coverage of what one Exam Board, Cambridge ESOL, does in this area. One of the few open and frank accounts of what goes on behind the scenes at one of the world's leading test deliverers.

Yang and Weir (1998) for a discussion of how parallel forms are achieved for the College English Test (CET) in China taken by over 10 million candidates a year.

11.6   Establishing evidence on *a posteriori* validities

Criterion-related validity	Compare the test scores with another measure of the same construct taken in close proximity
(a) Concurrent validity	Compare the test scores with another measure usually relating to later performance in the target situation
(b) Predictive validity	
Consequential (impact) validity	(1) Statistical analysis
(a) Differential validity (potential item, content and experience bias)	(2) Comparison with students' biodata and psychological characteristics:
	a) Detect bias in the test for or against groups of students defined by biodata characteristics
	b) Feedback from test takers (interview/ questionnaire)
(b) Washback in the classroom	Expert judgement
	Observation
	Interview
	Questionnaire
(c) Effect on society Value/Use	Stakeholder survey (Questionnaire/interview)

As we noted in Chapter 10, *criterion-related validity* is normally established by correlating performances on the test under review with an external measure you have some trust in as a valid indicator of the same construct. Correlations were dealt with in Chapter 9 and to check out this area of validity you are referred back to that chapter for details of how to calculate them. Accordingly, we will not discuss this validity any further here except to note that the context of the criterion test must also be comparable in terms of the elements we outlined in Chapter 6 (how to establish this context equivalence was also discussed in relation to parallel forms reliability in Case study 4 above). Examples of *criterion-related validity* studies are provided by Weir (1983a) Hughes *et al.* (1988) and Criper and Davies (1988), Cotton and Conrow (1998) and most recently Banerjee (2003).

Differential validity

We considered *differential* validity in the section on post-exam procedures entitled Scores, Grading and Post-exam Validation Procedures on pages 205–6, using the case study of the procedures adopted by Cambridge ESOL as an example. The main aim here is to ensure that no candidate suffers as a result of their gender or ethnic origin or other relevant background characteristics. At a basic level, descriptive statistics and ANOVA can be used to determine that a test is free from such bias. One would hope that no significant relationship occurs between levels of response on a background variable and the test results.

In Chapter 5 we laid out the potential test taker characteristics variables that might interact as moderator variables with test performance, under the headings:

- Physical/physiological
- Psychological
- Experiential

It is at the consequential validity stage that data on these individual test taker characteristics are used to determine impact on the testing process. Since they obviously can have a potential effect on test performance it is necessary to check no bias has resulted from the way we have written, conducted, scored or administered the test.

The individual researcher in the classroom might take any of the variables in these areas, either singly or in combination and determine whether test performance is affected by variation in the test population with respect to each. The most efficient way of doing this is probably by some pre- or post-checklist administered to the students in relation to these variables. Example questions relating to attitude towards English and learning preferences are presented below. These are taken from a wider background variable survey questionnaire used by Green (2003) in his research on the IELTS test, where he looked at a number of background variables relating to parts of the experiential and psychological domains we discussed in Chapter 5 and then looked at the effect they had on test performance. You might be interested in administering some parts of this questionnaire and comparing the responses with results on your own writing tests. Alternatively, you might construct questions employing a similar layout and scale to determine the effect of any of the other variables we discussed in Chapter 5 on background characteristics.

Green (2003) took the results of this questionnaire and used linear regression (a form of correlation) to determine whether any of these background factors impacted on performance on the IELTS writing test.

Questionnaire A (Green 2003: Appendix: 47 *et seq.*)

> ### Student Questionnaire A

In this questionnaire, we would like to find out about your experience of studying English, about what you expect to study on this course and about how you like to learn

*We hope these questions will also help **you** to think about how you study and about how to be successful*

The questions usually take about 20 minutes to answer

We will not use your name in our reports and we will not tell anyone about your personal answers, but we do need these details to help us to organize the information

If you have any trouble understanding a question, please ask your teacher or use a dictionary to help you. Thank you.

Section 1 [NOT INCLUDED]

⟹ SECTION 2

In this section, we would like to find out how you feel about learning languages and about taking tests.

		I definitely agree	I tend to agree	I tend to disagree	I definitely disagree	I don't know / I cannot answer this question
SC01	People say that I am good at language learning.	4	3	1	0	2
SC02	I feel happy about living in an English speaking country.	4	3	1	0	2
SC03	I usually did better than other students at my school in English classes.	4	3	1	0	2
SC04	I do NOT really like the British way of life.	4	3	1	0	2
SC05	I am NOT good at writing in English.	4	3	1	0	2
SC06	I feel I will never really enjoy writing in English.	4	3	1	0	2
SC07	Writing classes are difficult for me.	4	3	1	0	2

SECTION 2   (Continued)

SC08   I am pleased I chose to study at this school.   [4 | 3 | 1 | 0]   ②

SC09   I like writing down my ideas in English.   [4 | 3 | 1 | 0]   ②

SC10   If we had no tests, I think I would actually learn more.   [4 | 3 | 1 | 0]   ②

SC11   I usually enjoy meeting British people.   [4 | 3 | 1 | 0]   ②

SC12   I think learning languages is more difficult for me than for the average learner.   [4 | 3 | 1 | 0]   ②

SC13   During an important test, I often feel so nervous that I forget facts I really know.   [4 | 3 | 1 | 0]   ②

SC14   I DON'T think I write in English as well as other students.   [4 | 3 | 1 | 0]   ②

SC15   It is easy for me to write good English essays.   [4 | 3 | 1 | 0]   ②

SC16   Even when I'm well prepared for a test, I feel very worried about it.   [4 | 3 | 1 | 0]   ②

SC17   I don't study any harder for final exams than for the rest of my course work.   [4 | 3 | 1 | 0]   ②

SC18   I think the writing classes will be useful for me.   [4 | 3 | 1 | 0]   ②

SC19   I enjoy writing in English.   [4 | 3 | 1 | 0]   ②

Comments on your feelings about learning English and taking tests.

SECTION 4

In this section, we are interested in finding out about your general approach to studying (how you usually study). Do you learn best by seeing or doing, by reading or listening? Do you like to learn in a group or by yourself?

Instructions for Section 4.
You will see two sentences. Please decide which sentence better describes you.
Mark your choice on the scale.
If the first sentence describes you much better than the second sentence, mark 1.
If the second sentence describes you better, mark 9.
If both sentences are equally true about you, or if neither sentence is true for you, mark 5.

Example   I like listening to music while I study   I like to study in silence

| 1 | 2 | ● | 4 | 5 | 6 | 7 | 8 | 9 |

[The student usually likes to listen to music while she studies, but sometimes she likes to study in silence so she has marked 3.]

LP01   I prefer to study by making or building things   I prefer to study by looking at charts, maps or diagrams

| 1 | 2 | 3 | 4 | 5 | 6 | 7 | 8 | 9 |

LP02   I learn better when the teacher tells me something   I learn better when I can touch the things I am learning about

| 1 | 2 | 3 | 4 | 5 | 6 | 7 | 8 | 9 |

LP03   I learn better when I work alone on assignments.   I learn better when I work on group projects

| 1 | 2 | 3 | 4 | 5 | 6 | 7 | 8 | 9 |

LP04   I understand things better when I practise a new skill   I understand things better when the teacher gives a lecture

| 1 | 2 | 3 | 4 | 5 | 6 | 7 | 8 | 9 |

LP05   I understand more when I work on an assignment with two or three classmates   I understand more when I work by myself on assignments

| 1 | 2 | 3 | 4 | 5 | 6 | 7 | 8 | 9 |

LP06   Ilearn better by participating in role plays   I learn better when the teacher tells me something

| 1 | 2 | 3 | 4 | 5 | 6 | 7 | 8 | 9 |

LP07   I remember images and pictures   I remember things that I have heard people say

| 1 | 2 | 3 | 4 | 5 | 6 | 7 | 8 | 9 |

LP08   I understand better by reading books   I understand better by doing experiments or practical activities

| 1 | 2 | 3 | 4 | 5 | 6 | 7 | 8 | 9 |

LP09   I learn more when I write down my ideas   I learn more when I build something for myself

| 1 | 2 | 3 | 4 | 5 | 6 | 7 | 8 | 9 |

LP10   I enjoy reading for pleasure   I enjoy listening to people talking on the radio or on tape

| 1 | 2 | 3 | 4 | 5 | 6 | 7 | 8 | 9 |

LP11   I remember things better when I work with other students   I remember things better when I work independently

| 1 | 2 | 3 | 4 | 5 | 6 | 7 | 8 | 9 |

LP12   I learn more when someone tells me instructions   I learn more when I can make something for a class project

| 1 | 2 | 3 | 4 | 5 | 6 | 7 | 8 | 9 |

LP13   I learn when I write down my ideas   I learn more when the teacher gives a lecture

| 1 | 2 | 3 | 4 | 5 | 6 | 7 | 8 | 9 |

LP14   I prefer listening to the teacher   I prefer doing things in class

| 1 | 2 | 3 | 4 | 5 | 6 | 7 | 8 | 9 |

LP15   I understand better when someone tells me what to do   I understand better when I look at visual instructions

| 1 | 2 | 3 | 4 | 5 | 6 | 7 | 8 | 9 |

LP16   I remember better when I do experiments   I remember better when I look at diagrams or pictures
        or practical activities

| 1 | 2 | 3 | 4 | 5 | 6 | 7 | 8 | 9 |

LP17   I prefer to solve my problems by myself   When I have a problem, I usually ask for help from other people

| 1 | 2 | 3 | 4 | 5 | 6 | 7 | 8 | 9 |

LP18   I understand better when the teacher gives a lecture   I understand better when I read books

| 1 | 2 | 3 | 4 | 5 | 6 | 7 | 8 | 9 |

LP19   I enjoy making models or doing crafts   I enjoy reading for pleasure

| 1 | 2 | 3 | 4 | 5 | 6 | 7 | 8 | 9 |

LP20   I understand better by writing about a topic   I understand better by doing activities in class

| 1 | 2 | 3 | 4 | 5 | 6 | 7 | 8 | 9 |

Comments on how you like to learn:

Green also devised a very useful test awareness form (part of this is reproduced below) to enable him to investigate whether candidate's familiarity with the test impacted on their test scores. As we argued forcefully in chapter 5 it is critical that students are fully aware of and practised in the requirements of high stakes tests before they are entered in for it. It is the duty of responsible exam boards in high stakes tests to ensure that this is the case, but it is also a valuable preparatory task for teachers to provide to their own students who may be taking such tests.

IELTS Awareness Form A (Green 2003: Appendix, 36–7)

. . . .
SECTION 3 - English language tests
....
Are the following statements about the IELTS Writing Test true?

		Yes	*No*	*I don't know*
15.	The IELTS Writing test is 60 minutes long.	❏	❏	❏
16.	There are two sections in the Writing test.	❏	❏	❏
17.	The Writing test is worth more marks than the Speaking test.	❏	❏	❏
18.	The topic for one of the Writing tasks comes from one of the texts in the Reading test.	❏	❏	❏
19.	The Writing test also includes some grammar questions.	❏	❏	❏
20.	In Task 1, you should write 150 words.	❏	❏	❏

These questionnaires may not fit your own situation or your own tests exactly, but they provide a useful starting point. You should be able to customize them for your own context without too much difficulty.

For further more sophisticated methodologies and analysis the following studies are useful sources. Alderman and Holland (1981) looked at item performance on TOEFL across native language groups, as did Oltman *et al.* (1988). Chen and Henning looked at linguistic and cultural bias in proficiency tests. Kunnan (1990, 1994) and Ryan and Bachman (1992), Brown and Ishawita (1998) and Hill (1998) looked at differential item functioning (DIF) in terms of a number of background variables. Tittle (1990) discusses the contexts in which test bias can happen and details various methodologies for establishing whether it has occurred or not.

In addition, feedback questionnaires administered immediately after the test can elicit whether candidates perceived there to be bias in any aspect of the test. Weir (1983a), Cohen (1984), Bradshaw (1990), Brown (1993), Hill (1998), and Weir *et al* (2000) provide examples of a variety of methodologies to elicit test taker feedback for use in understanding and developing tests. Examples of some of the categories for such a questionnaire were provided in Case study 2 above.

Such test taker feedback studies are extremely valuable to test developers and teacher-researchers are ideally placed to carry out such studies. These studies can offer considerable information to test designers.

Washback validity

In investigating consequential validity we also need to consider the washback validity of the tests we develop or enter students for. This is primarily concerned with the effects of a test on what goes on in the preparation for the test and accordingly is likely to be an important aspect of test impact for most of the readers of this book (see Chapters 4 and 10).

Teachers in the classroom may not have the resources available to carry out fully the case study on washback validity described below, but at the very least they should be able to think about a number of questions relating to washback validity and check their views with those of their colleagues perhaps by using a common checklist. These questions would relate to both the content of the lessons as well as the methodological procedures obtaining in the classroom.

For those faced with practical constraints we first provide a short extract from a full questionnaire developed by Akmar Saidatul Zainal Abidin with the author for use in validating a spoken language test at University level in Malaysia. This portion is a short but effective checklist for staff on washback on teaching and learning. The speaking test consists of two parts: an oral presentation and a group discussion on the same topic area. Obviously, you will need to customize the questions to fit with the types of test task you employ.

Section C: Teaching and learning

This section concerns the effect the test has on teaching and learning in the English classroom. For each of the items below, circle the number that **reflects your viewpoint** on the five-point scale.
1 = Strongly disagree 2 = Disagree 3 = Undecided 4 = Agree 5 = Strongly agree
Note: DO NOT circle 3 unless you cannot understand OR really cannot answer the question.

1. Lecturers give students full details of all aspects of the tests tasks (e.g. goals, content, format and rating process of).   1   2   3   4   5
2. Lecturers spend time in class discussing with students various topics so students are familiar with information required in the test.   1   2   3   4   5

3. Lecturers spend time in class practicing past year questions with students so that students are familiar with structures, vocabulary and format used in the test.	1	2	3	4	5
4. Students spend a lot of time in class practicing individual speeches.	1	2	3	4	5
5. Students spend a lot of time in class practicing group discussions.	1	2	3	4	5
6. Students learn from their speech class how to present and support ideas in a presentation.	1	2	3	4	5
7. Students learn from their speech class how to:					
a) initiate a discussion	1	2	3	4	5
b) keep a conversation going	1	2	3	4	5
c) connect what they say to what has just been said	1	2	3	4	5
d) take turns appropriately	1	2	3	4	5
e) conclude a group discussion	1	2	3	4	5
8. Because students have had practice in individual presentations (task A) for the test, they are able to perform better in presentations in other classes.	1	2	3	4	5
9. Because students have had practice in group discussions (task B) for the test, they are able to participate better in group discussions in other classes.	1	2	3	4	5

Case study 5: Establishing washback validity

Green carried out a washback study as part of the ongoing IELTS research programme. As part of his study he looked at washback in IELTS preparation courses and compared these with University Pre-sessional Courses to determine where any differences might lie in the preparation of students for English medium study at tertiary level in the United Kingdom (the full study is described in detail in Green 2003, where additionally score gain on IELTS is related to course type and duration, and the influence of criterial background variables on performance is considered). The part of the study we are interested in arose from concern that IELTS scores (the same might be true for current TOEFL scores) for some students entering universities do not represent criterion abilities.

In order to test the claim that, 'by studying for IELTS you will not only be preparing for the test, but also for your future as a student in an English speaking environment' (McDowell and Jakeman 1996) against the counterclaims that scores for some students entering universities may not represent criterion abilities (Deakin 1997), the relevant comparison is seen to be between courses directed at IELTS and English for Academic Purposes (EAP) courses which are not directed towards the test, but are based more immediately on analyses of the university context and perceived student needs therein.

The hypothesis of particular interest to us in this case study is the following:

1. IELTS preparation courses do not reflect the EAP construct with respect to academic writing.

Methods/research methodology design – settings, subjects and methods

In investigating participant perceptions and learning processes you must triangulate both data sources and methods. This implies collecting data from different participant groups – teachers and students – and employing both qualitative and quantitative methods: interview, observation, documentation and questionnaires.

Sample of teachers and students might be interviewed regarding their courses, and these interviews could inform a questionnaire survey of participants in selected institutions providing IELTS (or TOEFL, TEEP or another acceptable academic purpose test) preparation on the one hand, and EAP courses on the other. One could also subject tests developed internally on EAP programmes to the same rigorous scrutiny. In this phase of the research, information on participant attitudes and beliefs can be supported by observational and documentary data drawn from the classroom as direct evidence of behaviour.

The methods might include:

- classroom observation
- analysis of teachers' written feedback to learners
- analysis of teaching materials such as text books and worksheets

All teacher participants and students can be administered a survey regarding their expectations and beliefs about their classes and what happens in them. A sample of teachers and students can be interviewed regarding their expectations and practices.

Quantitative comparisons between courses can be made based on the observational and survey data. The frequency of a variety of classroom activities associated with IELTS (or other specified test) and EAP can be counted and compared. Similarly, survey responses regarding the aims and practices of teachers and students can be used to make comparisons between the test and EAP courses.

Interview data in backwash studies have often proved to be limited because of the lack of comparability across contexts and between subjects in many ethnographic approaches. A potential failing of the heuristic, ethnographic procedure is that in an attempt not to influence the participant, data are allowed to emerge naturally. Because of the variability in the response of each individual generalizability on key issues may be thereby limited.

In a backwash study, such comparisons between treatments are highly desirable as the concern is with how students and teachers conceive of and approach their tasks as a result of the test as compared to how this might pan out in real life. A methodology which aims to capture the conceptualizations participants hold of a social context, their personal anticipatory theories about the world they are entering, is provided by Kelly (1955) on Personal Construct Psychology (PCP). The *repertory grid* technique in PCP offers the researcher the benefits of both focusing and quantifying interview data, allowing for estimates of the salient functional relationships within an individual's understanding of the setting: the language course (see http://repgrid.com/pcp/for useful advice and links to sites in this area). This method allows comparisons both between participants on the different courses and within groups. In essence it is a rather sophisticated form of the bi polar opposites that one often sees in questionnaires and respondents have to locate themselves on a continuum between these for each element of the construct. The sophistication emerges in the modes of analysis the programme lends itself to (see Roberts 1999).

Obviously, for use in the classroom or the school setting such sophisticated techniques may be over complex and a set of descriptors on a simple Likert scale might be the preferred alternative (see Case study 2) with calculation of basic descriptive statistics using EXCEL, ETA or SPSS sufficing. For research into high stakes test however resources should be available to take on board more advanced methodological procedures (see Roberts 1999 for a full discussion of PCP).

Further reading

Washback studies
Green (2003) provides a very good survey of the literature in the field, some useful data collection instruments, and some innovative methods of analyses.
Cheng (2004) provides a recent comprehensive study of the effect of the introduction of a new examination with a useful methodology section.
Cheng and Watanabe (eds.) (2004) provide a useful and varied set of papers on recent developments in this area
Wall (2004) provides an interesting account of washback in the Sri Lankan context and sets it in the context of change theory

Recommended reading
Recommendations for reading that relate specifically to the case studies have been included at the end of each case study. The following references relate to methodology or are of more general relevance to generating validity evidence:
Allan (1995) on questionnaires.
Allwright (1988) on observation.
Banerjee and Luoma (1997) on qualitative approaches to test validation.
Brown (1991) on research methods.
Cohen, Manion and Morrison (2000) on research methods in education.
Denicolo and Pope (eds.) (1997) on interviewing.
Foddy (1994) on constructing questions for interviews and questionnaires: language research.

Fulcher (2003: chapter 7) provides an accessible overview of correlation, factor analysis, multi-trait, multi-method studies, generalizability studies, multi-faceted Rasch analysis, expert judgement, questionnaires and interviews, discourse analysis and verbal protocol analysis

Hatch and Lazaraton (1997) on design and statistics for applied linguistics.

Miles and Huberman (1994) on qualitative data analysis.

Oppenheim (1992) on questionnaire design, interviewing and attitude measurement.

Patton (2002) on qualitative research methods.

Scwartz and Sudman (eds.) (1996) on the methodology for determining cognitive and communicative processes in survey research

Urquhart and Weir (1998: chapter 5) provide detailed accounts of how to do research in the area of reading and provide examples of instruments and analysis.

Weir and Roberts (1994) describe the advantages and disadvantages of a variety of survey instruments and how to construct and operationalize them

Weir, Yang and Jin (2000) investigate the construct of reading by a variety of methods.

Part 4

Further Resources in Language Testing

12
Key Sources

12.1 Books

The key references have been appended at the ends of chapters and you are recommended to look at these to obtain a reasonable overview of the field. A few of the core books of relevance to language testers are listed below.

Some key textbooks

Alderson, J. C. (2000). *Assessing Reading*. Cambridge: Cambridge University Press.

American Educational Research Association, American Psychological Association, and National Council on Measurement in Education (1999). *Standards for Educational and Psychological Testing*. Washington, DC: Author.

Association of Language Testers in Europe (ALTE) (1998). *A Multilingual Glossary of Language Testing Terms*.

Bachman, L. F. (1990). *Fundamental Considerations in Language Testing*. Oxford: Oxford University Press.

Bachman, L. F. and Palmer, A. S. (1996). *Language Testing in Practice*. Oxford: Oxford University Press.

Baker, R. (1997). *Classical Test Theory and Item Response Theory in Test Analysis*. Special Report 2: Language Testing Update, Centre for Research in Language Education.

Buck, G. (2001). *Assessing Listening*. Cambridge: Cambridge University Press.

Clapham, C. and Corson, D. (1997). *Language Testing and Assessment*. Volume 7, *Encyclopedia of Language and Education*. Dordrecht: Kluwer.

Council of Europe (2001). *Common European Framework of Reference for Languages: Learning, Teaching, Assessment*. Cambridge: Cambridge University Press.

Davies, A., Brown, A., Elder, C., Hill, K., Lumley, T. and McNamara, T. (1999). *Dictionary of Language Testing*. Studies in Language Testing, Volume 7. Cambridge: UCLES/Cambridge University Press.

Douglas, D. (2000). *Assessing Languages for Specific Purposes*. Cambridge: Cambridge University Press.

Fulcher, G. (2003). *Testing Second Language Speaking*. Harlow: Pearson.

Grabe, W. and Stoller, F. L. (2002). *Teaching and Researching Reading*. Harlow: Pearson.

Henning, G. (1987). *A Guide to Language Testing*. Cambridge, MA.: Newbury House.

Hughes, A. (2003). *Testing for Language Teachers*. Cambridge: Cambridge University Press.

Hughes, R. (2002). *Teaching and Researching Speaking*. Harlow: Pearson.

Hyland. K (2002). *Teaching and Researching Writing*. Harlow: Pearson.

Read, J. (2000). *Assessing Vocabulary*. Cambridge: Cambridge University Press.

Rost, M. (2002). *Teaching and Researching Listening*. Harlow: Pearson.

Spolsky, B. (1995). *Measured Words*. Oxford: Oxford University Press.

Urquhart, S. and Weir, C. (1998). *Reading in a Second Language: Process, Product and Practice*. London: Longman.

Weigle, S. C. (2002). *Assessing Writing*. Cambridge: Cambridge University Press.

Weir, C.J. 1993. *Understanding and Developing Language Tests*. Hemel Hemstead: Prentice Hall.

12.2   Journals

This section lists the main testing periodicals together with journals in related areas that sometimes contain relevant articles. Website addresses have been supplied but these may well change periodically.

Testing journals

Language Assessment Quarterly

https://www.erlbaum.com/shop/tek9.asp?pg=productsandspecific=1543-4303
From 2004, the LAQ will be dedicated to the advancement of theory, research, and practice in first, second, and foreign language assessment for school, college and university students; language assessment for employment; and language assessment for immigration and citizenship.

Language Testing

http://www.arnoldpublishers.com/Journals/pages/lan_tes/02655322.htm
http://www.ingenta.com/journals/browse/arn/lt?mode=direct
'*Language Testing* provides a forum for the exchange of ideas and information between people working in the fields of first and second language testing and assessment. This includes researchers and practitioners in EFL and ESL testing, and assessment in child language acquisition and language pathology. In addition, special attention is focused on issues of testing theory, experimental investigations, and the following up of practical implications.'

Melbourne Papers In Language Testing
The Working Papers of the Language Testing Research Centre. Information for Contributors. www.ltrc.unimelb.edu.au/mplt/mplt.html

Practical Assessment, Research and Evaluation (PARE)
'an on-line journal supported, in part, by the Department of Measurement, Statistics, and Evaluation at the University of Maryland, College Park. Its purpose is to provide education professionals access to refereed articles that can have a positive impact on assessment, research, evaluation, and teaching practice, especially at the local education agency (LEA) level'. http://pareonline.net/

Related journals

Applied Linguistics
http://www3.oup.co.uk/applij/

Assessing Writing
http://www.elsevier.nl/publications/store/6/2/0/3/6/9

English for Specific Purposes
http://www.elsevier.com/locate/esp

Journal of English for Academic Purposes
http://www.socscinet.com/linguistics/jeap/

Journal of Second Language Writing
http://icdweb.cc.purdue.edu/~silvat/jslw/index.html

Language Learning
http://www.blackwellsynergy.com/Journals/member/institutions/
issuelist.asp?journal=lang

System
http://www.elsevier.com

TESOL Quarterly
http://www.tesol.org

Written Communication
http://www.sagepub.co.uk

12.3 Professional associations

Specially devoted to testing

ALTE http://www.alte.org/
International Association of Applied Linguistics http://www.brad.ac.uk/
acad/aila/

ILTA International Language Testing Association
http://www.dundee.ac.uk/languagestudies/ltest/ilta/ilta.html

EALTA (European Association for Language Testing and Assessment)
http://www.ealta.eu.org/
'The purpose of EALTA is to promote the understanding of theoretical principles of language testing and assessment, and the improvement and sharing of testing and assessment practices throughout Europe.'

With an interest in testing

AAAL (American Association of Applied Linguistics)
http://www.aaal.org

BAAL (British Association of Applied Linguistics)
http://www.baal.org.uk

IATEFL (International Association for Teaching English as a Foreign Language)
http://www.iatefl.org

JACET (Japanese Association of College English Teachers)
http://www.jacet.org/

JALT (Japanese Association of Language Teachers)
www.jalt.org

TESOL
http://www.tesol.edu/

12.4   Principal testing conferences

Language Testing Research Colloquium (LTRC)
Conference held annually. The meeting for those with a serious interest in testing ESOL. Refereed papers, panel discussions, poster displays etc. provide a good overview of what is current in the field of language testing research. An introductory day provides in depth training in a relevant area of quantitative or qualitative methodology

East Coast Association of Language Testers
http://www.georgetown.edu/users/pmw2/ecolt/

Mid-West Association of Language Testers
http://www.uiowa.edu/~mwalt/

Language Testing Forum
A smaller gathering for testers in the UK and Europe held annually in Britain in November. Fairly informal and friendly with one session devoted to PhDs sharing the progress of their research with the group,

either in plenary or by poster, with participants providing feedback. Details are available at:
http://www.dundee.ac.uk/languagestudies/ltest/ltr.html.

12.5   Email lists and bulletin boards

LTEST-L is the discussion list of the International Language Testing Association. Its purpose is to encourage the discussion of language testing theory, research and practice. Membership is open to anyone who wishes to join.To join LTEST-L, send a **one-line** message to:
   listserv@lists.psu.edu
Which reads:
   subscribe 1test-1 [your first name] [your last name]

12.6   Internet sites

The best testing site by far is that run by Glenn Fulcher: *Resources in Language Testing Page* [On-line], available at:
http://www.dundee.ac.uk/languagestudies/ltest/ltr.html.
It deals with:

- types of tests available
- conferences
- organizations dealing with testing
- research studies
- numerous online resources reviewed for content and usefulness

It has been accurately described as a 'one-stop shop' for language testers and is an extremely valuable resource for testers everywhere. Pithy reviews are available on Fulcher's site for many of the websites listed below. All these sites were live at the time of going to press.

ACTFL
http://www.sil.org/lingualinks/languagelearning/otherresources/
actflproficiencyguidelines/contents.htm

American Association for Applied Linguistics (AAAL)
http://aaal.org/

American Educational Research association (AERA)
http://www.aera.net/

American Psychological Association (APA)
http://www.apa.org/

The Applied Linguistics WWW Virtual Library
http://alt.venus.co.uk/VL/AppLingBBK/welcome.html

Assessment Systems Corporation: Psychometric Software and Books and Electronic Tests
http://www.assess.com

BUROS Center for testing reviews
http://buros.unl.edu/buros/jsp/search.jsp

Cambridge ESOL Examinations research notes (UCRN)
www.CambridgeESOL.org

CAT tutorial
http://edres.org/scripts/cat

Center for Advanced Research on Language Acquisition
http://carla.acad.umn.edu/

Centre for Applied Linguistics (CAL)
http://www.cal.org/topics/tests.html

CAL foreign language testing database in Washington
http://www.cal.org/nclrc/fltestdb/

CITO http://www.cito.nl/e_index.htm

The Consortium for Equity in Standards and Testing http://wwwcsteep.bc.edu/ctest

Council of Europe European Language Portfolio
http://culture2.coe.int/portfolio/inc.asp?L = EandM = $t/208-1-0-1/ main_pages/../

Council of Europe (languages)
http://www.coe.int/T/E/Cultural_Co-operation/education/Languages/ Language_Policy/default.asp#TopOfPage

Defense Language Institute Testing
http://www.dlielc.org/testing/ecl_test.html

DIALANG
http://www.dialang.org/Education Standards and Testing
http://dir.yahoo.com/Education/Standards_and_Testing/

European Frame of reference
http://culture2.coe.int/portfolio//documents/0521803136txt.pdf

ETS (Testing Agencies)
http://www.sfsu.edu/~testing/testagnt.html

Educational Testing Service Network
http://www.ets.org

Fair Test
http://www.fairtest.org/

Foreign Languages in Tourism Training page (oddly named but highly recommended by Glenn Fulcher as a site for testers)
http://www.lingocity.com/flitt/

Hyperstat
http://members.aol.com/johnp71/javastat.html

Web pages that perform statistical calculations
IELTS
http://www.ielts.org/

The Interagency Language Roundtable
http://www.utm.edu/~globeg/ilrhome.shtml

Language Testing Research Centre, The University of Melbourne
http://www.ltrc.unimelb.edu.au/l

The Michigan English Language Assessment Battery (MELAB)
http://www.lsa.umich.edu/eli/melab.htm

National Centre for Research on Evaluation, Standards and Student Testing
http://www.cse.ucla.edu/index2.htm

National Council on Measurement in Education
http://www.ncme.org/

National testing in the USA
http://www.ed.gov/nationaltests/

Practical Assessment, Research and Evaluation

http://search.britannica.com/
frm_redir.jsp?query=assessmentandredir=http://ericae.net/

SearchEric
http://SearchEric.org – a privately operated website with information on what has happened to ERIC. See http://www.lib.msu.edu/corby/education/doe.htm for further information

Standards in Education
http://www.awesomelibrary.org/Office/Teacher/Standards/Standards.html

Standards and testing
http://dir.yahoo.com/Education/standards_and_testing/

TOEFL
homepage http://www.toefl.org/ – TOEFL research reports, many of which
are freely downloadable http://www.toefl.org/research/rtfldir.html

TOEFL Information on the Internet Linguistic Funland: http://
www.linguistic-funland.com/toefl.links.html

TOEIC
http://www.toeic.com/

University of Duisburg Research in Language Testing
http://www.uni-duisburg.de/FB3/ANGLING/FORSCHUNG/home.html

VOLTERRE-FR English and French Testing Services
http://www.wfi.fr/volterre/test.html

12.7   Databases

Dissertation abstracts on disc (US doctoral dissertations since 1861)
The ETS Test Collection
http://www.ets.org/testcoll/index.html – 'includes an extensive library of
20,000 tests and other measurement devices from the early 1900s to the
present. The collection is the largest in the world. It was established to make
information on standardized tests and research instruments available to
researchers, graduate students, and teachers. The tests contained in this
collection were acquired from a variety of U.S. publishers and individual test
authors. Foreign tests are also included in the collection, including some
from Canada, Great Britain, and Australia.'

Foreign Language Test Database
http://www.nclrc.org/fltestdb/ –
Index to theses (Britain and Northern Ireland)

12.8   Statistical packages

ETA
http://www.stet.co.uk –does both classical and IRT analysis and is moder-
ately priced

IRT
http://edres.org/irt/ – Include useful texts on IRT, references to other
websites and links to tutorial sites

Microsoft EXCEL spreadsheet and analysis program
http://www.microsoft.com/office/excel/default.asp

MINIFAC: Free Rasch measurement software. Student version of FACETS can be downloaded from: www.winsteps.com/minifac.

SPSS: the company website with detail of all its products including the good value student version can be found at:
http://www.spss.com/

Postscript

There is a clear need for validation of a test at both the *a priori* and the *a posteriori* stages of development, implementation, scoring and evaluation. Test providers need to consider validity in all its manifestations: context, theory-based, scoring, consequential and criterion-related.

Before the test is administered we want to know what steps have been taken to establish evidence relating to its theory-based and context validity. We also need to determine what information to collect on individual test taker characteristics so we can later use these data when analysing scores to determine whether, despite our best efforts to eliminate it at the test development stage, any bias has occurred. Once the test has been administered we need to investigate all aspects of scoring validity to determine the extent to which we can depend on the results. When grades have been awarded, attention shifts to the consequences of the test. We want to know about any previously undetected, residual bias and we also want to know the effects of the test on the teaching and learning process that precedes candidates sitting it. We might also wish to determine how the results of the test match any other available, reliable and valid external data we have on student ability in the construct under investigation. The need for such empirical validation should now be evident and a sine qua non for all high stakes tests.

Bachman (LTEST-L 13/11/02) among others has argued that the higher the stakes of the test, the higher the gravity of its impact, the stronger the argument for validation and the greater the amount of evidence that is called for. However, even low stakes tests, such as those in daily use in the classroom for formative purposes, should presumably be premised on some sort of validity argument and there should be some appropriate evidence to support such assumption. Determining how much evidence is necessary at differing levels of criticality is of course an area in urgent need of further investigation, the issue of who is to make the judgement notwithstanding.

It is hoped that this book will provide some help in clarifying the areas in test validity that we need to address and that it will encourage Examining Boards and all test developers to embark on a validity research agenda tailored to the level of stakes of the tests they are involved in. If they should fail to address these issues the test stakeholders have every right to know why. Tests without such validity evidence may not be worth the paper they are printed on.

Caveat emptor!

References

Alderman, D.L. and Holland, P.W. *Item Performance across Native Language Groups on the Test of English as a Foreign Language*. TOEFL research report No. 9. Princeton, N.J.: Educational Testing Service.

Alderson, J.C. (1978). A Study of the Cloze Procedure with Native and Non-Native Speakers of English. PhD Thesis. University of Edinburgh.

Alderson, J.C. (1990a). Testing reading comprehension skills. Part one. *Journal of Reading in a Foreign Language*, 6: 425–38.

Alderson, J.C. (1990b). Testing reading comprehension skills. Part two. Getting Students to talk about taking a reading test (a pilot study). *Reading in a Foreign Language*, 7(1): 465–503.

Alderson, J.C. (1991a). Dis-sporting Life. Response to Alistair Pollit's paper. In Alderson and North (eds.), pp. 60–7.

Alderson, J.C. (1991b). Bands and scores. In Alderson and North (eds.), pp. 71–86.

Alderson, J.C. (2000). *Assessing Reading*. Cambridge: Cambridge University Press.

Alderson, J.C. and Buck, G. (1993). Standards in testing: A study of the practice of UK Examination Boards in EFL/ESL testing. *Language Testing*, 10(2): 1–26.

Alderson, J.C., Clapham, C. and Wall, D. (1995). *Language Test Construction and Evaluation*. Cambridge: Cambridge University Press.

Alderson, J.C. and Hamp-Lyons, L. (1996). TOEFL preparation courses: a study of washback. *Language Testing*, 13(3): 280–97.

Alderson, J.C. and Hughes, A. (eds.) (1981). *Issues in Language Testing ELT Documents 111*. London: The British Council.

Alderson, C.J. and North, B. (eds.) (1991). *Language Testing in the 1990s*. London: Macmillan.

Alderson, J.C. and Urquhart, A.H. (eds.) (1984). *Reading in a Foreign Language*. London: Longman.

Alderson, J.C. and Urquhart, A. H. (1985). The effect of students' academic discipline on their performance on ESP reading tests. *Language Testing*, 2(2): 192–204.

Alderson, J.C. and Wall, D. (1993). Does washback exist? *Applied Linguistics*. 14(2): 115–29.

Alderson, J.C. and Wall, D. (1996). Special Issue: Washback. *Language Testing*, 13(3).

Allan, A.I.C.G. (1992). EFL Reading Comprehension Test Validation: Investigating Aspects of Process Approaches. Unpublished PhD thesis, Lancaster University.

Allan, A.I.C.G. (1995). Begging the questionnaire: instrument effect on readers' responses to a self-report checklist. *Language Testing*. 12(2): 133–56.

Allwright, D. (1988). *Observation in the Language Classroom*. New York: Longman.

American Educational Research Association, American Psychological Association, and National Council on Measurement in Education (1974, 1985, 1999). *Standards for Educational and Psychological Testing*. Washington, DC: Author.

Anastasi, A. (1988). *Psychological Testing* (6th edition). New York: Macmillan.

Anderson, N.J., Bachman, L. Perkins, K. and Cohen, A. (1991). An exploratory study into the construct validity of a reading comprehension test: triangulation of data sources. *Language Testing*. 8(1): 41–66.

Angoff, W.H. (1989). *Context Bias in the Test of English as a Foreign Language*. TOEFL Research Reports 29. Princeton, NJ: Educational Testing Service.

Association of Language Testers in Europe (ALTE) (1998). *A Multilingual Glossary of Language Testing Terms*.

Association of Language Testers in Europe (ALTE) (1994). *ALTE Code of Practice*.

Bachman, L.F. (1988). Problems in examining the validity of the ACTFL oral proficiency interview. *Studies in Second Language Acquisition*. 10(2): 149–64.

Bachman, L.F. (1990). *Fundamental Considerations in Language Testing*. Oxford: Oxford University Press.

Bachman, L.F. (2004). *Statistical Procedures in Language Assessment*. Cambridge: Cambridge University Press.

Bachman, L.F., Davidson, F., Ryan, K. and Choi, I.-C. (1995). *An Investigation into the Comparability of Two Tests of EFL: The Cambridge-TOEFL Comparability Study*. Cambridge: Cambridge University Press.

Bachman, L.F., Kunnan, A., Vanniarajan, S. and Lynch, B. (1988). Task and ability analysis as a basis for examining content and construct comparability in two EFL proficiency test batteries. *Language Testing*, 5: 128–59.

Bachman, L.F. and Palmer, A.S. (1981). A multitrait-multimethod investigation into the construct validity of six tests of speaking and reading. In A.S.P.J. Palmer Groot and F.A. Trosper (eds.), *The Construct Validity of Communicative Competence*. Washington, D.C.: TESOL.

Bachman, L. and Palmer, A. (1996). *Language Testing in Practice*. Oxford: Oxford University Press.

Bachman, L.F. and Savignon, S.J. (1986). The evaluation of communicative language proficiency: a critique of the ACTFL oral interview. *The Modern Language Journal*, 70(4): 380–90.

Bae, J. and Bachman, L. F. (1998). A latent variable approach to listening and reading: testing factorial invariance across two groups of children in the Korean/English two-way immersion program. *Language Testing*, 15(3): 380–414.

Bailey, K.M. (1996). Working for washback: a review of the washback concept in language testing. *Language Testing*, 13(3): 257–79.

Bailey, K.M. (1999). *Washback in Language Testing*. TOEFL Monograph Series 15. Princeton, NJ: Educational Testing Service.

Baker, R. (1997). *Classical Test Theory and Item Response Theory in Test Analysis*. Special Report 2: Language Testing Update, Centre for Research in Language Education.

Banerjee, J.V. (2003). Interpreting and Using Proficiency Test Scores. Unpublished PhD thesis. Univeristy of Lancaster.

Banerjee, J. and Luoma, S. (1997). Qualitative approaches to test validation. In C. Clapham and D. Corson (eds.), *Language Testing and Assessment, Encyclopedia of Language and Education*, Vol. 7. Dordrecht: Kluwer Academic Publishers, pp. 275–87.

Bensoussan, M. and Ramraz, R. (1984). Testing EFL reading comprehension using a multiple choice rational cloze *Modern Language Journal*, 68: 230–39.

Bereiter, C. and Scardamalia, M. (1987). *The Psychology of Written Composition*. Hillsdale, NJ: Lawrence Erlbaum.

Berman, R.A. (1984). Syntactic components of the foreign language reading process. In Alderson and Urquhart (eds.), pp. 139–59.

Berry, V. (1993). Personality characteristics as a potential source of language test bias. In Hutha, Sajavaara and Takala (eds.), pp. 115–24.

Berry, V. (1994). Current assessment issues and practices in Hong Kong: A preview. In Nunan, Berry and Berry (eds.), pp. 31–4.

Bond, Z.S and Garnes, S. (1980). Misperceptions of fluent speech. In R.A. Cole (ed.), *Perceptions and Production of Fluent Speech*. Hillsdale, NJ: Lawrence Erlbaum Associates, pp. 115–32.

Bradshaw, J. (1990). Test takers reactions to a placement test. *Language Testing*, 7: 13–30.

Bridgeman, B. and Carlson, S. (1983). *Survey of Academic Writing Tasks Required of Graduate and Undergraduate Foreign Students*. Princeton, NJ: ETS

Brindley, G. (1998). Describing language development? Rating scales and SLA. In L.F. Bachman and A.D. Cohen (eds.), *Interfaces between Second Language Acquisition and Language Testing Research*. Cambridge: Cambridge University Press, pp. 112–40.

Brindley, G. and Nunan, D. (1992). *Draft Bandscales for Listening*. IELTS research projects: project 1 NCELTR. MacQuarie University.

Brooks, L. (2003). Converting an observation checklist for use with the IELTS Speaking Test. *Cambridge ESOL Research Notes*, 11: 20–1.

Brown, A. (1993). The role of test taker feedback in the test development process: Test takers' reactions to a tape-mediated test of proficiency in spoken Japanese. *Language Testing*, 10: 277–304.

Brown, A. (2003). Interviewer variation and the co-construction of speaking proficiency. *Language Testing* 20: 1–25.

Brown, A. and Hill, K. (1998). Interviewer style and candidate performance in the IELTS Oral Interview. In S. Woods (ed.), *IELTS Research Reports 1997*, Volume 1. Sydney: ELICOS, pp. 173–91.

Brown, A., and Iwashita1, N. (1998). The role of language background in the validation of a computer-adaptive test. In A.J. Kunnan (ed.), *Validation in Language Assessment*. Mahwah, NJ: Lawrence Erlbaum Associates, pp. 195–208.

Brown, G., Anderson, A., Shillcock, R. and Yule, G. (1984). *Teaching Talk. Strategies for Production and Assessment*. Cambridge: Cambridge University Press.

Brown, G. and Yule, G. (1983). *Teaching the Spoken Language. An Approach Based on the Analysis of Conversational English*. Cambridge: Cambridge University Press.

Brown, J.D. (1991). *Understanding Research in Second Language Learning*. Cambridge: Cambridge University Press.

Bryman, A. and Cramer, D. (2001). *Quantitative Data Analysis with SPSS Release 10 for Windows: A guide for social scientists*. Hove: Routledge.

Buck, G. (1988). Testing listening comprehension in Japanese university entrance examinations. *JALT Journal*, 10(1): 15–42.

Buck, G. (1990). The Testing of Second Language Listening Comprehension. Unpublished PhD Thesis. University of Lancaster.

Buck, G. (1991). The testing of listening comprehension: An introspective study. *Language Testing*, 8: 67–94.

Buck, G. (2001). *Assessing Listening*. Cambridge: Cambridge University Press.

Burrows, C. (1998). Searching for washback: An investigation of the impact on teachers of the implementation into the Adult Migrant English Program of the assessment of the Certificates in Spoken and Written English. Unpublished PhD thesis, Macquarie University.

Butler, F.A., Eignor, D., Jones, S., McNamara, T. and Suomi, B.K. (2000). TOEFL (2000) Speaking Framework: A working paper. TOEFL Monograph Series 20. Princeton, NJ: Educational Testing Service.

Bygate, M. (1987). *Speaking*. Oxford: Oxford University Press.

Campbell, C. (1990). Writing with others' words: Using background reading texts in academic composition. In B. Kroll (ed.), *Second Language Writing: Research Insights for the Classroom*. Cambridge: Cambridge University Press.

Campbell, D.T. and Fiske, D.W. (1959). Convergent and discriminant validation by the multitrait-multimethod matrix. *Psychological Bulletin*, 56: 81–105.

Canale, M. and Swain, M. (1980). Theoretical bases of communicative approaches to second language teaching and testing. *Applied Linguistics*, I/I.

Candlin, C.N. and K. Hyland (eds.) (1999). *Writing: Texts, Processes and Practices.* London: Longman.

Carroll, B.J. (1980). *Testing Communicative Performance* London: Pergamon.

Carter, R. and McCarthy, M. (1995). Grammar and the spoken language. *Applied Linguistics*, 16: 141–58.

Carter, R. and McCarthy, M. (1997). *Exploring Spoken English*. Cambridge: Cambridge University Press.

Chalhoub-Deville, M. (ed.) (1999). *Computer Adaptive Tests of Reading Proficiency.* Cambridge: University of Cambridge.

Chalhoub-Deville, M. (2003). L2 interaction: current perspectives and future trends. *Language Testing* 20(4): 369–83.

Chalhoub-Deville, M. and Turner, C.E. (2000). What to look for in ESL admission tests: Cambridge certificate exams, IELTS, and TOEFL. *System*, 28(4): 523–39.

Chapelle, C. (1988). Field independence: a source of language test variation? *Language Testing*, 5: 62–82.

Chapelle, C. (1988). Construct definition and validity inquiry in SLA research. In L.F. Bachman and A.D. Cohen (eds.), *Interfaces between Second Language Acquisition and Language Testing Research*. New York: Cambridge University Press, pp. 32–70.

Chapelle, C. (1999). Validity in language assessment. *Annual Review of Applied Linguistics*, Vol. 19. New York: Cambridge University Press, pp. 254–72.

Chappelle, C. and Douglas, D. (eds.) (1993). *A New Decade of Language Testing Research*. Alexandria, VA: TESOL.

Chen, Z. and Henning, G. (1985). Linguistic and cultural bias in language proficiency tests. *Language Testing*, 2: 155–63.

Cheng, L. (1997/2004). The Washback Effect of Public Examination Change on Classroom Teaching: an Impact Study of the 1996 Hong Kong Certificate of Education in English on Classroom Teaching of English in Hong Kong Secondary Schools. Unpublished PhD, University of Hong Kong, Hong Kong and forthcoming in the Cambridge University Press.

Cheng, L. and Watanabe, Y. (eds.) (2004). *Context and Method in Washback Research: The Influence of Language Testing on Teaching and Learning*. Mahwah, NJ: Lawrence Erlbaum.

Chihara, T., Sakurai, T. and Oller, J.W. Jr. (1989). Background and culture as factors in EFL reading comprehension. *Language Testing*, 6: 143–51.

Clapham, C. (1996). *The Development of IELTS: A Study of the Effect of Background Knowledge on Reading Comprehension*. Cambridge: Cambridge University Press.

Clapham, C. and Corson, D. (1997). *Language Testing and Assessment*. Vol. 7, *Encyclopedia of Language and Education*. Dordrecht: Kluwer.

Clark, H.H. and Clark, E.V. (1977). *Psychology and Language: An Introduction to Psycholinguistics*. San Diego: Harcourt Brace Jovanovich.

Clark, J.L.D. and Swinton, S.S. (1979). *An Exploration of Speaking Proficiency Measures in the TOEFL Context*. Princeton, N.J. English Testing Services (TOEFL Research Reports 4).

Cohen, A. (1984). On taking language tests: What the students report. *Language Testing*, 1: 70–81.

Cohen, A. (1988). The use of verbal report data for a better understanding of test-taking processes. *Australian Review of Applied Linguistics*, 11: 30–42.

Cohen, A. (1994). *Assessing Language Ability in the Classroom* (2nd edition). Boston, MA: Heinle and Heinle.

Cohen, A.D. (1997). Towards enhancing verbal reports as a source of insights on test-taking strategies. In A. Huhta *et al.*, pp. 339–66.

Cohen, A. (1998). *Strategies in Learning and Using a Second Language*. Harlow: Longman.

Cohen, L., Manion, L. and Morrison, K. (2000). *Research Methods in Education* (5th edition). London: Routledge/Falmer.

Cotton, F. and Conrow, F. (1998). An investigation of the predictive validity of IELTS amongst a sample of international students studying at the University of Tasmania. In Wood (ed.), pp. 72–115.

Council of Europe (2001). *Common European Framework of Reference for Languages: Learning, Teaching, Assessment*. Cambridge: Cambridge University Press.

Crain-Thoreson, C., Lippman, M.Z. and McClendon-Magnuson, D. (1997). Windows on comprehension: Reading comprehension processes as revealed by two think-aloud procedures. *Journal of Educational Psychology*, 89(4): 579–91.

Criper, C. and Davies, A. (1988). *ELTS Validation Project Report*. London: The British Council.

Crocker, L. and Algina, J. (1986). *Introduction to Classical and Modern Test Theory*. San Diego: Harcourt Brace Jovanovich.

Cronbach, L.J. (1971). Test validation. In R.L. Thorndike (ed.), *Educational Measurement* (second edition). Washington DC: American Council on Education.

Cronbach, L.J. (1990). *Essentials of Psychological Testing* (fifth edition). New York: Harper and Row.

Cumming, A. (1997). The testing of writing in a second language. In Clapham and Corson, pp. 51–63.

Cumming, A. and Berwick, R. (eds.) (1996). *Validation in Language Testing*. Clevedon: Multilingual Matters Ltd.

Davies, A. (1977). The construction of language tests. In J.P.B. Allen and A. Davies (eds.), *Testing and Experimental Methods of Edinburgh Course in Applied Linguistics*, 4. Oxford: Oxford University Press, pp. 38–104.

Davies, A. (1983). The validity of concurrent validation. In A. Hughes and D. Porter, *Current Developments in Language Testing*. New York: Academic Press, pp. 141–45.

Davies, A. (1990). *Principles of Language Testing*. Oxford: Blackwell.

Davies, A. (ed.) (1997). *Language Testing* 14/3 (special issue on ethics in language testing).

Davies A. (2005). *The History of IELTS*. Cambridge: Cambridge University Press.

Davies A, Brown, A., Elder, C., Hill, K., Lumley, T. and McNamara, T. (1999). *Dictionary of Language Testing*. Studies in Language Testing, Vol. 7. Cambridge: UCLES/Cambridge University Press.

Deakin, G. (1997). IELTS in context: Issues in EAP for overseas students. *EA Journal*, 15(2): 7–28.

Denicolo, P. and Pope, M. (eds.) (1997). *Sharing Understanding and Practice*. Farnborough: EPCA Publications.

Douglas, D. (2000). *Assessing Language for Specific Purposes: Theory and Practice*. Cambridge: Cambridge University Press.

Dunkel, P. (1991). Listening in the native and second/foreign language: towards an integration of research and practice. *TESOL Quarterly*, 25(3): 431–59.

Ellerton, A.W. (1997). Considerations in the Validation of Semi-Direct Oral Testing. Unpublished PhD thesis, University of Reading.

Engineer, W.D. (1977). An Investigation of a Reading Model for English as a Second Language. Unpublished PhD thesis, University of Edinburgh.

Enright, M.K., Grabe, W., Koda, K., Mosenthal, P. Mulcahy-Ernt, P., Schedl, M. (2000). *TOEFL 2000 Reading Framework: A Working Paper*. TOEFL Monograph Series 17. Princeton, NJ: Educational Testing Service.

Ericsson, K.A. and Simon, H.A. (1993). *Protocol Analysis: Verbal Report as Data* (revised edition). Cambridge, MA: MIT Press.

Evans, T.D. (1988). A consideration of the meaning of the word 'discuss' in examination questions. In Robinson, pp. 47–52.

Farr, R., Pritchard, R. and Smitten, B. (1990). A description of what happens when an examinee takes a multiple-choice reading comprehension test. *Journal of Educational Measurement*, 27: 209–26.

Ferris, D. (1998). Students' views of academic aural/oral skills: a comparative needs analysis. *TESOL Quarterly*, 32(2): 289–318.

Ferris, D. and Tagg, T. (1996). Academic oral communication needs of EAP learners: What subject-matter instructors actually require. *TESOL Quarterly*, 30(1): 31–58.

Foddy, W. (1994). *Constructing Questions for Interviews and Questionnaires: Theory and Practice in Social Research*. Cambridge: Cambridge University Press.

Foster, P. and Skehan, P. (1996). The influence of planning and task type on second language performance. *Studies in Second Language Acquisition*, 18: 299–323.

Foster, P. and Skehan, P. (1999). The influence of source of planning and focus of planning on task-based performance. *Language Teaching Research*, 3(3): 215–47.

Freedle, R. and Kostin, I. (1994). Can multiple-choice reading tests be construct-valid? *Psychological Science*, 5: 107–10.

Freedle, R. and Kostin, I. (1999). Does the text matter in a multiple-choice test of comprehension? The case for the construct validity of TOEFL's minitalks. *Language Testing*, 16(1): 2–32.

Fulcher, G. (1993). The Construction and Validation of Rating Scales for Oral Tests in English as a Foreign Language. Unpublished PhD thesis, Lancaster University.

Fulcher, G. (1996a). Does thick description lead to smart tests? A data-based approach to rating scale construction. *Language Testing* 13(2): 208–38.

Fulcher, G. (1996b). Testing tasks: issues in task design and the group oral. *Language Testing*, 13(1): 23–51.

Fulcher, G. (2003). *Testing Second Language Speaking*. Harlow: Pearson.

Gass, S.M. and Mackey, A (2000). *Simulated Recall Methodology in Second Language Research*. Mahwah. N.J.: Lawrence Erlbaum

Ginther, A. and Grant, L. (1996). *A Review of the Academic Needs of Native English-Speaking College Students in the United States*. TOEFL Monograph Series 1. Princeton, NJ: Educational Testing Service.

Gollin, S. (1999). 'Why? I thought we'd talked about it before': collaborative writing in a professional workplace setting. In C.N. Candlin and K. Hyland (eds.), *Writing: Texts, Processes and Practices*. New York: Academic Press, pp. 41–58.

Grabe, W. (1991). Current developments in second language reading research. *TESOL Quarterly*, 25: 375–406.

Grabe, W. and Kaplan, R. (1996). *Theory and Practice of Writing*. London: Longman.

Grabe, W. and Stoller, F.L. (2002). *Teaching and Researching Reading*. London: Longman.

Green, A. (1998). *Verbal Protocol Analysis in Language Testing Research*. Cambridge: Cambridge University Press.

Green, A.B. (2003). Test Impact and English for Academic Purposes: A Comparative Study in Backwash between IELTS Preparation and University Presessional Courses. Unpublished PhD thesis. University of Surrey, Roehampton.

Hale, G.A. (1988). Student major field and text content: Interactive effects on reading comprehension in the TOEFL. *Language Testing*, 5: 49–61.

Hale, G.A. and Courtney, R. (1994). The effects of note-taking on listening comprehension in the TOEFL. *Language Testing*, 10: 133–70.

Hamp-Lyons, L. (1990). Second language writing: Assessment issues. In B. Kroll (ed.), *Second Language Writing: Research Insights for the Classroom*. Cambridge: Cambridge University Press, pp. 69–87.

Hamp-Lyons, L. (ed.) (1991). *Assessing Second Language Writing in Academic Contexts*. Norwood, NJ: Ablex.

Hamp-Lyons, L. (1997). Washback, impact and validity: ethical concerns. *Language Testing*, 14: 295–303.

Hamp-Lyons, L. and Condon, W. (2000). *Assessing the Portfolio: Principles for Practice, Theory and Research*. Cresskill, NJ: Hampton Press.

Hamp-Lyons, L. and Kroll, B. (1996). *TOEFL 2000 – Writing: Composition, Community, and Assessment*. TOEFL Monograph 5. Princeton: ETS.

Hasselgreen, A. (1998). Small Words and Valid Testing. PhD thesis. Bergen: Department of English, University of Bergen.

Hatch, E. and Lazaraton A. (1997). *The Research Manual: Design and Statistics for Applied Linguistics*. Boston, MA: Heinle and Heinle Publishers.

Hawkey R. and Barker, F. (2004). Developing a common scale for the assessment of writing. *Assessing Writing* 9(2).

Hawkey, R. (2004). *The Certificates in English Language Skills Exam: Development and Main Predecessors*. Cambridge: University of Cambridge Local Examinations Syndicate and Cambridge University Press.

Hayes, J.R and Flower, L.S. (1980). Identifying the organization of writing processes. In L.W. Gregg and E.R. Steinberg (eds.), *Cognitive Processes in Writing*. Hillsdale, NJ: Lawrence Erlbaum Associates, pp. 31–50.

Henning, G. (1987). *A Guide to Language Testing*. Cambridge, MA.: Newbury House.

Hill, K. (1997). The role of questionnaire feedback in the validation of the Oral Interaction Test. In G. Brindley and G. Wigglesworth (eds.), *Access: Issues in English Language Test Design and Delivery*. Macquarrie: NCELTR, pp. 147–74.

Hill, K. (1998). The effect of test taker characteristics on reactions to and performances on an oral English proficiency test. In Kunnan, pp. 209–30.

Hill, K., Storch, N. and Lynch, B. (1999). A comparison of IELTS and TOEFL as predictors of academic success. In Tulloh (ed.), pp. 52–63.

Horowitz, D.M. (1986). What professors actually require: Academic tasks for the ESL classroom. *TESOL Quarterly*. 20(3): 445–62.

Howatt, A.P.R. (1984). *A History of English Language Teaching*. Oxford: Oxford University Press.

Hughes, A. (1988a). Introducing a needs-based test of English into an English-medium university in Turkey. In A. Hughes (ed.), *Testing English for University Study*. London: Modern English Publications, pp. 134–53.

Hughes, A. (ed.) (1988b). Testing *English for University Study: ELT Documents 127*. Oxford: Modern English Press.

Hughes, A. (2003). *Testing for Language Teachers*. Cambridge: Cambridge University Press.

Hughes, A., Porter, D. and Weir, C.J. (1988). *Validating the ELTS Test: A Critical Review*. Cambridge: The British Council and the University of Cambridge Local Examination Syndicate.

Hughes, R. (2002). *Teaching and Researching Speaking*. London: Longman.

Huhta, A., Kohonen, V., Kurki-Suonio, L. and Luoma, S. (eds.) (1997). *Current Developments and Alternatives in Language Assessment*. Jyväskylä: University of Jyväskylä and University of Tampere, Finland.

Hyland, K. (2002). *Teaching and Researching Writing*. London: Longman.

Jacobs, H.L.S.A, Wingraf, D.R., Wormuth, V.F. Hartfield. and Hughey, J.B. (1981). *Testing ESL Composition: A Practical Approach*. Rowley, MA: Newbury House.

Jin, Y. (1998). An Applied Linguistics Model of Chinese Undergraduates' EAP Reading and its Operationalizations in the Advanced English Reading Test. PhD dissertation. Shanghai Jiao Tong University, China.

Johnson, M. (2001). *The Art of Non-conversation*. New Haven, CT.: Yale University Press.

Johnson, M. and Tyler, A. (1998). Reanalyzing the OPI: how much does it look like natural conversation? In R.Young and A Weiyun He (eds.), *Talking and Testing: Discourse Approaches to the Assessment of Oral Proficiency*. Studies in Bilingualism. 14. Amsterdam and Philadelphia; John Benjamins Publishing Company, pp. 27–51.

Johnston, P. (1984). Prior knowledge and reading comprehension in test bias. *Reading Research Quarterly*, 19: 219–39.

Jones, N. (2001). Reliability in UCLES' examinations. Unpublished internal UCLES' report.

Jordan, R.R. (1998). *English for Academic Purposes (EAP) and Needs Analysis: Implications and Implementation*. Cambridge: Cambridge University Press.

Just, M.A. and Carpenter, P.A. (1980). A theory of reading: from eye fixations to comprehension. *Psychological Review*, 87(4): 329–54.

Just, M.A. and Carpenter, P.A. (1987). *The Psychology of Reading and Language Comprehension*. Boston, MA.: Allyn and Bacon.

Kane, M.T. (1992). An argument-based approach to validity. *Psychological Bulletin* 122(3): 527–35.

Kelley, T.L. (1927). *Interpretation of Educational Measurements* New York: New World Book Company.

Kelly, G. (1955/1991). *The Psychology of Personal Constructs*. London: Routledge.

Kennedy, C., Dudley-Evans, T. and Thorp, D. (2001). *Investigation of Linguistic Output of Academic Writing Task 2*. British Council, IDP, UCLES IELTS Research Project 1999–2000, Final Report.

Khalifa, H. (1997). A Study in the Construct Validation of the Reading Module of an EAP Proficiency Test Battery: Validation from a Variety of Perspectives. PhD thesis. University of Reading.

Khalifa, H. (ed.) (2003). *Student Achievement Test Development Manual* (SATD). Egypt: USAID.

Khaniya, T.R. (1990). The washback effect of a textbook-based test. *Edinburgh Working Papers in Applied Linguistics*, 1: 48–58.

Kim, J.O. and Muller, C.W. (1978a). *Introduction to Factor Analysis: What it is and how to do it*. Newbury Park, CA: Sage.

Kim, J.O. and Muller, C.W. (1978b). *Factor Analysis: Statistical Methods and Practical Issues*. Newbury Park, CA: Sage.

Kintsch, W. (1998). *Comprehension: A Framework for Cognition*. Cambridge: Cambridge University Press.

Kintsch, W. and van Dijk, T.A. (1978). Toward a model of text comprehension and production. *Psychological Review*, 85: 363–94.

Kintsch, W. and van Dijk, T.A. (1983). *Strategies of Discourse Comprehension*. London: Academic Press.

Kintsch, W. and Yarborough, J.C. (1982). Role of rhetorical structure in text compre-hension. *Journal of Educational Psychology*, 74: 828–34.

Kroll, B. (1990). What does time buy? ESL student performance on home versus class compositions. In B. Kroll (ed.), *Second Language Writing: Research Insights for the Classroom*. Cambridge: Cambridge University Press, pp. 140–54.

Kunnan, A.J. (1990). DIF in native language and gender groups in an ESL placement test. *TESOL Quarterly*, 24: 740–6.

Kunnan, A.J. (1994). Modeling relationships among some test-taker characteristics and performance on EFL tests: An approach to construct validation. *Language Testing*, 11: 225–52.

Kunnan, A.J. (1995). *Test-taker Characteristics and Test Performance: A Structural Modelling Approach*. Cambridge: University of Cambridge Local Examinations Syndicate and Cambridge University Press.

Kunnan, A.J. (ed.) (1998). *Validation in Language Assessment: Selected Papers from the 17th Language Testing Research Colloquium, Long Beach*. Mahwah, NJ: Lawrence Erlbaum Associates.

Kunnan, A.J. (ed.) (2000). *Fairness and Validation in Language Assessment: Selected Papers from the 19th Language Testing Research Colloquium, Orlando*. Cambridge: University of Cambridge Local Examinations Syndicate and Cambridge University Press.

Lado, R. (1961). *Language Testing*. London: Longman.

Language Testing (1996). Vol. 13, No. 3. Special issue on backwash.

Lazaraton, A. (2002). *A Qualitative Approach to the validation of Oral Language Tests*. Cambridge: University of Cambridge Local Examinations Syndicate and Cambridge University Press.

Levelt, W.J.M. (1993). *Speaking: From Intention to Articulation*. Cambridge, MA.: MIT Press.

Lewkowicz, J.A. (1997). Investigating Authenticity in Language Testing. Unpublished PhD Thesis. University of Lancaster.

Lier, L. van (1989). Reeling, writhing, drawling, stretching and fainting in coils: oral proficiency interviews as conversation. *TESOL Quarterly*, 23: 489–503.

Loevinger, J. (1957). Objective tests as instruments of psychological theory. *Psychological Reports*, 3: 635–94.

Lumley, T. (1993). The notion of sub-skills in reading comprehension tests: An EAP example. *Language Testing*, 10: 21–234.

Lumley, T. and Brown, A. (1997). Interlocutor variability in specific-purpose language performance tests. In A. Huhta *et al.*, pp. 137–50.

Lunz, Mary E. and Wright, Benjamin D. (1997). Latent trait models for performance examinations. In Jürgen Rost and Rolf Langeheine (eds.), *Applications of Latent Trait and Latent Class Models in the Social Sciences*. http://www.ipn.unikiel.de/aktuell/buecher/rostbuch/ltlc.htm.

Luoma, S. (2004). *Assessing Speaking*. Cambridge: Cambridge University Press.

McDowell, C. and Jakeman, V. (1996). *Cambridge Practice Tests for IELTS 1*. Cambridge: Cambridge University Press.

McNamara, T.F. (1996). *Measuring Second Language Performance*. Harlow: Longman.

McNamara, T.F. (1997). 'Interaction' in second language performance assessment: Whose performance? *Applied Linguistics*, 18(4): 446–65.

McNamara, T. (2000). *Language Testing*, Oxford: Oxford University Press.

Mann, S.J. (1982). Verbal reports as data: A focus on retrospection. In S. Dingwall and S. Mann (eds.), *Methods and Problems in Doing Applied Linguistic Research*. Lancaster.

Mehnert, U. (1998). The effects of different lengths of time for planning on second language performance. *Studies in Second Language Acquisition*, 20: 83–108.

Messick, S. (1989). Validity. In R. Linn (ed.), *Educational Measurement*. New York: Macmillan, pp. 13–103.

Messick, S. (1992). Validity of test interpretation and use. In M.C. Alkin (ed.), *Encyclopedia of Educational Research* (6th edition). New York: Macmillan.

Messick, S. (1994). The interplay of evidence and consequences in the validation of performance assessments. *Educational Researcher*, 23(2): 13–23.

Messick, S. (1995). Validity of psychological assessment: Validation of inferences from persons' responses and performances as scientific inquiry into score meaning. *American Psychologist*, 50: 741–9.

Messick, S. (1996). Validity and washback in language testing. *Language Testing*, 13 (3): 241–56.

Miles, M.B. and Huberman, A.M. (1994). *Qualitative Data Analysis* (second edition). London: Sage Publications.

Moller, A.D. (1982). A Study in the Validation of Proficiency Tests of English as a Foreign Language. Unpublished PhD thesis. University of Edinburgh.

Moore, T. and Morton, J. (1999). Authenticity in the IELTS Academic Module Writing Test: A comparative study of Task 2 items and university assignments. In Tulloh (ed.), pp. 64–106.

Morrow, K. (1979). Communicative language testing: revolution or evolution? In C.J. Brumfit and K. Johnson (eds.), *The Communicative Approach to Language Teaching*. Oxford: Oxford University Press.

Murphy, R.J.L. (1979). *Mode 1 Examining for the General Certificate of Education. A General Guide to Some Principles and Practices*. Aldershot: AEB.

Myford, C.M. and Wolfe, E.W. (2000). *Monitoring Sources of Variability within the Test of Spoken English Assessment System*. TOEFL Research Report No. 65. Princeton, NJ: Educational Testing Service.

Myford, C.M. and Wolfe, E.W. (2003). Detecting and measuring rater effects using many-facet rasch measurement: Part 1. *Journal of Applied Measurement*, 4(4), 386–422.

Myford, C.M. and Wolfe, E.W. (2004). Detecting and measuring rater effects using many-facet Rasch measurement: Part 2. *Journal of Applied Measurement*, 5(2), 189–227.

Nevo, N. (1989). Test-taking strategies on a multiple-choice test of reading comprehension. *Language Testing*. 6: 199–215.

Nitko, A.J. (2001). *Educational Assessment of Students* (third edition). Upper Saddle River. NJ: Prentice Hall.

Norris, J, Brown, J.D., Hudson, T. and Yoshioka, J. (1998). *Designing Second Language Performance Assessments*. Technical Report No. 18. Hawai'i: University of Hawai'i Press.

Nystrand, M., Greene, S. and Wiemelt, J. (1993). Where did composition studies come from? An intellectual history. *Written Communication*, 267–333.

Oakeshott Taylor, J. (1977). Information redundancy and listening comprehension. In R. Dirven (ed.), *Listening Comprehension in Foreign Language Learning* Kronberg/Ts.: Scriptor.

Oller, J.W. (1979). *Language Tests at School*. London: Longman.

O'Loughlin, K. (2001). *The Equivalence of Direct and Semi-direct Speaking Tests*. Studies in Language Testing 13. Cambridge: Cambridge University Press.

Oltman, P.K., Stricker, L.J. and Barrows, T. (1988). *Native Language, English Proficiency and the Structure of the Test of English as a Foreign Language*. TOEFL Research Reports 27. Princeton, NJ: Educational Testing Service.

Oppenheim, A.N. (1992). *Questionnaire Design, Interviewing and Attitude Measurement*. London: Pinter.

Ortega, L. (1999). Planning and focus on form in L2 oral performance. *Studies in Second Language Acquisition*, 20: 109–48.

O'Sullivan, B. (2000). Towards a Model of Performance in Oral Language Testing. Unpublished PhD Dissertation. University of Reading.

O'Sullivan, B. (2004). *Issues in Testing Business English: The BEC Revision Project*. Cambridge: Cambridge University Press/Cambridge ESOL.

O'Sullivan, B. and Weir, C. (2002). *Research Issues in Testing Spoken Language*. Mimeo: Internal research report commissioned by Cambridge ESOL.

O'Sullivan, B., Weir, C. and Saville, N. (2002). Using observation checklists to validate speaking-test tasks. *Language Testing*, 19(1): 33–56.

Patton, M.Q. (2002). *Qualitative Research and Evaluation Methods*. Newbery Park, CA: Sage Publications.

Pavlou, P. (1997). Do different speech interactions in an oral proficiency test yield different kinds of language? In Huhta *et al*., pp. 185–202.

Pearson, I. (1988). Tests as levers for change. In D. Chamberlain and R. Baumgartner (eds.), *ESP in the Classroom: Practice and Evaluation*. ELT Documents 128. London: Modern English Publications.

Perkins, K. (1992). The effect of passage and topical structure types on ESL reading comprehension difficulty. *Language Testing* 9(2): 163–72.

Phakiti, A. (2003). A closer look at the relationship of cognitive and metacognitive strategy use to EFL reading achievement test performance. *Language Testing*. 20(1): 26–56.

Popham, W.J. (1990). *Modern Educational Measurement* (second edition). Englewood Cliffs, NJ: Prentice-Hall.

Pressley, M. and Afflerbach, P. (1995). *Verbal Protocols of Reading: The Nature of Constructively Responsive Reading*. Hillsdale, NJ: Lawrence Erlbaum.

Richards, J.C., Platt, J. and Platt, H. (1992). *Dictionary of Language Teaching and Applied Linguistics*. London: Longman.

Read, J.M. (1990). Responding to different topic types: a quantitative analysis from a contrastive rhetoric perspective. In B. Kroll (ed.), *Second Language Writing: Research Insights for the Classroom*. Cambridge: Cambridge University Press.

Read, J.M. (2000). *Assessing Vocabulary*. Cambridge: Cambridge University Press.

Riggenbach, H. (1998). Evaluating learner interactional skills: conversation at the micro level. In R. Young and A. Weiyun He (eds.), *Talking and Testing: Discourse Approaches to the Assessment of Oral Proficiency* Studies in Bilingualism, 14. Amsterdam and Philadelphia; John Benjamins Publishing Company, pp. 53–67.

Robb, T.N. and Susser, B. (1989). Extensive reading versus skills building in an EAP context. *Reading in a Foreign Language*, 5: 239–51.

Roberts, J. (1999). Personal construct psychology as a framework for research into teacher and learner thinking. *Language Teaching Research*, 3(2): 117–44.

Robinson, P.C. (ed.) (1988). *Academic Writing: Process and product*. Oxford: Modern English Publications.

Ross, S. (1992). Accommodative questions in oral proficiency interviews. *Language Testing*, 9(2): 173–86.

Ross, S. and Berwick, R. (1992). The discourse of accommodation in oral proficiency interviews. *Studies in Second Language Acquisition*, 14: 159–76.

Rost, D. (1993). Assessing the different components of reading comprehension: Fact or fiction? *Language Testing*, 10: 79–92.

Rost, M. (1990). *Listening in Language Learning*. London: Longman.

Rost, M. (2002). *Teaching and Researching Listening*. London: Longman.

Ryan, K. and Bachman, L. (1992). DIF on two tests of EFL proficiency. *Language Testing*, 9: 2–29.

Sarig, G. (1989). Testing meaning construction: can we do it fairly? *Language Testing*, 6: 77–94.

Saville, N. (2003). The process of test development and revision within UCLES EFL. In Weir and Milanovic (eds.), pp. 57–120

Sawilowsky, S.S. (2000). Psychometrics versus datametrics: comment on Vacha-Haase's 'reliability generalization' method and some EPM editorial policies. *Educational and Psychological Measurement* 60(2): 157–73.

Schank, R.C. and Abelson, R.P. (1977). Scripts, plans and knowledge. In P.N. Johnson Laird and P.C. Wason (eds.), *Thinking: Readings in Cognitive Science* Cambridge: Cambridge University Press.

Scwartz, N. and Sudman, S. (eds.) (1996). *Answering Questions: Methodology for Determining Cognitive and Communicative Processes in Survey Research*. New York: Jossey-Bass Publishers.

Shen, Z., Weir, C.J. and Green, R. (1998). *The Test for English Majors Validation Project*. Shanghai: Foreign Languages Education Press.

Shiotsu, T. (2003). Linguistic Knowledge and Processing Efficiency as Predictors of L2 Reading Ability: A Component Skills Analysis. Unpublished PhD dissertation. University of Reading.

Shohamy, E. (1984). Does the testing method make a difference? The case of reading comprehension. *Language Testing* 1(2): 147–70.

Shohamy, E. (1993). *The Power of Tests. The Impact of Language Tests on Teaching and Learning*. Washington, DC: NFLC Occasional Papers.

Shohamy, E. (2001). *The Power of Tests: A Critical Perspective on the Uses of Language Tests*. Harlow: Pearson Education.

Shohamy, E. and Inbar, O. (1991). Validation of listening comprehension tests: the effect of text and question types. *Language Testing*, 8(1): 23–40.

Skehan, P. (1996). A framework for the implementation of task based instruction. *Applied Linguistics*, 17: 38–62.

Skehan, P. and Foster, P. (1997). The influence of planning and post-task activities on accuracy and complexity in task-based learning. *Language Teaching Research*. 1(3): 185–211.

Smagorinsky, P. (1994). *Speaking about Writing: Reflections on Research Methodology*. Newbery Park, CA: Sage Publications.

Spolsky, B. (ed.) (1978). *Approaches to Language Testing. Advances in Language Testing Series: 2*. Arlington, VA: Center for Applied Linguistics.

Spolsky, B. (1995). *Measured Words*. Oxford: Oxford University Press.

SPSS Inc. (2002). *SPSS 11.5 for Windows*. Chicago, IL: SPSS Inc.

Storey, P. (1995). A Process Approach to Reading Test Validation. Unpublished PhD Thesis. University of Reading.

Storey, P. (1997). Examining the test-taking process: a cognitive perspective on the discourse cloze test. *Language Testing*, 14(2): 214–31.

Stratman, J.F. and Hamp-Lyons, L. (1994). Reactivity in concurrent think-aloud protocols. In P. Smagorinsky (ed.), *Speaking about Writing: Reflections on Research Methodology*. Newbery Park, CA: Sage.

Swinton, S.S. and Powers, D.E. (1980). *Factor Analysis of the Test of English as a Foreign Language for Several Language Groups*. TOEFL Research Reports 6. Princeton, NJ: Educational Testing Service.

Taylor, C., Jamieson, J., Eignor, D. and Kirsch, I. (1998). *The Relationship between Computer Familiarity and Performance on Computer-based TOEFL Test Tasks.* Research Reports 61. Princeton, NJ: Educational Testing Service.

Taylor, L.B. (2003). Responding to diversity: issues in assessing language learners with disabilities Paper presented at Language Testing Research Colloquium, Reading, 22–25 July 2003.

Tittle, C.K. (1990). Test bias. In H.J. Walberg and G.D. Haertel (eds.), *The International Encyclopedia of Educational Evaluation.* Oxford: Pergamon, pp. 128–33.

Tulloh, R. (ed.) (1999). *IELTS Research Reports Volume 2.* Canberra: IELTS Australia.

Urquhart, A.H. and Weir, C.J. (1998). *Reading in a Second Language: Process, Product and Practice.* Harlow: Longman.

Van Dijk, T.A. and Kintsch, W. (1983). *Strategies of Discourse Comprehension.* New York: Academic Press.

Wall, D. and Alderson, J.C. (1993). Examining washback: the Sri Lankan impact study. *Language Testing,* 10(1): 41–69.

Wall, D. (2004). *The Impact of a High-Stakes Examination on Classroom Teaching: A Case Study Using Insights from Testing and Innovation Theory.* Cambridge: Cambridge University Press.

Watanabe, Y. (1996). Does grammar translation come from the entrance examination? Preliminary findings from classroom-based research. *Language Testing,* 13(3): 318–33.

Watanabe. Y. (1997). *The Washback Effects of the Japanese University Entrance Examinations of English – Classroom-based Research.* Unpublished PhD thesis. University of Lancaster.

Waters, A. (1996). *A Review of Research into Needs in English for Academic Purposes of Relevance to the North American Higher Education Context.* TOEFL Monograph 6. Princeton: ETS.

Weigle, S. (1994). Effects of training on raters of ESL compositions. *Language Testing* 11(2): 197–223.

Weigle, S.C. (2002). *Assessing Writing.* Cambridge: Cambridge University Press.

Weir, C.J. (1983a). Identifying the Language Problems of Overseas Students in Tertiary Education in the UK. Unpublished PhD dissertation. University of London.

Weir, C.J. (1983b). The Associated Examining Board's test of English for academic purposes: An exercise in content validation. In A. Hughes and D. Porter (eds.), *Current Developments in Language Testing.* London: Academic Press, pp. 147–53.

Weir, C.J. (1988a). Construct validity. In A. Hughes, D. Porter and C. Weir (eds.), *ELT Validation Project: Proceeding of a Conference Held to Consider the ELTS Validation Project Report.* The British Council and the University of Cambridge Local Examination Syndicate.

Weir, C.J. (1988b). Academic writing – Can we please all the people all of the time? In Robinson, pp. 17–35.

Weir C.J. (1988c). The specification, realisation and validation of an English language proficiency test. In Hughes, pp. 45–110.

Weir, C.J. (1990). *Communicative Language Testing.* New York: Prentice Hall.

Weir, C.J. (1993). *Understanding and Developing Language Tests.* New York: Prentice Hall.

Weir, C.J. (2001). The formative and summative uses of language test data. In Elder *et al.* (eds.), 117–26.

Weir, C.J. (2003). A survey of the history of the Cerificate of Proficiency in English (CPE) in the twentieth century. In Weir and Milanovic (eds.), 1–56.

Weir, C.J., Hughes, A. and Porter, D. (1990). Reading skills: hierarchies, implicational relationships and identifiability. *Reading in a Foreign Language,* 7: 505–10.

Weir, C.J. and Milanovic, M. (eds.) (2003). *Continuity and Innovation: The History of the CPE 1913–2002*. Cambridge: Cambridge University Press.

Weir, C.J. and Porter, D. (1996). The multi-divisible or unitary nature of reading: the language tester between Scylla and Charybdis. *Reading in a Foreign Language*, 10: 1–19.

Weir, C.J. and Roberts, J.R. (1994). *Evaluation in ELT*. Blackwell: Oxford.

Weir, C.J. and Wu, J. (2005). Parallel-form Reliability – A Case Study of the GEPT Intermediate Spoken Performance Test.

Weir, C., O'Sullivan, B. and Jin Yan (2004). *Does the Computer Make a Difference? An Investigation into the Differences between Writing on Computer and on Paper*. Report on IELTS research project.

Weir, C.J., Yang, H. and Jin, Y. (2000). *An Empirical Investigation of the Componentiality of L2 Reading in English for Academic Purposes*. Studies in Language Testing 12. Cambridge: Cambridge University Press.

Widdowson, H.G. (1978). *Teaching Language as Communication*. Oxford: Oxford University Press.

Wigglesworth, G. (1997). An investigation of planning time and proficiency level on oral test discourse. *Language Testing*, 14(1): 85–106.

Williams, E. and Moran, C. (1989). Reading in a foreign language at intermediate and advanced levels with particular reference to English. *Language Teaching*, 22: 217–28.

Wood, R. (1993). *Assessment and Testing*. Cambridge: Cambridge University Press.

Wu Yi'an (1998). What do tests of listening comprehension test? A retrospection study of EFL test-takers performing a multiple-choice task. *Language Testing* 15(1): 21–44.

Yang, H. and Weir, C.J. (1998). *Validation Study of the College English Test*. Shanghai: Shanghai Foreign Language Education Press.

Young, R. and Milanovic, M. (1992). Discourse variation in oral proficiency interviews. *Studies in Second Language Acquisition*, 14: 403–24.

Index